Praise for *Recollec*

M000238623

"Lucy Fischer's *Recollecting Collecting* is one of the most ~~~~~~~~~~~~ film and media collecting from a scholarly point of view. Featuring the work of scholars whose collections have inspired, tested, or extended their research, Fischer provides a rare and compelling look into film and media collecting and the ways that it has shaped professional lives."

—Patrice Petro, professor of film and media studies,
University of California, Santa Barbara

"Gathering a range of first-rate scholars and inventive topics, Lucy Fischer's fascinating collection orchestrates three contemporary theoretical currents—focused on material culture, thing theory, and collecting—to make a clear case for the vibrancy of current debates in film and media criticism."

—Timothy Corrigan, professor emeritus of cinema and
media studies, University of Pennsylvania, and author of
The Essay Film: From Montaigne, After Marker

"In addition to its erudition and scholarly value, *Recollecting Collecting* will produce sighs of pure pleasure among readers who have always viewed their assorted and cherished treasures as a tangible means of connection with the past, real or imagined. In fact, the only thing 'wrong' with this volume is that I am not in it."

—Adrienne L. McLean, author of *All for Beauty:
Makeup and Hairdressing in Hollywood's Studio Era* and
Being Rita Hayworth: Labor, Identity, and Hollywood Stardom

"This is a wonderful 'collection' of essays devoted to a subject many readers can relate to but perhaps have not quite come to terms with. For any scholar there is surely an element of autobiography in the reading of this engaging, important, and wonderfully accessible collection. Indeed, the first-person narratives are fascinating whether one knows the writers personally or not at all. One wants often to say, 'that's interesting!' or 'me, too!' and the deft integration of theoretical underpinning or scholarly revelations only makes this sharper, clearer, and more inviting. It is surprising that there has been no significant work on personal collecting by film and media scholars. Thus, Lucy Fischer, one of the true pioneers in the field, has done it again, offering up a book that, somehow, we didn't realize but now insist that we absolutely need."

—Frances Gateward, professor of communication, culture, and media studies, Howard University

"In *Recollecting Collecting*, Lucy Fisher gathers an eclectic selection of scholars who cannily explore the ways affective attachment to material objects can contribute to the widening of film and media research. Engaging Black cinema collectibles, Hollywood fan magazines, TV-inspired fashion, and comic books, among other artifacts, this timely anthology urges a nuanced questioning of the roles ownership, access, and power have accrued in the writing of media historiographies. By dwelling on the intersection of fandom and scholarship, this collection of essays further prompts an important reconsidering of what emerges when a scholar falls in love with their primary sources."

—Diana W. Anselmo, author of *A Queer Way of Feeling: Girl Fans and Personal Archives of Early Hollywood*, and assistant professor of critical studies, California State University, Long Beach

RECOLLECTING COLLECTING

Contemporary Approaches to Film and Media Series

A complete listing of the books in this series can
be found online at wsupress.wayne.edu.

GENERAL EDITOR

Barry Keith Grant
Brock University

RECOLLECTING COLLECTING

A Film and Media Perspective

Edited by

LUCY FISCHER

WAYNE STATE UNIVERSITY PRESS
DETROIT

Library of Congress Control Number: 2022946468

ISBN 9780814348550 (paperback)
ISBN 9780814348567 (hardcover)
ISBN 9780814348574 (e-book)

Cover design by Philip Pascuzzo

Wayne State University Press rests on Waawiyaataanong, also referred to as Detroit, the ancestral and contemporary homeland of the Three Fires Confederacy. These sovereign lands were granted by the Ojibwe, Odawa, Potawatomi, and Wyandot Nations, in 1807, through the Treaty of Detroit. Wayne State University Press affirms Indigenous sovereignty and honors all tribes with a connection to Detroit. With our Native neighbors, the press works to advance educational equity and promote a better future for the earth and all people.

Wayne State University Press
Leonard N. Simons Building
4809 Woodward Avenue
Detroit, Michigan 48201-1309

Visit us online at wsupress.wayne.edu.

CONTENTS

INTRODUCTION

Collecting My Thoughts

Lucy Fischer

> What academic doesn't collect things?
>
> —Dean R. Snow[1]

THIS SERIES OF ESSAYS BY film and media scholars draws on three vibrant currents of contemporary critical studies. The first is an interest in *material culture*, which is commonly understood as "the aspect of social reality grounded in the objects and architecture that surround people. It includes the usage, consumption, creation, and trade of objects as well as the behaviors, norms, and rituals that the objects create or take part in."[2] Clearly, material culture has had a strong influence on the field of film and media studies especially in relation to screen costumes and decor, the sites of film exhibition, the role of fan magazines, and the presence of consumer "tie-ins" produced to accompany movie releases. That this area has become a prominent aspect of academic discourse is demonstrated by the existence of an entire publication dedicated to the topic: *Journal of Material Culture*, which released its first issue in 1996.[3]

The second, though less pervasive, current of thought that has influenced this volume is *thing theory*, which attends to the status and role of objects in human life—a corrective to the alleged academic privileging of ideas. Thus, in 2001, a complete issue of *Critical Inquiry* was devoted to the subject. In it, the volume's editor, Bill Brown, asks, "Is there something perverse, if not archly insistent, about complicating things with theory?" Clearly, he thinks not, since a group of commissioned essays follow his introduction. For Brown, things "precipitate a new materialism that takes objects for granted only to grant them their potency—to show how they organize our private and public affection."[4]

The third (most obvious and dominant) current of thought related to this volume is the scholarly investigation of the social and psychological aspects of *collecting*. While in the past this topic concentrated primarily on the established inventories of museums, libraries, and other recognized institutions, in the contemporary era the focus has shifted to the activity of individual people. Just recently, for instance, the *New York Times* ran an article by musician Questlove, who admits that he has "been collecting things for as long as [he] can remember" as "a way to prevent the past from slipping away." For him, it is "an act of devotion."[5]

All three of these intellectual branches come together in this anthology through an examination of (1) collecting by film and media scholars whose acquisitions have direct ties to their work as researchers and teachers, (2) the film- and media-related collections of others as examined by scholars, and (3) collecting as a subject of film and television representations. Beyond this, the volume gives the reader a rare opportunity to delve into the minds of academics outside the narrow confines of the university to understand how the personal habit of collecting relates to their professional lives. In some cases, childhood collections of film-themed materials prove early harbingers of careers to come. In others, collections started for purely aesthetic reasons eventually find resonances in filmic texts. In still others, crossovers are forged between collections in different media (music or comics) and the cinema. And finally, in some cases links are made between collections of toys and the movies in which they are animated. Thus, in addition to being introduced to film scholars who collect, this volume helps us understand how such individuals come to research, write, and teach about the subjects that they do.

COLLECTING

In the last several decades, there have been a plethora of scholarly tomes that consider the nature of collecting as a societal act and form. As Susan Pearce states, "The study of collecting is a growth point in cultural studies."[6] Similarly, Peter Monaghan notes how "a new wave of scholarship examines the centuries-old 'mental landscape' of collectors."[7] However, while collecting has become a familiar topic in university discourse, no one has examined in depth the manner in which academics themselves constitute collectors. Yet as Dean Snow asks in this chapter's epigraph, "What academic doesn't collect things?" This would not be especially interesting in the case of a professor who accrued material unrelated to her own research or teaching (the literature professor who collects fishing lures). But it becomes intriguing when an academic's collecting habits dovetail with her own field. We should not be surprised that this frequently occurs since, as Werner Muensterberger states, "Often people's preference [for certain objects] is linked to their professional occupation."[8] Similarly, Susan Pearce finds (through her demographic study) that at least 10 percent of collectors feel that their collections have ties to their employment (e.g., the postal worker who collects stamps).[9]

My own interest in the subject stems from a long-standing collecting obsession (discussed in chapter 2), which came to be tied to my academic career in film and media studies. My exploration of the intersection of cinema and the design movements of Art Deco and Art Nouveau (which resulted in two monographs)[10] was born of my prior accrual of artifacts in those modes—for instance, a souvenir trylon and perisphere from the 1939 New York World's Fair and an Art Nouveau peacock-themed brooch. Like so many, when I began amassing these objects, it was purely for pleasure, without any practical notion of where it might lead.

This volume focuses on the personal collections of Anglo-American scholars who work in film and media studies. It fills several gaps in the critical literature by publishing (1) firsthand accounts by film and media

A souvenir trylon and perisphere indicative of the Art Deco style in the author's collection from the 1939 New York World's Fair

academics whose collections are tied to their discipline, highlighting how such items have sparked, tested, or augmented their research or teaching practices; (2) articles by scholars who have examined film and media collecting by others; and (3) discussions (in the introduction and in chapter 9) of the image of the collector in various moving image texts. As the chapter summaries make clear, the volume references

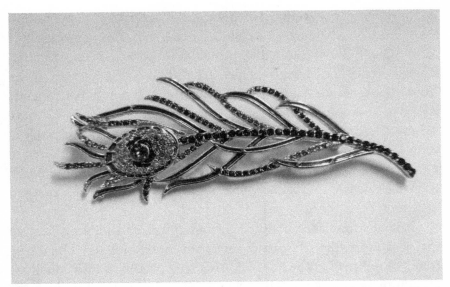

A reproduction Art Nouveau Tiffany peacock feather brooch in the author's collection that reflects the bird's popularity with the movement due to its beauty

collections of films, videos, toys, fan magazines, comics, movie or television memorabilia, recordings, jewelry, objets d'art, movie posters, stills, and broader artifacts of popular culture.

THEORIZING COLLECTING IN GENERAL

Before proceeding, however, it is first necessary to define collecting and understand its varied emotional qualities and motives as well as the diverse nature of collectors and collections themselves. Muensterberger understands collecting as "the selecting, gathering, and keeping of objects of subjective value."[11] Russell Belk is more expansive in his phrasing, seeing it as "the process of actively, selectively, and passionately acquiring and possessing things removed from ordinary use and perceived as part of a set of non-identical objects or experiences."[12]

So let us unpack these definitions and extend them by cataloging the important stages of the practice. First, of course, is the element of acquisition. Sometimes an individual obtains an object that only later becomes part of a collection (when she recognizes a desire to get more of the same). As Belk remarks, a collection seldom begins purposefully.[13] Most often, however, an item is gained in order to augment a particular grouping. For Muensterberger, acquisition is characterized by an "unrelenting need, even hunger."[14] Similarly, Belk sees it as frequently entailing "a desire and longing for specific material things"—a "'have to have it' feeling."[15] Susan Stewart makes clear that "it is not acceptable to simply purchase a collection *in toto*; the collection must be acquired in a serial manner. . . . 'Earning' the collection simply involves *waiting*."[16] For Walter Benjamin, obtaining objects grants them a "rebirth" and even "freedom."[17]

Belk distinguishes collecting from ordinary shopping, stating that it is more like a "treasure-hunt, adventure, a quest" characterized by the "thrill of the hunt."[18] It is also typically an individualistic pursuit marked by competitiveness with others involved in the same activity.[19] Furthermore, most scholars agree that collecting is different than mere accretion. As Jean Baudrillard says, "What makes a collection transcend mere accumulations is not only the fact of its being culturally complex but the fact of its incompleteness, the fact that it *lacks* something"[20]—hence, the continual need to enlarge it. Other writers have observed that collections must also display order and system.[21]

Once an item has been procured, it likely produces a sense of pride, accomplishment, and achievement in its owner,[22] though this is only temporary—as "repetition is mandatory."[23] On the other hand, repetition has its limits. Thus, for Baudrillard, "the collection is never really initiated in order to be completed" *since* "the acquisition of the final item would in effect denote the death of the [collector]."[24] Belk agrees: "Given notions of extended self, what is being completed is really the collector."[25] Though exciting, collecting can also result in feelings of "guilt or dis-ease." For Muensterberger, it can also entail the shameful behavior "of a compulsive gambler."[26]

Some theorists see the placement of the new object within the series as a kind of ritual act; as Belk states, "The owner must perform the alchemy of transforming it into a part of the collection."[27] In a similar vein, Muensterberger notes that such possessions "are imbued with 'magic,'"[28] and Benjamin talks of their owner placing them in a "magic circle."[29]

For Benjamin, the "interior" (as opposed to the outside world) is the collector's realm, his "casing," and he is its true "inhabitant."[30] It is not only a world "far-off in distance and in time, but . . . also [one imagined as] a better one."[31] Furthermore, he sees collecting as a battle between "the poles of disorder and order" and collectors as "the physiognomists of [their] objects."[32]

The things a person acquires tend to be ones of "particular significance" to the individual and "reflect certain aspects of his own personality, his taste, his sophistication or naïveté."[33] Putting it more bluntly, Baudrillard states, "it is invariably *oneself* that one collects."[34] Belk adds that people can also "express fantasies of the self" through collecting.[35]

As Belk's definition makes clear, collectibles are generally taken out of the realm of ordinary use; thus, if I acquire antique kitchen implements, it is unlikely that I will use them for everyday cooking. Baudrillard sees this as a process that stamps the object with the individual sign of the collector. As he observes, "The object pure and simple, divested of its function, abstracted from any practical context, takes on a strictly subjective status."[36] But we need to qualify Baudrillard's assertion, since book collectors often read the volumes they own; similarly, jewelry collectors often wear their pins, earrings, cuff links, or necklaces. Pearce sees the collected object a bit differently from Baudrillard, not so much as involving the personalization of use value but rather its "total aestheticization."[37] Thus, an antique pen is no longer prized for its function but for its beauty.

Several writers remark on the unique sense of time associated with a collection. For Pearce, it "replaces history with *classification*, with order beyond the realm of temporality."[38] Likewise, for Baudrillard: *"The setting up of a collection itself displaces real time."*[39] Thus, in grouping a collection of Depression-era glass, the particular date in which each was produced may be lost in the display logic of the collection. Benjamin, however, sees a sense of time entailed in the "spring tide of memories" that collections spark in their owners. Thus, he recounts his experiences of book auctions, as well as the sightseeing he did in the cities he visited in order to purchase the volumes.[40]

Once assembled, the collection tends alternately to be exhibited or sequestered, for as Pearce observes, it "must move between the public and the private, between display and hiding."[41] Concealment may occur because one is guilty about how many objects she has acquired and what she has spent on them. In fact, Belk asserts that by establishing a collection, one "legitimizes acquisitiveness as art or science."[42] One may also conceal a collection because she does not want to signal to competitors the extent of her possessions. Furthermore, she may have more artifacts than she can exhibit at any one time. Reasons for exhibiting items include a collector's desire to enjoy them or her wish to be admired or envied for owning them.

Drawing on a Marxian vocabulary, some writers see collecting as the process of consumption masquerading as production. As Pearce states, it "generates a fantasy in which it [the self] becomes producer of those objects, a producer by arrangement and manipulation."[43] Likewise, Mieke Bal introduces Marx's notion of "commodity fetishism" to describe the collected article.[44] In its simplest classic formulation, that concept involves "the mistaken view that the value of a commodity is intrinsic and the corresponding failure to appreciate the investment of labour that went into its production."[45] Hence, the claim is that, in collecting, one masks the work of the object's creator with one's own efforts in acquiring and arranging it.

As to who collects, it is not surprising that the enterprise is popular among the upper or middle classes as opposed to the lower economic tiers (who have no extra funds to expend on such a hobby). Most theorists assume a male collector (using the pronouns "he" and "his" in writing on the topic), and this is due to traditional conceptions of gender. Collecting entails voyaging outside the home, which in prior generations was the prerogative of the male (as was the control of family funds). Furthermore, success in collecting requires such traits as aggressiveness and competitiveness, also associated with men.[46] In the modern era, however, both genders are represented (and now women may actually exceed men).[47] Furthermore, certain traditional female traits are beneficial to collecting, including care, creativity, nurturance, and preservation.[48] Often the type of collection follows rigid social stereotypes—with men acquiring military or sports items, clocks, stamps, guns, coins and knives, and women purchasing decorative articles, jewelry, animal figurines, or household goods.[49] Men are often relieved of the charge of trivial consumption by being thought more likely than women to collect for "investment" purposes.[50]

For Pearce, gender informs not only the type of objects collected but also the meaning and use of the collection.[51] She finds that women are generally more interested in remembering where a piece was acquired than men, as they are in having their items displayed attractively.[52] Furthermore, they are more likely to feel guilty about their collecting habits than their male counterparts.[53]

Pearce identifies three basic "modes" of collecting that individuals practice. Some acquire "souvenirs" tied to a particular occasion (e.g., a trip) or to an individual or group (e.g., family photos, greeting cards, inherited jewelry or clothing, pressed flowers, theater programs, etc.). Second is "fetishistic" collecting (whose less tendentious name is "devoted" collecting). Here, people acquire more and more of a particular type of object that has personal meaning and emotional worth to them (e.g., wine bottle labels or World War II medals). The final and less romantic mode of collecting is the "systematic" one that "depends upon principles or organization which are perceived to have external reality beyond the specific material under consideration, and which are held to derive from general principles." While "devoted" collectors acquire samples, "systematic" ones accrue examples.[54]

But we might ask, *why* do people collect? Again, cultural critics have proposed myriad hypotheses, as there is no single generic collector. Muensterberger sees the motives in negative psychological terms, collecting being "molded by irrational impulses" that may have originated from "physical hurt or emotional trauma or actual neglect . . . or . . . states of alarm and anxiety." By granting power to the objects obtained, the collector's mental suffering is somehow ameliorated.[55] He also finds potentially "pathological" elements in certain collectors' preference for objects over human beings.[56] Similarly, Pearce admits that a collector's fixation on systematizing objects can bespeak domination or control.[57] Finally, Belk mentions that collecting can also be associated with obsessive-compulsive behaviors.[58]

Lincoln Geraghty sees nostalgia as a "driving force" in the urge to collect, especially among media fans, and notes that this has often been viewed in an adverse light—since allegedly it causes individuals to forget the real past in favor of a mythic one.[59] However, he argues against this notion, citing Svetlana Boym who states, "Nostalgia is not always about the past; it can be retrospective but also prospective."[60] Thus, for Geraghty, "collecting objects that form a visual and physical biography of the self is an act of improvement not loss; it is not about mourning the past but about creating a reflexive and tangible identity in the present."[61]

For Baudrillard, collecting has its mental roots in childhood and the period of latent genital sexuality. Thus, an adult's collection has "the strong whiff of the harem" about it.[62] Similarly, for Pearce, "the language of collecting parallels that of sexual activity" as "objects of desire are pursued with passion."[63] She notes as well that often collecting is seen as a "perverted form" of sexuality, with the material object viewed as a kind of "fetish" (used here in a different sense than the Marxian one).[64] In Freudian discourse, of course, a fetish is something that functions as a symbolic substitute for the missing penis that the male views with alarm in confronting the female body. Pearce, however, distances herself from this interpretation given that her study of actual collectors has revealed few with any erotic attachment to their artifacts. Furthermore, given that (at least in Great Britain) she has found more female collectors than male, she wonders at the applicability of the concept of fetishism, which has classically attached to men.[65]

For Bal, collecting is an ersatz autobiographical form, with the collector as narrative "agent" and her objects telling the tale.[66] Thus, "collecting is a story" that "everyone needs to tell."[67] Drawing on the work of Pearce, Bal mentions sixteen other broad motives for the practice: "leisure, aesthetics, competition, risk, fantasy, a sense of community, prestige, domination, sensual gratification, sexual foreplay, desire to reframe objects, the pleasing rhythm of sameness and difference, the desire to achieve perfection, extending the self, reaffirming the body, producing gender-identity, [and] achieving immortality."[68] Additionally, Pearce speaks of collecting as a playful act[69] as well as one that (in its reframing of objects) has inventive impulses.[70] "The collector's aesthetic disposition," she notes, "engages in an artist's play with his world."[71]

Geraghty sees collecting not as an isolating act, as do some theorists, but one that involves communication with others. As he remarks (in speaking of media fans), "Once collected, . . . objects become talking points and allow for social exchange between individuals as they become highly valued and desirable within the wider fan community."[72] Finally, Belk finds that "collections can say things about us that it would be socially unacceptable to express aloud";[73] thus, a Jewish person may not wish to admit that she has collected Egyptian Revival jewelry emblazoned with images of the Pharoah (as have I), or a Black

An Egyptian Revival brooch decorated with the head of the Pharaoh (ca. 1920s–early 1930s) from the author's collection

person to admit that she has collected Aunt Jemima cookie jars. Here, the credit sequence of Spike Lee's 2000 film *Bamboozled* (about some frustrated Black writers who propose a television minstrel show and are shocked when it is optioned and successful) seems especially relevant, as it is illustrated with racist memorabilia.

For Belk, regardless of psychological motivation, there are two basic types of collectors. Type A "employs affective criteria to choose items" but has "no sense of a series needing completion." Alternatively, Type B "uses cognitive criteria to choose items that add to a series and help improve their knowledge rather than the beauty of the collection."[74]

There is a final issue to consider in the discourse of collecting—how the collection itself is organized and the rationale for its constitution. According to Brenda Danet and Tamar Katriel there are five basic strategies. The first involves "completing a series or set." This could entail collecting "all of something" (e.g., multiple editions of a single book) or "exemplars of subcategories" (e.g., one of each book written by Ernest Hemingway). The second strategy involves "filling a space"

The author reflected in the mirror behind a group of her glass vases, candlesticks, and bowls displayed on a living room shelf (e.g., collecting enough decorative glass pieces to fill a particular display cabinet). A third involves "creating a visually pleasing, harmonious display" (e.g., arranging those pieces in an aesthetic fashion). The latter two techniques are ones I employ in positioning my collection of my 1930s–50s American glass vases, candlesticks, and bowls on a shelf in my living room. The fourth entails "manipulating the scale of objects" (e.g., collecting only miniatures). Finally, the fifth strategy involves "aspiring to perfect objects" (e.g., collecting only mint-condition items or collecting progressively more flawless items of a certain type).[75]

As this review of theoretical tracts has made clear, there is no single type of collector, motivation for collecting, or collection, a point that will be obvious in the personal essays that follow.

SURVEYING THE LITERATURE: FILM AND MEDIA COLLECTING

While there has been no significant work on personal collecting by film and media scholars, there have been some articles or books on relevant collections of others. Here, I will first consider those in the popular press.

In 1970, historian Kalton C. Lahue published a how-to book, *Collecting Classic Films*, on acquiring works from the silent era through the 1930s.[76] It came out at a time when 16 mm films were available for rental to schools and community groups, and movies in both that gauge and 8 mm were obtainable for purchase. So it was possible for someone without great wealth to amass a significant film collection. As Lahue notes, "Rich man, poor man, young or old—it matters little. Classic films have become the newest objects of a leisure-oriented society."[77] The introduction to the volume by Frank Leon Smith hails the reader encouragingly: "You are about to embark on a hobby which will bring you many hours of enjoyment. . . . You will acquire new knowledge and an insight into the spirit that made America loved, respected, and even feared across the globe."[78] Lahue informs us that at the time of publication about fifty thousand people in the United States and Canada collected classic films. Furthermore, "Countless others around the world also collect, giving this rapidly growing hobby a world-wide fraternity of interest."[79] The various chapters of the volume consider film reproduction and size;

the projector and related equipment; care, repair, and storage of films; adding color to the classics (with color wheels); and adding sound to silent movies. There is also a section on purchasing movie memorabilia and three appendices that list classic film distributors, sources of musical scores, and selected works of film history.

In considering the world of 16 mm film collectors, I cannot help but recall a former professor of mine in the New York University Department of Cinema Studies—William K. Everson—both a historian and a collector. Unlike so many collectors, he was generous with his films—lending them out to students and others without so much as a slip of paper documenting the loan. I remember that his living room (which was outfitted with rows of old wooden theater seats) was lined with shelving stacked with 16 mm prints. I recall going to his apartment on the Upper West Side to borrow a compilation print of Busby Berkeley production numbers for a paper I was writing for class—one that would eventually be published.

But platforms for film viewing radically changed in the decades following the 1970s. A 2005 article in the *New York Times* by Edward Lewine examined a group of people who buy video, media, or time-based art.[80] (Note that this kind of collecting is discussed in more depth in an essay by Erika Balsom in chapter 11.) Primary among them are Pam and Dick Kramlich of San Francisco who own some 250 such works, including some by Nancy Holt and Robert Smithson. Part of the article focuses on the differences between collecting this kind of art and other more traditional types. As Lewine notes of the Kramlich home, "When all the art is activated, the house hums, thrums, squeaks and squawks, gibbers, moans and shouts. In fact, the effect is so overwhelming that the Kramlichs are more or less forced to leave most of their expensive, impeccably chosen collection turned off most of the time." Therefore, such collectors often have blank black screens on the walls of their domiciles. Some have built media rooms for their art, while others have converted garages into screening rooms. The works that collectors tend to keep activated are often calm, meditative pieces. An interview with Pam Kramlich (by Rachel Corbett) also appears in a 2013 issue of *Artspace*.[81]

But by far the greatest number of books or articles on media collecting involve movie memorabilia. *Starstruck: The Wonderful World of Movie Memorabilia* by Robert Heide and John Gilman offers both personal remembrances of collecting, an encyclopedia of types of things collected, and a discussion of the movies and stars around whom collections are most often built.[82] Author Robert Heide discusses his childhood in New Jersey, his frequent trips to the movies, and his collection of star-laden Dixie Cup lids and "autographed" pictures of actors. The lives of other collectors are also featured (e.g., Jo Ann Janzen, a member of the [Shirley] Temple Collectors Club).[83] Most interesting is the chapter "Kenneth Anger, Film Mystic, Valentino Collector Extraordinaire."[84] Anger is deemed the "true collector as artist whose primary concern is not for the value of the thing collected but for the inherent magic that can emanate from Hollywood memorabilia."[85] We learn of how his collection is "artfully arranged" in his Manhattan apartment and that it contains such items as a *Son of the Sheik* lamp, a 1930 Valentino calendar, a Valentino slot machine, and a Valentino box of cigars.[86] Other sections of the book concern various types of collectibles: movie posters, lobby cards, press books, souvenir programs, campaign books, scene stills, dolls, autographs, toys, comic books, tin boxes, and so forth. Among the stars featured as icons of collectability are Greta Garbo, Jean Harlow, Carole Lombard, Bette Davis, Joan Crawford, Marilyn Monroe, and James Dean.

A September 1995 piece in the *Los Angeles Times* discusses how the chain restaurant Planet Hollywood decorates each of its branches with authentic movieland artifacts. The Beverly Hills location, for instance, contains a jacket worn by Charles Chaplin in *The Great Dictator* (Charles Chaplin, 1940), costumes worn by Clark Gable and Vivian Leigh in *Gone with the Wind* (Victor Fleming, 1939), an ensemble worn by Rita Hayworth in *Gilda* (Charles Vidor, 1946), and a carousel horse from *Mary Poppins* (Charles Vidor, 1964). The article also notes how collecting such materials can be a high-stakes pursuit, with the red slippers from *The Wizard of Oz* (Victor Fleming, 1939) having sold for a six-figure sum.[87]

A year later, a *New York Times* article, "Movie Memorabilia: Every Little Souvenir is Collectible," remarks on how the market for such items "grows with each new film release," reporting that "within the past five years . . . prices for collectibles in this genre have increased sharply." Especially popular at this time were autographs of Hollywood greats (like Humphrey Bogart) and contemporary stars (like Tom Cruise). Also desirable were *Star Wars* action figures, old Mickey Mouse pocket watches, and costumes and props from both classic and contemporary films (e.g., the white suit worn by John Travolta in *Saturday Night Fever* [John Badham, 1977]).[88]

A 2003 piece in *Variety* notes how "auctions thrive on [the] hunger for [movie] memorabilia." Author Ben Fritz sees three factors as leading to a growth in collecting such materials: the introduction of auction internet sites, more careful accounting by studios of their property, and growing awareness among film executives that their "detritus" is worth a lot to fans. In terms of genre, often the most dedicated collectors are aficionados of horror and science fiction. Summing up, Doug Haase says, "Hollywood has done an extremely good job of marketing movie magic, so when you have a piece of it in your home, it's as much a great conversation piece as memorabilia."[89]

A 2004 article in the *Los Angeles Business Journal* discusses how eBay has become a prime venue for the auction of movie props. Thus, for instance, Twentieth Century Fox has sold items there from *Planet of the Apes* (Franklin J. Schaffner, 1968) and *Moulin Rouge* (Baz Luhrmann, 2001). Evidently, the company Bidmachine manages the auctions for Fox and other corporations. Selling items on eBay not only provides revenue for studios but also publicity for their movies.[90]

Daniel Cohen's *The Official Price Guide to Movie Autographs* (2004) falls into the category of a how-to book about memorabilia collecting.[91] It contains detailed chapters on the history of autograph collecting and guidelines for determining the value of one, starting a collection of them, authenticating them, and preserving them. It also attends to a range of classical-era stars (e.g., James Dean, Greta Garbo, Jean Harlow) and the legacy of their signed letters or photographs.

A 2012 piece in the Arts section of the *New York Times* presents an interview with the rock group Metallica's lead singer, Kirk Hammett, about his collection of horror movie memorabilia—which includes films, posters, costumes, dolls, masks, and original artwork. Some of it has been reproduced in the book *Too Much Horror Business* published by Abrams.[92]

A 2013 article in the *San Fernando Business Journal* focuses on Joe Maddalena, who founded and manages Profiles in History, a business that sells movie costumes, photos, and props. An auction in December 2012 raised nearly $4 million. He also collaborated on two seasons of the television reality show *Hollywood Treasure* (discussed further below). According to him, most of his movie artifacts come directly from the studios, the costume houses that supply them, and film actors. He sells to collectors not only in the United States but all over the world as well.[93]

A 2016 article by David Goran in *The Vintage News* discusses the case of Forrest J. Ackerman who, during his lifetime, amassed a collection of thousands of objects associated with the horror, fantasy and science fiction film genres. Furthermore, he housed them in a succession of Los Angeles homes that he converted into informal museums which he periodically opened to the public. It is estimated that from 1951 to 2002, some fifty thousand fans visited there. Between 1958–1983, he also published the magazine *Famous Monsters of Filmland*.[94]

Clearly, to be valuable, movie memorabilia must be authentic, but unfortunately there are always numerous fakes up for sale. In a 2018 article in *The Hollywood Reporter*, Gary Baum confronted this problem—one that has become especially critical as the popularity of such collecting has skyrocketed. "Hollywood collectibles," he reports, "are on the verge of a major wave of canonization in the permanent displays of L.A.'s Academy Museum of Motion Pictures and Lucas Museum of Narrative Art."[95] He remains amazed that, while wealthy collectors scrupulously investigate the provenance of other items that they consider for purchase, with Hollywood memorabilia they do not—perhaps due to their nostalgic longing for these objects and their "own aching desire to believe."

Though many purveyors of Hollywood treasures remain anonymous, one well-known individual was screen actress Debbie Reynolds, who owned a famed collection of precious movie costumes that she began in the 1970s. It included Charlie Chaplin's bowler hat, the ruby red slippers and cotton dress from *The Wizard of Oz*, Scarlett O'Hara's "drapery" dress from *Gone with the Wind* and Marilyn Monroe's halter-neck outfit from *The Seven Year Itch* (Billy Wilder, 1955). For decades, she attempted to find a museum to house the collection, but a deal was never struck. Finally, in 2011, some of Reynold's costumes were auctioned off to private individuals.[96] Years later, with plans to build the Academy Museum of Motion Pictures in Hollywood, the industry was suddenly anxious to purchase her remaining collection, which still included her own iconic costumes from *Singin' in the Rain* (Stanley Donen and Gene Kelly, 1952) as well as screen garments created for Mary Pickford, Deborah Kerr, and Cyd Charisse and rare memorabilia from classics like *The Maltese Falcon* (John Huston, 1941).[97]

While there has been considerable coverage of film and media collecting in the popular press, there has been little scholarly writing about the topic. A major exception is a section of Barbara Klinger's 2006 book, *Beyond the Multiplex: Cinema, New Technologies and the Home*, which focuses on contemporary DVD collectors—mostly males, whom she deems today's cinephiles.[98] She opines that DVDs are acquired because they are considered visually pristine, and their purchase gives individuals a sense of ownership of materials that were originally restricted. Furthermore, it allows them to classify films as they see fit. She makes much of the aficionados' tendency to purchase special "collectors' editions" (e.g., those distributed by Criterion) and "boxed sets"—both of which offer bonus material (e.g., stills, interviews, trailers, newsreels of premieres)—as well as "directors' cuts." By doing so, collectors cultivate a sense of connoisseurship and membership in an elite group. Klinger asserts that often individuals favor purchasing foreign or silent films that would otherwise be unavailable to them at their local theaters. Also acquired are film "classics," works by established "auteurs," and action- and special-effects-laden movies that show off a collector's cutting-edge home-viewing technology.

A scholarly article on the topic takes the form of a 2016 interview by Timothy P. A. Cooper with Guddu Khan, a collector of Pakistani film memorabilia from the 1960s and '70s—the heyday of that nation's film production.[99] His collection is particularly important since no official

Pakistani film archive exists.[100] Given this, it is not surprising that Khan's material is denigrated within his country, viewed as *raddi,* or scrap.[101] This is due to a rampant sense of cinephobia that obtains in Pakistan.[102] Hence, Khan's acquisition process involves not so much contacting other collectors as dealing with salvage and scrap merchants.[103] His collection has been viewed mostly by those actors to whom he has gifted packets of material related to their careers (posters, clippings, photographs, press kits, etc.). On at least one occasion, however, through pressure from the Karachi Alliance de Française, parts of his collection were displayed publicly.[104]

A second relevant scholarly interview was published in *The Moving Image* in 2017 (though it took place in 2005–6). In that piece, Ed Carter (a curator at the Academy Film Archive) interviews the late film historian and preservationist David Shephard about his life's work. As part of the broad-ranging discussion, Carter asks Shephard about the history of his film collecting. Shephard recalls that as a child in New Jersey he was an avid film viewer and owned a few prints that he had purchased from vendors like National Cinema Service, Abbe Films, Blackhawk Films, Crawford Film Service, and Rieger's Camera Store.[105] His collecting habit continued through college and into adult life, which included a variety of jobs in the media world (e.g., teaching film at Penn State and working with Peter Bogdanovich on *Directed by John Ford* [1971]). Like many, however, Shephard had ambivalent feelings about amassing a collection: "A couple of times I either gave away or sold most of my film collection, but I made the mistake of keeping—'Well, I think I'll keep fifty films'—so that if somebody comes over, and we decide we want to see a movie, there'll be something to look at. But you put those fifty films in a dark room—and they breed! And soon, there's a thousand of them again. Then it's time to dispose of the collection again."[106] Eventually, he gave a large donation of films to the University of Southern California. When, later, he visited the archives, he had mixed feelings about ever having owned the films:

I was down at USC earlier this week looking for a film that I need and they can't find. And standing in this vault with an enormous number of films was very depressing. It was as if some other person from some other life had invested such passion—not to mention money—in acquiring all these films, which hadn't really been in my physical possession for twenty years. I looked at them and said, "Did I do this? How could this be? Who was I?" It just seemed as if it was the product of a different mind. . . . I no longer can see my nature in that collection.[107]

In 2018, Anthony Slide, author of some sixty books on film history, published *Magnificent Obsession: The Outrageous History of Film Buffs, Collectors, Scholars, and Fanatics*. Part of the volume deals with the history of media-related collecting, the types of material collected, the publications addressed to collectors, and the stores in which such memorabilia could be purchased.[108] Thus, he considers the tie-in materials so popular in the classical film era (e.g., Famous Film Star cards enclosed in British cigarette packs), the strategies of autograph hounds, the newsletters/magazines aimed at film collectors (*National Screen Service, 8mm Collector, Classic Film Collector, Big Reel, Movie Collector's World*), and the establishments oriented to film book and memorabilia enthusiasts (e.g., Larry Edmunds and Collectors Bookstore in Los Angeles).[109] He also discusses famous scholars (Everson) and actors (e.g., Roddy McDowall, Rock Hudson) who were collectors of movies and film-related material.[110]

Another piece written by Peter Jewell and published in *Film History*, speaks personally about a collection of "film fiction" that he amassed with his friend, the late filmmaker Bill Douglas.[111] Under this rubric, Jewell considers a variety of subcategories of the form: books of the film (reprints or novelizations of movies), film fiction by literary greats (e.g., Nathanael West's *The Day of the Locusts*), crime fiction set in Hollywood (e.g., Joseph Wambaugh's *The Glitter Dome*), movie-related children's books and comics (e.g., Lee Hope's *The Moving Picture Girls* or *The Charles Chaplin Scream Book*), romances about Hollywood (e.g., Berta Ruck's *A Star in Love*), Hollywood-themed science fiction (e.g., Harry Harrison's *The Technicolor Time Machine*), and movieland romans à clef (e.g., F. Scott Fitzgerald's *The*

Last Tycoon). Jewell asserts that film fiction is an understudied aspect of the broader institution of cinema.

There have been a handful of other scholarly publications on collectors of media-related material, several of which are included in this volume (e.g., those by Leah M. Kerr on Black film collecting, Josh Stenger on collectors of *Buffy the Vampire Slayer* memorabilia, and Erika Balsom on how limited-edition films and art videos began to be collected in the 1990s). (See chapters 10–12 in this volume.)

THE MEDIA LANDSCAPE: THE IMAGE OF THE COLLECTOR ONSCREEN

Given the cultural fascination with collecting, it is not surprising that beyond print formats, the subject has entered the realm of movies and television, though not always concerning media acquisition specifically. In each of the works discussed below, *an image of the collector is presented*, although the import of collecting varies from peripheral to central by title.

The Collector in Fiction Feature Films

One movie that Lincoln Geraghty highlights is *The 40-Year-Old Virgin* (Judd Apatow, 2005), a comedy whose main character, Andy Stitzer (Steve Carell) is an avid collector of toys (many of which are linked to movies or television programs). His type of collection relates to his portrayal as a somewhat juvenile, sexually inexperienced nerd. In many scenes, aspects of his collection are pictured, including action figures, boxed toys, and life-size movie cutouts. They are stored on the floor of his apartment, on shelves in his bathroom, by his bed, and in various cabinets throughout. In some sequences, we see him repairing tiny action figures while looking through a magnifying glass. Specific toys are mentioned by name, including Aquaman, Iron Man, and Steve Austin (the latter from *The Six Million Dollar Man* [1973–78]). Significantly, when he finally has a girlfriend and they begin to make love on his bed, boxes of his toys fall to the ground. He is so upset about possibly damaging them that he stops his romancing, and a fight between the couple breaks out. Eventually, the two reconcile, and because his girlfriend runs a store that boxes items to sell on eBay, Andy decides to auction off his collection—leading to significant financial gain. Geraghty finds a positive message in the film's narrative arc in that it "stresses that there is real worth in the collecting activities that fans carry out and in which they invest heavily. . . . While Stitzer starts out a loner, confirming the fan stereotype, his transformation to professional collector and businessman suggests that being a fan is about capital consumption and defining an identity and social life with others through the popular culture texts on offer in contemporary society."[112]

Several other films deal with more traditional collectors of items recognized by society to have cultural value. The Italian drama *Conversation Piece* (Luchino Visconti, 1974) concerns an aging, retired American professor and art collector (Burt Lancaster) residing in Rome. He lives alone in an old, luxe residence that is dark and seemingly airless. He is surrounded by Old Masters on the walls and myriad books on ubiquitous shelving. The title of the film refers in part to a specific genre of artwork like some of those he owns: informal group portraits of people engaged in genteel conversation or some other activity, very often outdoors.

In the first scene, we see him examining a painting with a magnifying glass that a gallerist has brought for him to consider purchasing. Into his calm and solitary life comes the Marchesa Brumonti (Silvana Mangano) who insists on renting his upstairs apartment even though it is not for lease. Barging in anyway, she arrives with her entourage—her daughter, Lietta (Claudia Marsani); her daughter's fiancé, Stefano (Stefano Patrizi); and her much younger lover, Konrad (Helmut Berger). They are all obnoxious and spoil the tranquility of the professor's life (renovating the upstairs apartment without permission, having orgies in his apartment, talking on his phone, eating his food, and blasting music). Thrown into the mix are some entirely unconvincing discussions of art and politics, and against all odds, the lonely professor seems to adopt the group (and particularly Konrad) as his ersatz "family." The film portrays collectors stereotypically as isolated individuals sealed hermetically in their interior domains, more comfortable with things than people. "I'm accustomed to being alone," says the professor at one point. "The sense of another person in my house disturbs me." Further-more, on one occasion, he talks of how he prefers to be "surrounded by the calm people in his paintings." *New York Times* reviewer Vincent Canby called the film "fatuous" and "a disaster, the kind that prompts giggles from victims in the audience."[113]

The Thomas Crown Affair (John McTiernan, 1999) is also about an art collector but a different kind from the one represented in the Visconti film. Rather than a lonely hermit, Thomas Crown (Pierce Brosnan) is a suave, charming playboy who owns an art acquisitions company and whose home is liberally adorned with costly paintings and sculptures. Not only is he a collector, but he is also a shrewd art thief. We first see him in a museum, admiring works in the impressionist gallery. On the same day, a heist takes place there, and although it is foiled midway, a famous Monet painting is stolen. We later see Crown in his home, removing a Monet from his briefcase and hiding it on a wall behind a secret mobile panel. In a later scene, at a reception, museum officials thank Crown for donating one of his own paintings (a Pissarro) to fill the spot left vacant by the purloined Monet. The police and a beautiful insurance agent investigate the crime, and the latter, Catherine Banning (Renee Russo), begins an affair with Crown. When she and the cops rummage through his home, they find what they think is the lost Monet, but it turns out to be a fake. Eventually, it is learned that Crown returned the Monet (concealed beneath the painting he loaned to the museum) but then stole another (one conveniently not covered by Banning's company). He gifts it to Banning, but she returns it to the police. As the film closes, the couple fly off together to distant lands.

A collection of another sort marks the French film *Summer Hours* (Olivier Assayas, 2008), which concerns Hélène (Edith Scob), an aging matriarch who is heir to a treasure trove of expensive Art Nouveau objects. During scenes of a family birthday celebration with her extended family at her home, the camera shows us specific items in her beloved collection: a wooden desk and a vitrine by Louis Majorelle, a vase by Antonin Daum, a Josef Hoffmann cabinet, two decorative panels by Odilon Redon, a Georg Jensen silver tea service, and a Christofle silver tray. After Hélène dies, the drama revolves around whether or not her children wish to possess these heirlooms or give them to a state museum (for tax purposes). Ultimately, they choose the latter option—their aesthetic tastes differing from that of their mother and their financial situations benefiting from a donation. Thus, the film makes clear how a cherished collection belonging to one individual may not be as dear to those who inherit it, underscoring the very personal nature of collecting. As Belk asserts, "Post-mortem distribution problems are significant to collectors and their families."[114] In a final scene, we see the Majorelle desk housed in the Art Nouveau section of the Musée d'Orsay as visitors pass by.

Some films about collectors cast those individuals as extremely perverse or dangerous. One of the first of these is the thriller *The Collector* (William Wyler, 1965). It concerns a shy and lonely working-class young man, Freddie Clegg (played against traditional casting by the handsome Terence Stamp) who has collected butterflies since his youth and won awards for so doing. He is a misfit and a recluse, and a flashback shows him mocked by his fellow workers in a bank because of his eccentric hobby. He wins a great deal of money in a "pool" (or lottery) and buys an old Tudor house in a rather deserted area outside of London that has an attached stone shed with a cellar. We see him stalk and then kidnap a beautiful woman, Miranda Grey (Samantha Eggar), whom he holds hostage there. He does not hurt or molest her (because he "respects" her too much) but wants to keep her captive so that she can get to know and love him. Of course, she tries numerous times to escape but ends up dying and being buried in the grounds outside his home—boxed like one of his prized insects. Clearly, here, the image of the collector is a grotesque one—that of a repressed, virginal man who believes that he can force a woman's affections. Parallels are, of course, made to his capturing beautiful butterflies, whose fate is to lie pinned and dead in glass cases. He is, in fact, upset when he shows his collection to Miranda; she finds it only morbid and sad. Freddie's mode of collecting also speaks to Walter Benjamin's notion of the interior as being the center of a collector's world—enclosed, airless, and barred from reality. To this end, all windows in Freddie's home are boarded up and all doors locked to prevent Miranda's exit.

The Collector (Marcus Dunstan, 2009) is also about a man who imprisons humans, but it is a far darker movie than Wyler's and fits firmly within the horror genre. Arkin (Josh Stewart) is a handyman at work on a huge mansion. He desperately needs money to help his ex-wife pay off her debts and support their daughter. Along with another man, he cooks up a scheme to enter the mansion when the family is on vacation, open their safe, and steal its contents. He enters the house without any initial problem but then begins to hear footsteps and screaming. He learns that the family never left the home and instead are being held prisoners of a serial murderer known as the Collector (Juan Fernande). The Collector generally kills all victims save one that he "collects" and keeps in a red box. We know this because in the opening shots of the film, before being introduced to Arkin, we have already seen a couple arrive home surprised to find a red box in their bedroom. Within short order, an intruder clasps his hand around the man's face as the film cuts elsewhere. Later, we find him in the selfsame red box.

Upon hearing the noises, Arkin abandons his plan for theft and tries to escape, finding various victims along the way, chained, bound, and bloody. He soon realizes that the entire house is booby-trapped with wires that, when tripped, cause impalement by knives, nails, or fishhooks. He fights against the black-clothed and -masked Collector and eventually gets away along with the family's youngest child, who has been hidden all this time. He is placed in an ambulance, but it overturns and the Collector captures him and sequesters him in a red box—augmenting his ongoing human collection.

This is a rather bad horror film of the "torture porn" variety with an illogical plot full of myriad holes. Despite its negative critical reception, Dunstan was able to direct a sequel—*The Collection* (2012)—in which Arkin escapes from the box and is enlisted to help save a young woman who has been confined by the Collector in a hotel. Evidently, a third film in the series, *The Collected*, is currently in the works.

Beyond the fiction feature films discussed above, there are others covered in depth in a chapter of Kara Andersen's *Immaterial Materiality: Collecting in Live-Action Film, Animation, and Digital Games*. As she writes, "Roman Polanski's *The Ninth Gate* (1999) exhibits fears about the obsessive nature of collectors in a neo-noir story about a satanic book collector. . . . Steven Spielberg's *Indiana Jones* series (1989–2008) takes a different tactic, centering on the tomb raider extraordinaire (despite Jones's assertions to the contrary) who is not himself a collector, merely an 'obtainer' of rare objects for museums."[115]

The Collector in Documentary Films

Finally, there are a few feature-length documentaries about collecting, though the nature of the act profiled in each varies tremendously. *Herb & Dorothy* (Megumi Sasaki, 2008) concerns the Vogels, a couple of modest means (he was a postal clerk, she a librarian) who managed to accrue one of the most important contemporary American art collections in history. They began frequenting art galleries and studios in the 1960s, befriending artists before they had become famous. Working within a budget and paying cash for paintings, gradually they built a significant collection of minimalist art and eventually donated some forty-seven hundred works to the National Gallery. A sequel to the film by the same director, *Herb & Dorothy 50 × 50* (2013), begins where the last one ended and follows the couple as they donate ten of their works to a series of different museums in each of the fifty states.

On a more macabre note, the film *Collectors* (Julian Hobbs, 2000) profiles two serial killer enthusiasts, Rick Staton (a funeral director by trade) and Tobias Allen, who amass art and artifacts relating to such murderers. The two have collaborated in curating several gallery shows of serial killer art, and we see one such installation featuring the paintings and drawings of Elmer Wayne Henley. Attending the event are both other collectors and curiosity seekers and also those who vehemently protest it. One man buys a $600 work in which Henley (a molester, torturer, and killer of young boys) pictures a nude boy. The purchaser then proceeds to burn the canvas on the street outside the gallery. We also hear from Henley himself, his mother, victim rights advocates, and the father of one of Henley's victims. Much of the film, however, focuses on Staton's collecting habits (contacting imprisoned serial killers and asking them to send him various items, such as artworks or, in the case, of Charles Manson, a lock of hair). Staton keeps many of the items he procures for his own collection but also exhibits or sells them—giving the prisoners a share of the profits. We watch as both Staton and Allen take a road trip to Texas to visit some of the sites of Henley's (and his collaborator, Dean Corll's) crimes—a candy store where the latter lured his prey and a boat shed under which he hid his deceased victims. At each location, they take soil samples to add to their collections. We also see them visit the house in Los Angeles where Sharon Tate was murdered; there, they steal a brick, rationalizing it because the house is soon to be demolished. The documentary considers two contrasting points of view—one voiced by Allen and Staton that a fascination with the macabre is normal and harmless and another expressed by opponents that the impulse is sick and exploitive.

THE COLLECTOR IN TELEVISION PROGRAMS

In addition to films that feature collectors, there are also television shows that do so. Geraghty mentions the character of Comic Book Guy on the animated series *The Simpsons* (1989–) and observes, "As seen in numerous episodes his shop, The Android's Dungeon, is home to a vast array of comics, toys and other media merchandise that are, more often than not, objects from his own personal collection. They are on display but not for sale."[116] In a 1999 episode (season 11, episode 4), much like the male characters in the 1965 and 2009 films *The Collector*, Comic Book Guy seeks to acquire a human being. He attends a *Xena: Warrior Princess* convention and abducts Lucy Lawless (the actress who plays the heroine of the series), not understanding that she is a performer and not the fictional character. He then displays her in his home in a mylar pouch alongside his other collectibles.[117] Bart and Lisa Simpson show up to rescue Lawless, and Comic Book Guy tries to fight them off. Among the weapons he uses is his *Star Wars* light saber, and he is distressed when he realizes that because it has now been unboxed, it will no longer be worth very much. Eventually, Bart and Lisa triumph and Lawless is saved.

However, most of the television programs about collecting fall within the reality TV genre. The Syfy channel website advertises *Hollywood*

Treasure (2010–) in the following way: "Get an inside view from the life of Joe Maddalena, owner of Profiles in History and the world's largest auctioneer of original movie, television and pop culture relics. *Hollywood Treasure* follows Joe as he navigates his way through the intricate world of collecting showbiz and pop culture memorabilia, from the Wicked Witch of the West hat and the vintage *Chitty Bang* car to Mary Poppins' carpet bag and other unforgettable props and costumes."[118] Thus, it is a show specifically about collecting media-related materials, starring the man whom we previously discussed as featured in a 2013 newspaper article.

In one episode (Season 2, #6, 2012), Joe Maddalena visits Greg Cannom, a makeup and special effects artist who worked on the 1992 film *Bram Stoker's Dracula* (Francis Ford Coppola). He is ready to auction off his archive of maquettes, facial masks, wigs, decapitated character heads, and full body suits from the movie. Eventually, it nets him $82,500. In another segment, Maddalena spends $5,000 to purchase a stunt sword from *Braveheart* (Mel Gibson, 1995), unsure of its authenticity. When it is proven to be legitimate, he auctions it for $45,000. Finally, Maddalena convinces a movie poster collector to sell his one-sheets for such movies as *Rear Window* (Alfred Hitchcock, 1954), *To Catch a Thief* (Alfred Hitchcock, 1955), *The Incredible Shrinking Man* (Jack Arnold, 1957), *Goldfinger* (Guy Hamilton, 1964), and *Singin' in the Rain*—netting some $42,000 at auction.

Similarly, the lineup of the MeTV network includes *Collectors Call* (2018–). As its website proclaims, "The 13-episode unscripted series will introduce you to some of the biggest collectors of pop culture memorabilia in the country."[119] In one segment, Maria Spadafora describes her fascination with 1970s American television memorabilia, which harkens back to her youthful viewing habits. She shows off her stash of *Starsky and Hutch* (1975–79) dolls and fanzines; *The Six Million Dollar Man* action figures, backpack radios, and remote-control cars; as well as a pink *Charlie's Angels* (1976–81) toy car. She states that her eleven-year-old son now watches and enjoys reruns of the programs she loved.

Collection Complete (2018–19) is a reality series (produced by Gemr, an online e-commerce social platform for collectors) that provides a detailed look into the lives of filmmakers and artists and the collections that inspire their work.[120] In one episode, talent agent and producer Sean Clark talks about his collection of horror movie paraphernalia. He is proudest of his possession of the chainsaw used in *Texas Chainsaw Massacre 2* (Tobe Hooper, 1986), which was autographed for him by Bob Elmore, the actor who played Leatherface during most of the movie. He opines that a collection is only "complete" when you give up on it. In another episode, actress and producer Micheine Pitt discusses her collection of materials related to *The Creature from the Black Lagoon* (Jack Arnold, 1954)—including a full-size resin replica of the Creature (which she unboxes on camera). She claims that at one time she also had a *Creature*-themed pinball machine, which she sold and regrets losing. She remarks on how she cannot foresee the end of her collecting practice.

Perhaps the reductio ad absurdum of the collector is the hoarder, who takes the practice to the extreme—often deludedly collecting things "with a pretense of utilitarian purpose."[121] Hoarders also fail to discriminate between objects, having no clear system for organizing or displaying them. The A&E television show *Hoarders* (2009–) documents such individuals. However, some hoarders do "specialize" in certain types of material in ways that approach the logic of a collector. Thus, for example, season 10, episode 2 (2019) focuses on Dale, a man who has crammed his Alaska property with over a hundred vehicles.

CHAPTER INTRODUCTIONS

Personal Collections

In the first nine chapters, consisting of original essays, scholars discuss their own collections and how they have informed their personal lives as well as their experiences as teachers and researchers in the area of film and media studies. These articles give us the opportunity to glimpse the manner in which scholars develop ideas for their professional work, sometimes drawing on their personal attraction to certain types of materials.

In chapter 1, "Collecting Doris Day Magazines . . . and More," Tamar Jeffers McDonald discusses her collection of movie fan magazines, which began with a "casual purchase" of *Movie Life* while researching publications referencing Doris Day for her doctoral work. She soon realized, however, that beyond examining particular articles, it was important to understand the magazine as a whole and the article's placement in relation to ads, other pieces, illustrations, photographs, captions, choice of graphics, font, and color palette. The employment of her collection of movie magazines has become a vital part of McDonald's publishing and pedagogy and she has argued for their value as a primary and legitimate research tool in film and media studies.

In chapter 2, "Material Girl: Design Objects Collected and Screened," I discuss my collections of Art Deco and Art Nouveau objects, which started purely for pleasure and comprise decorative pieces (e.g., vases, statuettes, candlesticks, bowls, ashtrays) and jewelry (e.g., brooches, earrings, rings). Beyond being valued as beloved objets d'art and, in some cases, fashion accessories, these items eventually functioned as artifacts of research for my two books on the role of Art Deco and Art Nouveau in cinematic production design—providing illustrations of the aesthetic qualities of the movement. In addition, these collections have influenced my writing, teaching, and lecturing on broader issues of the ties between cinema and art and design history.

In chapter 3, "My Record Collection and the Making of a Discipline," Krin Gabbard discusses how he began collecting jazz recordings as a teenager in the era of vinyl LPs—amassing some ten thousand by the time he was a professor of literature and film. It then occurred to him to merge his love of jazz with his professional life and consider it within an academic framework, and he published two volumes on the subject—one taking the perspective of its place within the cinema. Though he eventually sold his material collection (due to problems of space and weight), he now has access to all the recordings he desires in digital form, technology shifting his listening habits.

In chapter 4, "Animate Objects," Joanne Bernardi discusses her collection of objects and ephemera related to her teaching and researching of Japanese culture and film history. It includes souvenir film programs, glass lantern slides, stereographs, advertisements, sheet music, tourism materials, small-gauge films and postcards. These items help animate the vision of twentieth-century Japan pictured in the movies that she teaches and writes about. With the help of institutions like the George Eastman Museum, she has utilized her collection to create a vast collaborative digital archive (Re-envisioning Japan: Japan as Destination in 20th Century Visual and Material Culture) that is employed by students and researchers of Japanese culture and cinema.

In chapter 5, "Godzilla on the Shelf: Spectacle and the Gigantic in Miniature," Mark Best focuses on three interrelated topics concerning collecting giant monster toys and figures (e.g., Godzilla, Gamera). First is the relationship of the toys to the films from which they are licensed and the basic assumption of play as an extension of the film's story line into the everyday lives of children who create their own narratives. Second, he examines some of the contrasts suggested in the tension between "play" and "display" that come with collecting toys and action figures, by not only children but also adults. Third, he frames his discussion within the context of his own monster toy collection and academic work.

In chapter 6, "Ape and Essence," Adam Lowenstein discusses a collection that grew from a preteen fixation on *Planet of the Apes*, a film made before he was born but that he saw on TV. Taken with the film, he tracked down all the film posters, trading cards, comic books, model kits, and action figures he could find in an attempt to turn his childhood bedroom into his personal version of the planet. Lowenstein sees his later scholarly interests in fantasy, horror, and surrealism as prefigured in his choice of youthful collection, which he now keeps in the basement of his home and has begun to introduce to his daughter.

In chapter 7, "Collecting and Thinking Generically," Barry Keith Grant reveals certain similarities in his collecting habits to Gabbard since, for a time, he too collected records—though his stash included rock 'n' roll as well as jazz. But he also collected comics ranging in type from superhero (*Superman*), to humorous (*Mad* magazine), to horror (*Weird Tales*), to literary (*Classics Illustrated*) and was as fascinated by the aesthetics of the comic artwork as by their narratives, an interest that prepared him for looking closely at film. Two through-lines in Grant's collecting habits are strongly linked to his later academic work in media studies: a focus on popular culture and on genre studies.

In chapter 8, "To Be Continued: Collecting Comics as Ouroboros / Ouroboros as Comics Collecting," we return to the subject of comics, a medium that has recently gained influence, as has its academic study. Blair Davis's collection, which began in the 1980s, comprises many formats: single issues, fancy hardcovers, and digital editions. He sees collecting as a cyclical process, and over time he has bought, sold, and replaced some of his collection (as finances have dictated) over platforms like eBay. He brings his collection into class for his students to examine and handle. Moreover, he teaches and writes about comics as a medium in their own right as well as their adaptation into blockbuster movies.

In Chapter 9, "The *Lego* Movies, a LEGO Collector, and the Problem with Representations of Collecting in Film," Kara Lynn Andersen takes a two-pronged approach to discussing collecting—analyzing its representation in the movies (in particular, the two LEGO movies) and also examining her own collection of LEGOs and their playful use in a household containing two young children. Andersen finds that most portrayals of collectors in films are negative and apocryphal, and in the LEGO movies, play with such toys is deemed appropriate only for children. This does not square with her own collecting and love of LEGOs over the years, which has continued into adulthood but which contrasts in a frustrating way with the manner in which children engage with them.

Collections of Others

In the three final chapters, reproduced from academic journals, scholars discuss the film- and media-related collections of other individuals. These articles represent prior work in the field, antecedent to the group of original essays published here. They also fill in certain "gaps" in areas not otherwise covered in the volume: Black cinema and television, collections of "memorabilia" (e.g., costuming and props), and collections of video art.

In chapter 10, Leah M. Kerr first quickly summarizes the early history of African Americans' relationship to the cinema as subjects of the camera, moviegoers, and, in rare cases, filmmakers of so-called race movies. She then goes on to highlight several important collectors of memorabilia (e.g., posters, lobby cards) and of films made by and/or featuring Black Americans: Pearl Bowser, Dr. Mayme A. Clayton, and Dr. Henry T. Sampson Jr. In addition to acquiring films (and often saving them from oblivion), several of these individuals (e.g., Bowser and Clayton) have made sure that such rare films are available to the public through festivals and museum screenings. The work of others (like Dr. Sampson) has led to the publication of important source books on African American film.

In chapter 11, "Original Copies: How Film and Video Become Art Objects," Erika Balsom first discusses the sale of film and video as a means of establishing the moving image's viability as an art medium. She then examines the post-1990s boom in collectors purchasing limited-edition films and videos. These formats cultivate rarity and assure owners both the control and uniqueness associated with other prestigious art acquisitions. Finally, she considers the reasons for the ascendance of this collecting model in the 1990s as well as the criticisms that have been directed toward it.

In chapter 12, "Clothes Make the Fan: Fashion and Online Fandom when *Buffy the Vampire Slayer* Goes to eBay," Josh Stenger first examines how the television show *Buffy the Vampire Slayer* (1997–2003), about a high school girl, highlighted fashion and achieved a huge cult fan base. He then discusses how, upon the show's end, Twentieth Century Fox auctioned off the program's props. Objects like candleholders or flowerpots were sold, but the mainstay constituted wardrobe items that fans might display, wear, or role-play with. Stenger sees this auction as an intersection point for online fandom, television, consumerism, and internet collecting.

NOTES

1   Dean R. Snow, "What Academic Doesn't Collect Things?," *Chronicle of Higher Education*, August 9, 2002, www.chronicle.com/article/what-academic-doesnt-collect-things/.

2   "Material Culture," Wikipedia, last edited February 8, 2022, en.wikipedia.org/wiki/Material_culture.

3   *Journal of Material Culture*, journals.sagepub.com/loi/mcua.

4   Bill Brown, "Thing Theory," in "Things," ed. Bill Brown, special issue, *Critical Inquiry* 28, no. 1 (2001): 1–22, 7.

5   Ahmir Questlove Thompson, "Collecting Things as an Act of Devotion," *New York Times*, March 25, 2022, 10.

6   Susan Pearce, "General Preface to Series," in *The Collector's Voice: Contemporary Voices*, vol. 4, ed. Susan Pearce and Paul Martin (London: Routledge, 2002), viii–x, viii.

7   Peter Monaghan, "Collected Wisdom," *Chronicle of Higher Education*, June 28, 2002, www.chronicle.com/article/collected-wisdom/.

8   Werner Muensterberger, *Collecting: An Unruly Passion* (Princeton, NJ: Princeton University Press, 1994), 242.

9   Susan M. Pearce, *Collecting in Contemporary Practice* (London: Sage, 1998), 54.

10   Lucy Fischer, *Designing Women: Cinema, Art Deco, and the Female Form* (New York: Columbia University Press, 2003); and Lucy Fischer, *Cinema by Design: Art Nouveau, Modernism, and Film History* (New York: Columbia University Press, 2003).

11   Muensterberger, *Collecting*, 4 (italics in original).

12   Russell Belk, *Collecting in a Consumer Society* (London: Routledge, 2001), 67.

13   Russell Belk, "Collectors and Collecting," in *Interpreting Objects and Collections*, ed. Susan M. Pearce (London: Routledge, 1994), 317–26, 318.

14   Muensterberger, *Collecting*, 3.

15   Belk, *Collecting*, 73.

16   Susan Stewart, *On Longing, Narratives of the Miniature, the Gigantic, the Souvenir, the Collection* (Baltimore: Johns Hopkins University Press, 1984), 166.

17   Walter Benjamin, *Illuminations*, trans. Harry Zohn (New York: Schocken, 1973), 61, 64.

18   Belk, *Collecting in a Consumer Society*, 65, 72, 92.

19   Belk, 68.

20   Jean Baudrillard, "The System of Collecting," in *The Cultures of Collecting*, ed. John Elsner and Roger Cardinal, (London: Reaktion Books, 1994), 7–24, 23.

21   Susan M. Pearce, "The Urge to Collect," in *Interpreting Objects and Collections*, ed. Susan M. Pearce (London: Routledge, 1994), 158–59, 158.

22   Belk, *Collecting in a Consumer Society*, 68.

23   Muensterberger, *Collecting*, 11.

24   Baudrillard, "System of Collecting," 13.

25   Belk, "Collectors and Collecting," 323.

26   Muensterberger, *Collecting*, 4, 6.

27   Belk, *Collecting in a Consumer Society*, 74.

28   Muensterberger, *Collecting*, 15.

29   Benjamin, *Illuminations*, 60.

30   Walter Benjamin, *Charles Baudelaire: A Lyric Poet in the Era of High Capitalism*, trans. Harry Zohn (London: NLB, 1973), 168, 169.

31   Benjamin, 169.

32   Benjamin, *Illuminations*, 60.

33   Muensterberger, *Collecting*, 4.

34   Baudrillard, "System of Collecting," 12.

35   Belk, "Collectors and Collecting," 317–26, 322.

36   Baudrillard, "System of Collecting," 8.

37   Pearce, *Collecting in Contemporary Practice*, 151.

38   Pearce, 151.

39   Baudrillard, "System of Collecting," 16 (italics in original).

40   Benjamin, *Illuminations*, 60.

41   Pearce, *Collecting in Contemporary Practice*, 155.

42   Belk, "Collectors and Collecting," 320.

43   Pearce, *Collecting in Contemporary Practice*, 158.

44   Mieke Bal, "Telling Objects: A Narrative Perspective on Collecting," in *The Cultures of Collecting*, ed. John Elsner and Roger Cardinal (London: Reaktion Books, 1994), 97–115, 104.

45   "Commodity Fetishism," Oxford Reference, www.oxfordreference.com/view/10.1093/oi/authority.20110810104638104.

46   Russell W. Belk and Melanie Wallendorf, "Of Mice and Men: Gender Identity in Collecting," in *Interpreting Objects and Collections*, ed. Susan M. Pearce (London: Routledge, 1994), 240–53, 241–42.

47   Pearce, *Collecting in Contemporary Practice*, 26, 126.

48   Belk and Wallendorf, "Of Mice and Men," 242.

49   Belk and Wallendorf, 242–43.

50   Belk, *Collecting in a Consumer Society*, 99.

51   Susan M. Pearce, *Museums, Objects and Collections: A Cultural Study* (Leicester: Leicester University Press, 1992), 59.

52   Pearce, *Collecting in Contemporary Practice*, 139, 141.

53   Pearce, 148.

54   Susan M. Pearce, "Collecting Reconsidered," in *Interpreting Objects and Collections*, ed. Susan M. Pearce (London: Routledge, 1994), 195–201, 196.

55   Muensterberger, *Collecting*, 8–9.

56   Muensterberger, 255.

57 Pearce, *Museums, Objects and Collections*, 51.

58 Belk and Wallendorf, "Of Mice and Men," 240.

59 Lincoln Geraghty, *Cult Collectors: Nostalgia, Fandom and Collecting Popular Culture* (Routledge, 2014), 9.

60 Svetlana Boym, quoted in Geraghty, 10.

61 Geraghty, 10.

62 Baudrillard, "System of Collecting," 9–10.

63 Pearce, *Collecting in Contemporary Practice*, 126.

64 Pearce, 126–27.

65 Pearce, 132–33.

66 Bal, "Telling Objects," 99, 101.

67 Bal, 103.

68 Bal, 103.

69 Pearce, *Museums, Objects and Collections*, 50.

70 Pearce, 52.

71 Pearce, 52.

72 Geraghty, *Cult Collectors*, 10.

73 Belk, *Collecting in a Consumer Society*, 90.

74 Belk, "Collectors and Collecting," 320.

75 Brenda Danet and Tamar Katriel, "No Two Alike: Play and Aesthetics in Collecting," *Play and Culture* 2, no. 3 (1989): 253–77, 000.

76 Kalton C. Lahue, *Collecting Classic Films* (New York: American Photographic Book, 1970).

77 Lahue, 11.

78 Frank Leon Smith quoted in Lahue, 10.

79 Lahue, 11.

80 Edward Lewine, "Art That Has to Sleep in the Garage," *New York Times*, June 26, 2005, www.nytimes.com/2005/06/26/arts/design/art-that-has -to-sleep-in-the-garage.html.

81 Rachel Corbett, "Pam Kramlich on Pioneering the Market for Video Art," Artspace, July 3, 2013. www.artspace.com/magazine/interviews_features/ how_i_collect/how_i_collect_pam_kramlich-51428.

82 Robert Heide and John Gilman, *Starstruck: The Wonderful World of Movie Memorabilia* (Garden City, NY: Doubleday), 1986.

83 Heide and Gilman, 24.

84 Heide and Gilman, 90–114.

85 Heide and Gilman, 92.

86 Heide and Gilman, 93.

87 Chuck Crisafulli, "A Hollywood Museum with Mustard, Mayo. Memorabilia: Planet Hollywood May Be the Closest Thing to a Movie Museum

in Film Capital," *Los Angeles Times*, September 19, 1995, www.latimes
.com/archives/la-xpm-1995-09-19-ca-47753-story.html.

88   Barbara Wall, "Movie Memorabilia: Every Little Souvenir Is Collectible," *New York Times*, May 4, 1996, www.nytimes.com/1996/05/04/your
-money/IHT-movie-memorabilia-every-little-souvenir-is-collectible
.html.

89   Ben Fritz, "Bidding Biz: Auctions Thrive on Hunger for Memorabilia,"
Variety, August 31, 2003.

90   Karey Wutkowski, "eBay Economy Makes Bidmachine a Movie of 'Cast-
away' Movie Props," *Los Angeles Business Journal*, May 10, 2004, 3.

91   Daniel Cohen, *The Official Price Guide to Movie Autographs* (n.p.: House
of Collectibles, 2004).

92   Erik Piepenburg, "Movies, Memorabilia and Metallica" *New York Times*,
November 27, 2012, www.nytimes.com/1996/05/04/your-money/IHT
-movie-memorabilia-every-little-souvenir-is-collectible.html.

93   Mark R. Madler, "Real History," *San Fernando Business Journal*, January 7,
2013, 7.

94   David Goran, "Erm, Yeah, the Ackermansion—A Horror Museum Hidden Away in a Private Home," *The Vintage News*, May 23, 2016, https://
www.thevintagenews.com/2016/05/23/erm-yeah-the-ackermansion-a
-horror-museum-hidden-away-in-a-private-home/.

95   Gary Baum, "Real Crimes, Fake Stuff: Taming the Wild West of Movie
Collectibles," *The Hollywood Reporter*, June 6, 2018.

96   Cari Beauchamp, "The Girl with the Golden Wardrobe," *Wall Street
Journal*, May 26, 2011, www.wsj.com/articles/SB1000142405274870373
08045763213517134388800.

97   Brooks Barnes, "Academy Museum Gives Debbie Reynolds Her Due
as a Costume Conservator," November 16, 2020, www.nytimes.com/
2020/11/16/movies/academy-museum-debbie-reynolds-costumes
.html.

98   Barbara Klinger, *Beyond the Multiplex: Cinema, New Technologies and
the Home* (Berkeley: University of California Press, 2006).

99   Timothy P. A. Cooper, "*Raddi* Infrastructure: Collecting Film Memorabilia
in Pakistan: Guddu Khan of Guddu's Film Archive," *Bioscope* 7, no. 2
(2016): 151–71.

100 Cooper, 153.

101 Cooper, 151.

102 Cooper, 153.

103 Cooper, 158.

104 Cooper, 153.

105   Ed Carter and David Shepard, "David Shepard: Excerpts from an Oral History," *The Moving Image* 17, no. 1 (2017): 89–121, 91–92.

106   Carter and Shephard, 99.

107   Carter and Shephard, 99.

108   Anthony Slide, *Magnificent Obsession: The Outrageous History of Film Buffs, Collectors, Scholars, and Fanatics* (Jackson: University Press of Mississippi, 2018).

109   Slide, 34, 135, 137.

110   Slide, 96, 97.

111   Peter Jewell, "Collectors' Tales: A Personal Overview of Film Fiction at Bill Douglas Centre," *Film History* 20, no. 2 (2008): 149–63.

112   Geraghty, *Cult Collectors*, 21.

113   Vincent Canby, "Film Festival: *A Conversation Piece*," *New York Times*, September 27, 1975, timesmachine.nytimes.com/timesmachine/1975/09/27/83680184.html?pageNumber=21.

114   Belk, "Collectors and Collecting," 321.

115   Kara Andersen, *Immaterial Materiality: Collecting in Live-Action Film, Animation, and Digital Games* (PhD diss., University of Pittsburgh, 2009).

116   Geraghty, *Cult Collectors*, 21.

117   Discussed by Geraghty, 21.

118   SyFy channel website, www.syfy.com/hollywoodtreasure (URL inactive).

119   MeTV website, metv.com/shows/collectors-call.

120   *Collection Complete*, Instagram, www.instagram.com/p/B398zrPFM4c/, accessed June 18, 2022.

121   Pearce, "Urge to Collect," 158.

I

PERSONAL COLLECTIONS

1

COLLECTING DORIS DAY MAGAZINES . . . AND MORE

Tamar Jeffers McDonald

IN 2000, I WAS WORKING full-time for a social science journal as an editorial assistant and studying part-time for my doctorate in film at the University of Warwick, with a thesis on Doris Day. My initial investigations into her enduring star persona were beginning to resolve themselves into a more defined single research question: Why was it popularly believed that she always played a virgin? I was pondering both how one would go about crafting a performance that made legible such an invisible quality, a not-yet occurrence, and why critics said this of Day. Having read the not-vast scholarly literature on the star, most of which seemed to take the virginal pose as so obvious it needed no exploration, I felt I needed to find out what was being said about Day when her career was active. When did the aged maiden tag originate, and whence? In seeking to answer this, I found myself one lunchtime on eBay, contemplating the purchase of a movie magazine . . . and my life changed. It sounds dramatic, but buying the May 1961 issue of *Movie Life* turned out to alter the way I looked at Day, historical evidence, and stardom; I can trace back to that single acquisition a major career change and, eventually, innovations in the way I teach, research, and enjoy stars, Hollywood, and movies themselves.

It seems important to acknowledge that my first exposure to movie magazines was to *Movie Life*, an American monthly, but never the most popular or glamorous of publications; as I removed my purchase from its packing, I noted the rather poor-quality paper and smudgy pictures. Later I would realize that this issue from 1961 was published when the heyday of the movie magazines was over: my first purchase was not from the golden age of the fan periodicals, which I would date from 1914 to 1950, when the spectacular oil painting of one fabulous Hollywood star tended to grace the cover of the best-selling magazines *Motion Picture*, *Photoplay*, and the like. On my issue of *Movie Life*, Elvis and Doris Day share the cover space, while five lines of text in various fonts, sizes, and colors all jostle for attention, blurting out names I didn't then know. With its top headline—"Gulager: 50 New Pix/McBain-Hamilton Life Stories"[1]—it seems almost to be in some kind of code. And then the color photographs of Elvis and Doris appear to have been treated to make them more intense; though they have the same blue eyes, their arrangement on the cover seems to set them up as Manichean opposites:

Male	Female
Black hair	Blonde hair
Looking away	Looking at us
Brooding	Smiling

While Elvis is mysterious, looking off into the distance, refusing our gaze, Doris placates us, meeting our eyes with cheerful sincerity. The stars' existing personae are, then, further perpetuated on the cover. The designers for *Movie Life* could perhaps be seen hedging their bets with this pair of images, opting not solely for the teen idol or the established top box-office female star, but featuring both, thus widening their potential catchment of purchasers. Although it is interesting that while the Elvis story is mentioned here, it involves other "Hollywood teens" and therefore does not give him the same focused attention Day receives. On the other hand, there is no hint of the negative story

Cover of *Movie Life*, May 1961

about her that the magazine contains until the contents information.[2] The magazine cover maximizes its appeal with its dual-star portrait, and indeed, I know now that this was one of the regular features of the *Movie Life* format: from its first major year of production, the magazine had maintained a regular rotation of solo stars, couples, and ensembles.

Even if, at the time, I did not realize quite how significant my findings were, I understand now that I learned so much from studying the *Movie Life* issue. My purchase of the magazine was driven by the fact it contained an article, "Doris Day: The Rumors and the Facts!,"[3] which alluded to a schism between appearance and reality, precisely the area I was investigating. Reading the article as soon as the issue arrived in the mail, I remember being frustrated that the anonymous author seemed to waste time dwelling on mere unsubstantiated gossip about the star, whereas I now know this was precisely the point of the article.

I read, made notes on, and filed the issue. The next eighteen months saw me buying more, locally whenever possible, but usually from the States, rejoicing every time I found a pertinent bargain and then wincing when I realized the cost of the postage to the United Kingdom. But nevertheless I began to build up a collection. The point of the acquisitions still remained finding out the ways in which Day was discussed during her active career, so my searches had me concentrating on the years 1948–68, with another decade at the end when she was engaged in her TV series and specials and still very much a fixture in the movie magazines. In pursuit of more information, I visited the British Film Institute Library and the British Library which have some holdings of American movie publications, and I started to amass another collection, this time of photocopied extracts, specific articles on Day, which I carefully annotated with source publication, year, page reference and library. My attendance in 2002 at the then Society for Cinema Studies conference led to a visit to the excellent Denver Public Library where I found bound volumes of *Photoplay* on the main reading room shelf, to my delight.

By 2004, when I submitted my dissertation and been awarded my PhD, I had amassed about twenty magazines and hundreds of pages of articles. I had a chart showing years of maximum coverage of the star and a table that recorded article titles chronologically. I left the social science journal, became a university lecturer, wrote my first book.[4] This made little use of the collection, but the second, on the costume transformation motif in Hollywood,[5] drew heavily on it, and the third, my book-length exploration of Doris Day and the virgin persona, relied on it even more.[6] By then, I had visited the Margaret Herrick Library, the library of the Academy of Motion Picture Arts and Sciences in Los Angeles, and found my way to the LA Public Library, too, both proving fruitful sources of material and the former, in particular, swelling my collection of photocopies by the score. And then I made another major discovery. The photocopies were of limited use. I had over fourteen hundred individual articles on Doris Day, *and they were of limited use!*

A magazine issue published much earlier than the one I first purchased was responsible for this revelation. In working on my monograph on Day, I had bought an August 1948 copy of *Motion Picture*: I'd seen it online and realized it contained one of the earliest pieces to hail Day as a star, granting her this significant endorsement after she had appeared in just one movie, *Romance on the High Seas* (Michael Curtiz and Busby Berkeley, 1948). Given what I was beginning to appreciate about publishing lead times, the article, "The Most 'Everything' Girl In Hollywood" by Laura Pomeroy,[7] must have been filed in June, when the film was in movie theaters, meaning that readers would have had a chance to see and judge the newly minted star themselves. Apart from being one of the first to extol Day's star quality, remarking on the ease with which she had transitioned from a big band singer to a film performer, however, the article was significant for another reason. While Day received the biggest push in the magazine of all the actors discussed, the cover featured another star: Shirley Temple, seen with her small child, Linda Susan. At the top of the cover appeared a mysterious command: "See page 25 . . . YES, PAGE 25 . . . look on page 25 . . . NOW! PAGE 25." The alternation of lowercase and uppercase lettering, with the implied urgency of the repetition, served to intrigue and urge the reader to turn to the mentioned page. But what was on that page? A letter from the editors of *Motion Picture*, with the signature of each in facsimile, urging the reader to accept their joint assurance that a genuine new film star

Cover of *Motion Picture*, August 1948

had arrived—and to turn to page 38. To find out the name of this star, then, the reader again had to turn over pages, before the Laura Pomeroy article was finally found and Doris Day revealed to be the veritable marvel. The editors' attempts to arouse curiosity and create suspense were extreme—I haven't seen another buildup like this again. But more important to me, the trail they laid out, urging the reader to search on through the pages of the magazine, revealed the importance of reading an article in the context of the entire issue. A photocopy of the Pomeroy article alone would be lacking in the most important part of the piece's message: that Day was deemed worthy of having an elaborate pathway created for her through the magazine, with each mysterious withholding of her name building interest through the anticipation wrought by delayed gratification.

My magazine acquisitions, begun in pursuit of contemporaneous views about Day, had become a research interest, and now it had brought me to comprehend that the wider context for any article—its location in the magazine, its placement on the page or pages, the surrounding material, such as advertisements, use of color, font, graphics—was key in finding meaning. In learning to read a film, I had come across semiotics; now I was learning the semiotics of magazine reading.

Armed with this new insight, I went back to my first *Movie Life* issue. It was now clear that the various means of font choice, size, and placement; page layout; and article placement, were all intentional. Before the main text is even read, through the visual cues it gives, the piece on Day seems resolved on undermining her, even as its first paragraph states the opposite: "Just mention the name Doris Day and most people think of a sunny smile, a bouncy personality and a glamour-girl-next-door with a heap of talent and not a care in the world. But a few people don't think of these things–the images that cross their minds include temperament, lingering illness, fakery, coldness and offbeat ideas! From time to time during her long career, strange stories have circulated about Doris Day. After you read these rumors be sure to turn to page 60 for the facts."[8] The beginning of this article appears across two pages in about the middle of the magazine, not only giving it the significant space that befits an established star but also assigning prominence to four "rumors" while contesting only one. The four negative stories published on these pages, the first of thirteen in all, are also given emphasis through their visual layout: three are arranged, eye-catchingly, in black boxes with white text, and one appears in bold black in the main text, and only the content of this last "rumor" is disputed on the same page.

Movie Life, May 1961

As Sally Stein[9] has indicated was traditional in magazines, and not just movie fan publications, the rest of the story was displaced toward the back of the issue, ensuring that the reader needed to turn over various pages—and be exposed to various advertising material as well as other stories—in order to secure the pleasure of finishing the narrative. Significantly, the reader of this Day story would also need to persist to the back of the issue to read the refutations of the rumors supplied upfront.

In addition to the written element of the story, the accompanying photographs also subtly add to the weight given the negative stories. Traditionally, in Western printing, the verso page is given less emphasis in a page spread.[10] In this article's layout, opposite the text-bearing page is a full-page black-and-white photograph, seemingly unposed, of a smiling Doris Day. The fact that her gaze is directed away from the camera implies that the picture captures a candid moment; this varies from the magazine's cover image of the star, where she very much seems to acknowledge her audience.

But while Day's wide unforced smile and look of pleasure serve to some extent to counter the belligerent appearance of the adverse text on the opposite page, this is reduced by the left-page positioning of the large photograph. Of the three smaller photos carried on the recto page, two also feature Day smiling, but the cheerful aspect of the star in these is undermined by the rumors' captions, which directly reference her male companions and cast doubt on the successfulness of her relationships with them. The fourth small picture is an image from *Midnight Lace* (Miller, 1960), at that point the star's most recent vehicle, which shows her character, Kit Preston, looking startled and anxious as she holds a telephone; the caption next to it mentions Day's Christian Science faith and alludes to the "cancer scare" she suffered in 1956. The specific image from *Midnight Lace* pictured seems thus to have been chosen to illustrate the notion of Day being *scared*, even though in the film's narrative her character's anxiety had nothing to do with health worries.

The rather random-seeming collage effect of the placement of images and text, boxed captions, and story column, I now realized, was fully in keeping with the magazine's rather chaotic visual style at this time—a hectic mix of fonts, use of capitals, and stylistic formatting throughout, presumably in an attempt to maintain reader interest. However, that three of the four disparaging stories about Day placed here appear in bold, and are thus given extra emphasis, is not random. The use of bold for the "rumors" continues throughout the story, even in the concluding columns on pages 60–62, while the countering "facts" are printed in regular text, giving the former more immediate visual emphasis even if the latter ostensibly exposed them as fictions.

Just as the use of boldface type to give visual prominence to the negative, salacious parts of the story is not random, so none of the details in the text itself are accidental either. The story works via a version of the rhetorical device of *apophasis*, where a topic is raised by the very act of refusing its mention. Thus, while the article concludes that Doris Day is not, for example, hiding her son, Terry, from the public because he undermines her image as "a perennial twenty-two year old ingenue,"[11] readers initially perceive that this is the reason for his absence from the star's publicity because the plausibility of this explanation is suggested to them before the more nuanced facts are revealed.

As I was later to discover, and subsequently write about in detail,[12] movie magazine editors had long employed article *titles* to hint at salacious details in order to arouse reader interest and ensure sales, while the actual story content denied the sensational in order to avoid litigation. The *Movie Life* piece fits this pattern but here extends the presentation of negative possibilities into the "rumors," using them as mini titles and then having each subsequent section of the text roll back on undesirable imputations.

One of these pieces of gossip reverses, at least to contemporary eyes, the usual pattern of ugly rumor/mitigating fact; here the suggestion is that Day was an astute entrepreneur, fully in charge of her own career:

RUMOR: Doris rose from nowhere to become a top singer and the top movie box-office draw because she is one of the shrewdest business women around—and everything she touches turns to gold.

FACT: Nothing could be further from the truth! Doris leaves all the details of her life to her husband Marty, who was her agent before they were married and now is her personal manager. Doris, who started her fantastic career with a non-paying job, attributes a lot of her success to luck: "Things just happened and I had to go along."[13]

It is interesting that the story moved immediately to quash the notion that Day could be actively, and expertly, involved in making both money and wise career moves. Presumably this was, in 1961, being posited as unwomanly or, perhaps, just not a good fit with the persona associated with the performer. Beyond this contemporaneous sexism, however, is another point of interest: the fatalism inherent in the quotation ascribed to Day. While the article parses her words as attributing her success to luck rather than any design of her own, they actually hint more at a passivity and resignation that very much chimes with the lyrics of the Academy Award-winning song "Que Sera Sera,"[14] which she first sang in the 1956 Alfred Hitchcock film *The Man Who Knew Too Much*. The song became associated with Day to the point where it could be used as a metatextual reference invoking the star's own persona and career in *The Glass Bottom Boat* (Frank Tashlin, 1966). It later became the theme song for her television show (1968–73), but also, most significantly for the *Movie Life* piece, it was sung by Day to her costar David Niven in her other 1960 vehicle, *Please Don't Eat the Daisies* (Charles Walters). The echo in the magazine piece of this fatalistic philosophy may have been either conscious or unconscious but certainly accorded with the Day image.

My first movie magazine purchase, then, turned out to be invaluable despite the shabbiness of its journalism, paper, and photographs. It taught me that a star could be acknowledged, by her placement on the cover, as important enough to sell an issue but that this importance was no guarantee of respectful treatment inside. It taught me the need to read all the information—both visual and verbal—in the presentation of an article and that a story could be built around an established part of the star persona, or even its adjuncts (as with the theme song "Que Sera Sera"), perhaps in an attempt to give credence to rumors or facts, or both, by evoking a well-known association.[15] And it taught me the truth that magazine editors used all the rhetorical tools they could muster perennially to suggest and deny, working toward having their cake and eating it too.

I think it was really important to my work as a Hollywood historian who analyzes movie magazines that my first encounter with these periodicals was with a relative outlier in popularity terms. *Movie Life* began with two issues at the end of 1937 and managed to stagger on into the 1980s, but despite the success implied by this longevity, it was never in the top five best-selling movie magazines. Certainly by 1961 it had suffered a decline in quality that was marked as much by its very pulpy paper as its very pulpy contents. Even just six years beforehand, it had been printed on better-quality paper stock and contained color advertising and editorial features (such as the "crescent diamond rings" ad opposite page 28 and the extended "What Hollywood Wears" multipage piece), both in September 1954's issue.[16]

By first becoming acquainted with the movie magazine through an issue of *Movie Life*, I was fortunate in missing out on the "*Photoplay* bias,"[17] which tends to assume *that* magazine is representative of the other movie fan publications instead of an anomaly in terms of subscriptions, industry dominance, cost, and even sometimes size. By starting with a more modest publication, I began my exploration of the world of movie magazines with few assumptions. The important if somewhat tardy realization that any one issue can always be put into a wider environment, arising from my collection, has directly impacted my research; now, I seek to read an issue in the context of other issues of the same magazine, or different publications from the same year, or different issues and magazines that tell same story or focus on the same star . . . At the same time, I am always alert to find in the single issue a path that sends the reader on a trail to discover a star's secret and have yet to find one as extravagant in deferring its disclosure as *Motion Picture*'s for Day.

Besides movie magazines now succeeding in pushing my other topics of interest in research terms to the margins, they have also made their way into my teaching in the last decade. I used them first in writing my own lectures, but by 2010 they had emerged as explicit topics and research sources, both in a master's course I teach on methods for historical research. I had an early skirmish with a colleague from another institution who refused to accept the magazines as a valid resource since they could only ever be unreliable *secondary* sources; subsequently, I have learned that getting students to recognize that the fan publications are worth studying as primary sources, even though we don't go to them for "the truth," is a good thing, since it then spurs the students to examine other written pieces with the same healthy skepticism. Most recently, I have even begun to nudge my first-year undergraduates toward appreciating the significance of the movie periodicals when teaching them about the Hollywood studio system and, of course, stardom. I have supervised to successful completion several PhD theses that used movie magazines as their central source reservoir, drawing on them to interrogate stars and stardom, and I've proudly seen their authors publish their work. With one of these postgraduates

I founded NoRMMA (Network of Research: Movies, Magazines and Audiences),[18] a research network for those working on movie magazines, and it has produced conferences, symposia, exhibitions, and an edited collection, *Star Attractions: Twentieth-Century Movie Magazines and Global Fandom.*

Thus the casual purchase of an issue of *Movie Life* has led to changes in my job, research, methodologies, teaching, conference attendance, and even where I go on vacation. Having finished my Doris Day book (the first one, anyway), I have moved on to collecting publications from all periods and countries. Hollywood movie magazines are my main passion and the focus of my collection, but a new exhibition I was curating for 2021 before the pandemic struck[19] had me scouring eBay also for publications from the United Kingdom, France, the Netherlands, Japan, India, Malaysia . . . and, in fact, I can't see an issue without wanting to craft a research project around it. There is always the hunger for just one more issue, even though the now two-hundred-strong collection continually outgrows the receptacle housing it: although I always reference the magazines' cheapness and ubiquity, they are precious and anything but commonplace to me.

NOTES

1   While the text of the article on television actor Clu Gulager focuses on his ambitions to become a star while yet maintaining "a certain amount of dignity," the "50 NEW PIX!" highlights his body in tight jeans and a loosely buttoned shirt. "When an Artist Ceases Being a Dreamer . . . ," *Movie Life*, May 1961, 32–37. Nascent film stars George Hamilton and Diane McBain are depicted as trying "to avoid the reputation they're building up in Hollywood as the town's Gold Dust Twins!" "Please, Stop Making Us the Kids in the Yacht Next Door!," *Movie Life*, May 1961, 42–47.

2   Contents, *Movie Life*, May 1961, 4.

3   "Doris Day: The Rumors and the Facts!," *Movie Life*, May 1961, 30–31, 61, 62, 63.

4   Tamar Jeffers McDonald, *Romantic Comedy: Boy Meets Girl Meets Genre* (New York: Columbia University Press, 2007).

5   Tamar Jeffers McDonald, *Hollywood Catwalk: Exploring Costume and Transformation in American Film* (London: I.B. Tauris, 2010).

6   Tamar Jeffers McDonald, *Doris Day Confidential: Hollywood, Sex and Stardom* (London: I.B. Tauris, 2013).

7   Laura Pomeroy, "The Most 'Everything' Girl in Hollywood," *Motion Picture*, August 1948, 38–39, 76.

8   "When an Artist Ceases Being a Dreamer," 31.

9   Sally Stein, "The Graphic Ordering of Desire: Modernization of a Middle-Class Woman's Magazine, 1919–1939," *Heresies* 18 (1985): 6–16.

10 "Advertisers have long preferred right-hand facing positions in newspapers and magazines. The argument was that people read newspapers from front to back and therefore were first exposed to advertisements on the right hand page." Ruth Rettie and Carol Brewer, "The Verbal and Visual Components of Package Design," *Journal of Product and Brand Management* 9, no. 1 (2000): 56–70, 69.

11 "Doris Day," 63.

12 Tamar Jeffers McDonald, "Come-On Covers and Climb-Down Contents: Salaciousness and Timidity in the Movie Magazines," in *Star Attractions: Twentieth-Century Movie Magazines and Global Fandom*, ed. Tamar Jeffers McDonald and Lies Lanckman (Iowa City: University of Iowa Press, 2019), 29–44.

13 "Doris Day," 31.

14 Written by Jay Livingstone and Ray Evans, "Que Sera Sera" received the Academy Award for Best Original Song in 1956.

15 I profited from this insight when I came across another article that builds itself around the same song and its associations with the star. See "Doris Day" and "Sex Isn't Everything," *Motion Picture*, May 1956, 26–27, 67; Jeffers McDonald, *Doris Day Confidential*, 101–10.

16 "What Hollywood Wears," *Movie Life*, September 1954, 28–47.

17 Anne Helen Petersen, "The Politics of Fan Magazine Research," In Media Res, November 13, 2013, mediacommons.org/imr/2013/11/04/politics-fan-magazine-research.

18 NoRMMA, www.normmanetwork.com/.

19 See "Design and Desire: The Glamorous History of the Movie Magazine," NoRMMA, March 8, 2020, www.normmanetwork.com/design-and-desire-design-and-desire-the-glamorous-history-of-the-movie-magazine/.

2

MATERIAL GIRL

Design Objects Collected and Screened

Lucy Fischer

I HAVE TITLED THIS ESSAY "Material Girl," because that is what I am. Though a professor, author, and holder of a doctorate, my life has also been enriched by the world of things. One need only step inside my house to be surrounded by them. My attachment to these objects has sometimes embarrassed me, as it seems (in the popular imagination) that such an impulse stands in contrast to the "intellectual" one—unless, of course, you collect books, which I do not. I have learned, however, that the two drives are not necessarily opposed, and, in fact, my material life as a collector has informed, enhanced, and invigorated my life as a scholar.

I find my interest in objects especially relevant to my discipline of film and media studies since theorists have long asserted that cinema, as a medium, prioritized them in a manner unlike other art forms. As André Bazin opined, "On the screen man is no longer the focus of the drama. . . . The decor that surrounds him is part of the solidity of the world. For this reason . . . man in the world enjoys no a priori privilege over . . . things."[1] Siegfried Kracauer agreed. He saw one of cinema's special capacities as "redeeming" parts of physical reality that would otherwise go unnoticed in daily life.[2] Finally, filmmaker Abram Room opined: "In the cinema, on the screen, a thing grows to gigantic proportions and acts with the same force (if not a greater force) as man himself."[3]

In my introduction to this volume, I also mentioned the novel academic area of "thing theory," in part a reaction against the supremacy of ideas in intellectual discourse. Writing hyperbolically in his groundbreaking 1942 book, *The Voice of Things*, poet Francis Ponge observes that ideas "give me a queasy feeling, nausea" whereas "objects in the external world . . . delight me."[4] While, as a scholar, I am devoted to the world of ideas, I am also enmeshed in the world of things and wish to acknowledge their importance in both our theorizations and lives.

ART DECO-DENCE

While I have no talent in producing art, I have always been drawn to the visual arts and design. But that interest piqued when I discovered antiques fairs in the late 1970s. This occurred following my reluctant move out of New York City to a small Pennsylvania college town where, in the absence of many other cultural options, "swap meets" became alluring. Attending them, I soon began purchasing old jewelry and decorative objects. Here, I find myself conforming to female gender stereotypes about collecting. Furthermore, my interest in design entailed a fascination with the past (a concern that would also mark my scholarly work on "primitive" and silent film).

At first, I had no idea how to even name the styles of the things I procured. Neither did I care about that—since mine was not, initially, an academic pursuit nor one that I imagined as an investment. It was pure fun and time away from finishing my film studies dissertation. Moreover, as with most would-be collectors, I was not consciously setting out to start a "collection," only to purchase some things that appealed to me.

I ultimately became aware of the label for the design modes to which I was attracted from my interactions with others. A friend visited me in Pennsylvania and when we went to an antiques show, she hunted for Fiestaware—a colorful brand of table service originally produced by the Homer Laughlin China Company of West Virginia in 1936.[5] I learned that it emerged in the Art Deco period but mocked her interest in such "clumsy" dinnerware. My second introduction to Art Deco came when my husband's cousin from Los Angeles visited us years later in Pittsburgh and we stopped at a shabby antiques store. She admired a classic Deco metal lamp, amazed at its low price (compared to the price she would have found on the West Coast). But she did not buy it, and the next week I found myself returning to the store and purchasing it myself—perhaps out of the competitive urge that theorists have noted can attach to collecting. This became the first of myriad Art Deco items I amassed that featured sleek, metal-crafted women (both nude and clothed); others included vases, ashtrays, figurines, candlesticks, and other lamps.

My love of the Art Deco style soon expanded to include jewelry—already a great passion of mine since childhood. I have always viewed my love of adornment as entirely selfish and narcissistic, but I have been comforted by the words of Georg Simmel who saw it as involving reciprocity. As he writes, "One adorns oneself for oneself, but can do so only by adornment for others. It is one of the strangest sociological combinations that an act, which exclusively serves the emphasis and increased significance of the actor, nevertheless attains the goal just as exclusively in the pleasure, in the visual delight it offers to others, and their gratitude."[6] My Art Deco jewelry collection does not primarily comprise expensive baubles but rather modest items of sterling, base metal, plastic, glass, semiprecious stones, and the like. What I particularly admired about the jewelry that I sought was the geometry of the pieces—whether squares, rectangles, triangles, or circles. This attraction also translated to decorative items. Thus, I collected such things as chrome and blue-mirrored glass globular candlesticks as well as geometrically embossed boxes and vases.

My Art Deco collection grew while I was a doctoral student in cinema studies at New York University. Interestingly, one of my comprehensive exam areas was the coming of sound, an era that coincided with the rise of Art Deco. So my scholarly and collecting habits were beginning to meld. But the true intersection of the two came with my publishing an essay on production numbers by Busby Berkeley in the movie *Dames* (Ray Enright, 1934) in which myriad quasi-identical women were posed in a manner consonant with my Deco lamps and candlesticks.[7] Moreover, the abstract black-and-white sets used for the dance numbers as well as the geometric patterns in which the women were arranged also smacked of a Deco aesthetic.

However, it was only much later in my career that I consciously connected my acquisitions with my scholarly work. Perhaps it was a lecture given at my university that touched on the topic[8] or a decision as a senior scholar to allow myself to work on an area linked to a personal passion. It also bespoke my urge to investigate a highly original subject. Although critics and scholars over the years had made passing (but rather superficial) reference to the influence of Art Deco on the cinema, there was no serious study of it.

This was the beginning of my writing *Designing Women: Cinema, Art Deco, and the Female Form*[9]—a volume that considered the ties between the design style and film costumes and decor in genres like the melodrama (*The Kiss* [Jacques Feyder, 1929]), the musical (*Swing Time* [George Stevens, 1936]), the South Sea adventure film (*Tabu* [F. W. Murnau, 1931]), and the fantasy (*Lost Horizon* [Frank Capra, 1937]). Beyond this, I considered the unique image of woman in the Art Deco mode—the importance of which had already been clear to me from my collected objects and earlier work on *Dames*. Hence, I found the Deco female identified both with modernity and a body type consonant with the sleek, tubular forms of the era.

Throughout the writing process, my collection meshed with and inspired my scholarly work. First, had I not been a "material girl," interested in things, my study would not have recognized the import of mise-en-scène and set decoration in the vision of women in movies. Second, my collection led me beyond the screen to the design culture of the era. Hence, one chapter of the book considered magazine ads and articles concerning modernist home furnishings. Another was devoted to the spectacular and exotic Art Deco architecture of a major picture palace—the 1931 Oakland Paramount Theatre, designed by Timothy L. Pflueger. Third, had I not owned of so many female-adorned objects, I might not have focused on the issue of woman in my writing. Fourth, the wide stylistic range of items that I owned alerted me to Art Deco's multivalent form, including "Orientalist," geometric, and Egyptian Revival modes (the latter sparked by the discovery of King Tut's tomb in 1922). Furthermore, my familiarity with certain materials used in crafting the objects also factored into my analyses of films. For instance, the Bakelite jewelry and boxes that I owned led me to understand the plastic's function as the polished flooring used in many Fred Astaire/ Ginger Rogers' dance numbers.[10]

I also realized that my interest in Art Deco had clear autobiographical roots—echoing several theorists' (e.g., Jean Baudrillard's) claims that collection often has its beginnings in childhood. I grew up in Manhattan, an architectural wonderland of the style. As a kid, the skyline I sometimes viewed included the majestically austere Empire State Building as well as the jewel-capped Chrysler building. I occasionally attended shows at Radio City Music Hall, an internationally regarded Art Deco shrine. Furthermore, in accumulating material that eventually inspired my scholarly writing, I became one of many individuals whose collection had associations with their professional life—a fact noted by thinkers like Muensterberger and Pearce.[11] It would not, however, be the last time that this was the case.

ART NOUVEAU AND A NOUVEAU COLLECTION

As I reconstruct the trajectory of my interest in Art Nouveau, I realize that it began around the same time as my love of Deco but was tabled for a period of time. In the 1970s, a painter friend gave me some coasters decorated with images of works by Alphonse Mucha, which I very much liked. I was ignorant of the artist as well as the movement he participated in, but I now realize the coasters' production was part of the Art Nouveau revival in that era. Years later, a visit to Vienna found me a fan of the work of Gustave Klimt and the Secessionists. The opening of New York City's Neue Galerie in 2000 (focusing on early twentieth-century German and Austrian art and design) afforded me other opportunities to see extraordinary works with ties to Art Nouveau, including those of the Weiner Werkstätte.

However, with my research and writing concentrating on Art Deco, attention to this earlier movement faded into the background. Only after I had published *Designing Women* did my appetite for Art Deco wane and a new one for Art Nouveau grow, with the associated collecting appetite. In this respect, I am, perhaps, typical. While I had not yet officially "completed" a collection of Art Deco (since there was still much to acquire), finishing the book represented another kind of "closure." But the collecting habit itself did not diminish, and like an "addict," I moved on to other things.

Once again, it was the image of woman in Art Nouveau that initially fascinated me—especially the "close-up" renditions of her face with flowing hair that adorned so many silver brooches I bought. Beyond this, there were the full-bodied representations of the female in candlesticks and vases, posed gracefully in cascading gowns. While Deco spoke of the geometric and the tubular, Art Nouveau celebrated the asymmetric and curvilinear.

Since I had already been able to tie my personal love of Deco to film history, I sought to do so with Art Nouveau, which meant taking a step backward in time, to the mid- and late nineteenth century through the early twentieth century. Research on this topic proved more difficult. While Art Deco had occasionally been mentioned in works of film history (albeit sketchily), there were almost no references to Art Nouveau. This only whetted my appetite to pursue the issue, a task that years later resulted in the publication of my book *Cinema by Design: Art Nouveau, Modernism, and Film History.*[12]

As I began the project, I hunted for cinematic works that displayed the movement's influence based on a hunch that morphed into a conviction. In the silent era, I focused on the trick films of Segundo de Chomón—realizing that the bevy of women that surrounded his films' magical occurrences were much like my decorative Art Nouveau maidens. Furthermore, the movement was known for its colorful hues and the work of Chomón was redolent with hand-colored chromatic splendor. Beyond that, Chomón was from Barcelona—a city famous for the creations of Antoni Gaudí, one of the premier Art Nouveau architects. Similarly, I realized that Raoul Walsh's 1924 version of *The Thief of*

Bagdad created a curvilinear fantasy with ties to the Islamic roots of Art Nouveau. Furthermore, there existed a literal example of a bona fide Art Nouveau film, *Salomé*, directed by Charles Bryant in 1922. Primarily conceived by actress Alla Nazimova and costumer/art director Natacha Rambova, the look of the film drew directly from the prints of Aubrey Beardsley that had accompanied an edition of the original Oscar Wilde play.

I soon realized that because Art Nouveau was popular only briefly (and soon considered passé), I had to look beyond the years of its ascendance. This brought me to another autobiographical moment—my youth in the 1960s and early 1970s and "psychedelic" art, which was influenced by Art Nouveau—with its bright Day-Glo colors and endless circles and spirals (as in so many rock posters). I then thought of the animated film *Yellow Submarine* (George Dunning, 1968) as an instance of Art Nouveau graphics translated to cinema (reminiscent of those of Winsor McCay in the 1900s) and, therefore, undertook an analysis of it. I also recalled seeing Michelangelo Antonioni's *The Passenger* (1975) when it came out in the 1970s (which had scenes shot in Barcelona) and being stunned by the protagonists' visit to a certain architectural site. I had no idea at the time that it was a famous Gaudí building (Casa Milà/La Petrera) or that it was linked to Art Nouveau. But in rediscovering the film (and in managing later to visit the site), I saw it as another instance of the movement's influence on later cinema and devoted a chapter of the book to it. I also realized again how I was already attracted to Art Nouveau in the 1970s, at the same time I cherished those Mucha coasters—planting seeds for a collection and research to come in decades following.

Underlying my writing project was the wish to champion Art Nouveau in the face of its omnipresent detractors who conceived the style as excessive, "girlish," sentimental, kitsch, or camp. This, of course, was also an attempt to defend my own collection of objects, which could be tarred with the same brush, a denigration of my sense of taste. I researched all the early references to Art Nouveau in the *New York Times* in order to demonstrate the ambivalence toward the movement at the time of its birth. One critic of the era, in fact, deemed the style grotesque and "horrible"—which led me to consider how, in certain contemporary horror films (e.g., *Deep Red* [Dario Argento, 1975], *The Abominable Doctor Phibes* [Robert Fuest, 1971], and *The Strange Color of Your Body's Tears* [Bruno Forzani and Hélène Cattet, 1975]), the houses in which ghastly events take place are often marked by an Art Nouveau aesthetic.

Ultimately, I tried to reclaim the movement as a pioneering modernist mode that was rejected primarily because of its allegedly "feminine" traits (its curves, female imagery, and appeal to surface beauty)—the opposite of the austere, much-vaunted Bauhaus and International styles to come. Even Art Deco was deemed superior to Art Nouveau, since it was sleek, elegant, aerodynamic, and restrained—in other words more "masculine."

ARTIFACTS AND FILMS

Since collecting concerns material objects, no essay on the topic would be complete without discussing and displaying some of them. So here I will highlight particular items in my Art Deco and Art Nouveau collections and investigate them in a more granular way—underscoring their ties to my writing as a film and media scholar.

Dancers

Several of the Art Deco pieces that I collected represent female dancers. This figure was ubiquitous in the era with its most famous iterations in the chryselephantine sculptures produced in France by Dimétre Chiparus immortalizing such performers as the Dolly Sisters, Hungarian American twins who appeared in vaudeville and the theater during the 1910s and 1920s. While Chiparus's work was very expensive and well beyond my budget, I acquired more mundane examples of the form, for instance some figurines and bookends depicting chorines. One, made of colorful pottery, depicts a dancer posed with an outstretched scarf. Similarly, a set of chrome bookends portrays dancers (heads thrust back and one leg raised) holding balls in their outstretched arms. Here, I am reminded of a production number in Busby Berkeley's *Dames* in which

A chrome Art Deco bookend of a dancer from the author's collection reminiscent of chorines in the films of Busby Berkeley

the chorus girls hold black balls as they "fly up" to the camera. Also interesting are two pieces I own that constitute parts of what would have been lamps (the light fixture missing). They both depict posed dancers (in bronze-tone metal), set within decorative frames and positioned against frosted glass through which an electric lightbulb would have shone. One can still get a sense of their potential illumination by simply positioning them before a window—revealing the women simultaneously in silhouette and three dimensions. They remind me of a Busby Berkeley production number in *Footlight Parade* (Lloyd Bacon, 1933) that involves a water ballet occurring in a backlit pool. When illuminated, the dancers appear in silhouette on the surface; their white bathing suits are turned black. Also relevant is a portion of a production number from *Dames*. Here, a female dancer (Ruby Keeler) stands within a decorative frame dressed in white, her outline underscored by a black background. Though the female dancer figure was not as prominent in the Art Nouveau era, it did arise in the film *Salomé*. When Nazimova performs the dance of the seven veils, she is sometimes outlined through backlighting, like the figures in my lamps.

Geometry

Aside from representations of female dancers, Berkeley production numbers are known for the strict geometry of their sets and the placement of women in them—another hallmark of Deco aesthetics. Once while visiting Paris, I purchased two Deco metal vases made of polished aluminum. Both are covered with triangular designs on their surface, rendered in a three-dimensional fashion with contrast established by some dull, textured sections. They are representative of the abstract strain of Art Deco that favored geometric shapes. Also, in keeping with this style are two rings from my collection (fashioned by Theodor Fahrner, a German jewelry designer of the early twentieth century). Both are made of sterling silver, marcasite, and semiprecious stones. In one, blue chalcedony is cut into three rectangular pieces and worked into the silver, and in the other, floral carved coral is attached in two square panels. A third ring (of unknown provenance) is made entirely of silver and marcasite and is an assemblage of ovals and rectangles.

A geometric Art Deco glass earring and necklace set from the author's collection

Finally, a green-and-rust-colored Deco glass necklace and earring set displays a similar devotion to geometric shapes. When I think of a similar design mode in the cinema, a film that comes to mind is *The Kiss*, which I examine in depth in *Designing Women* (with art direction by Cedric Gibbons at MGM). Both the sets in which Greta Garbo performs and the outfits she wears are conceived in terms of geometric patterns.

The Natural World

Nature was a very important theme in Art Nouveau, an element that some have seen as a reaction against the burgeoning industrial environment. Thus, we find multitudes of dragonfly or butterfly brooches in the era and hybrids of women merged with insects. We also see in the glass pieces crafted by the Daum family in France objects adorned with images of leaves and flowers. While, again, the latter items have always been beyond my price point, I have accumulated less expensive objects that demonstrate the movement's love of nature. One is a brass curved letter opener with raised lilies as part of its handle. Two others are plates. The first is French Limoges and quite ornate. Its center is white, but its wide border is gold and portrays graceful pink and green lilies and lily pads. The second is German and depicts raised white, green, and tan lilies and lily pads against a vibrant turquoise background bordered by a tan-and-green curvilinear ribbon. The imagery of this plate resonates strongly with a film I examined in *Cinema by Design* as part of discussing an Art Nouveau revival—*The Tales of Hoffman* (Michael Powell and Emeric Pressburger, 1951). The relevant sequence is "The Enchanted Dragonfly Ballet" where Moira Shearer, costumed as the beloved insect, danced on a surface depicting a pond sprouting lily pads. Another beloved member of the animal world during the Art Nouveau era was the peacock, a colorful, sumptuous bird. Like the dragonfly, it was often associated with the female due to, one suspects, its astounding beauty (despite the most gorgeous specimens of the species being male). Here, my collection echoes this trend in the form of a small silver and marcasite peacock pendant decorated with ivory or bone as well as amethyst stones. The movie that most reverberates with this figure (and

An Art Nouveau German Limoges plate from the author's collection that emphasizes the movement's love of Nature

one I have written about in depth) is *Madame Peacock* (Ray Smallwood, 1920), again starring and influenced by Nazimova. In it, she appears as a cold, selfish career-driven actress who leaves her husband and abandons her child. Throughout the film, sets and clothing identified with her are decorated with peacock imagery. Particularly noteworthy are the decorative screens and panels in her home that are emblazoned with peacock motifs.

Female Figures

In both my books on Art Deco and Art Nouveau, I examined the look of the typical woman associated with each movement. In Art Deco, she was sleek and pared down—somewhat androgynous (rather than voluptuous) and streamlined (rather than curvaceous). Several objects in my collection represent this vision. One is a small metal statuette of a woman holding a circular tray. She is quite boyish, has closely cropped hair, and seems fashioned more to project a silhouette than a full figure. Another item is a gold-toned bookend that depicts a seated woman—knees up, with arms around her ankles. She bears a smooth, rounded surface and displays minimal breasts and bobbed hair. In my writing on Art Deco, I found this type of woman embodied in the actress Greta Garbo (both on- and off-screen) and investigated her role films like *The Kiss* and *The Single Standard* (1929, John Robertson). In contrast, the Art Nouveau female was typically Rubenesque in bodily shape, with flowing gowns, pinched waist, and long sinuous hair. Here, an antique metal vase in my collection depicts such a woman in gilt tones, holding and surrounded by flowers—the latter a highly romantic symbol. A similar vision of woman is found in an Art Nouveau glass pin I own, as well as in a bonze ashtray. Furthermore, since I had devoted a section of *Cinema by Design* to a biopic of Klimt (*Klimt*, Raúl Ruiz, 2006), I bought a kitsch, modern-day Klimt Barbie doll based on a woman he had famously painted, Adele Bloch Bauer. Turning to cinema, we can also see hints of the Art Nouveau woman in publicity stills for silent screen actresses like Mary Pickford.

Female Faces

In both Art Deco and Art Nouveau, the female countenance is a visual fixation. Thus, one item in my Deco collection (perhaps a paper weight) is made of brass and depicts a female face along with a typical architectural element of the era. Its lines are simple and stark, and the head is portrayed with almost no hair. Another Deco item that I own is a pair of bookends comprising female heads. The fixation on the female face was even more obsessive in Art Nouveau where it appears on endless silver brooches, necklaces, and boxes in my collection. Here,

An Art Nouveau vase from the author's collection that depicts the movement's version of the idealized female form—hair flowing and adorned with flowers

the female face is more rounded and is framed by swirling locks of hair. Of course, these pieces have direct relevance to film through the import of the cinematic close-up. Significantly, the cover of my book on Art Nouveau displays a close-up of Nazimova wearing a peacock headdress in *Salomé*.

Egyptian Revival

Within both the Art Nouveau and Art Deco movements there was a fascination with the culture and history of Egypt due to the discovery of King Tut's tomb during in the second decade of the twentieth century. As stated in the introduction, I too became captivated with this style and sometimes collected items with Pharaonic iconography. I find my attraction to this rather bizarre since I am Jewish, and Egyptian rulers were oppressors of my people. While I never really confronted that fact when purchasing such artifacts, I am now somewhat embarrassed to own them. Some of the objects I acquired were decorative pieces, like a brass letter opener topped with a Pharaoh's head. But others were jewelry pieces: an ornate metal belt buckle decorated with colored rhinestones and the face of Pharaoh, a metal pendant adorned with two red plastic inserts of Pharaoh's head, and a more elaborate brass brooch that supplemented the Pharaonic face with other Egyptian symbols (e.g., the falcon). Some acquisitions of this type sported more neutral representations. A green Art Nouveau pottery vase, for instance, was ornamented only with a gold scarab (another beloved Egyptian icon). Finally, some bookends and lamps depict Egyptian slave girls (items that, as a feminist, should have shamed me as well). Beyond discussing the Egyptian Revival in *Designing Women* and *Cinema by Design*, I also wrote an article that traced its appearance in such films as *The Mummy* (Karl Freund, 1932).[13]

Orientalism: Chinoiserie

As part of Art Deco's interest in the exotic, imagery influenced by Chinese arts and crafts flourished, and several items in my collection bear the mark of this. I own a green imitation jade necklace with a floral medallion at the bottom and green and pearl beads on the strand. I also

An Egyptian Revival 1920s brooch from the author's collection emblazoned with Pharaonic imagery

have a silver and enamel bracelet with seven geometric links adorned with turquoise-colored figures of Chinese people. This use of enamel is carried out as well in a small bronze-toned metal planter with turquoise enamel on the interior and multicolored Asian figures, trees, and houses pictured on the sides. Also in my collection is a silver bracelet with links of carved red cinnabar—the latter being a mineral commonly used in Chinese arts and crafts (and one I first saw in a brooch owned by my mother that I admired as a child). Finally, I have a pin with a central white ivory or bone abstract Oriental design surrounded by a multicolored border. A focus on Orientalism also played a part in my research on Art Nouveau in *Cinema by Design*. Specifically, I considered the film *The Red Lantern* (Albert Capellani, 1919), which takes place in China during the Boxer Rebellion. It again stars Nazimova, this time as a Eurasian woman who, at one point, pretends to be a mythical goddess to help the revolutionaries.

Hollywood Memorabilia

Strangely, while I am a film scholar, I am not a collector of movie memorabilia. I own only one item of this type, and it fits in with my love of Art Nouveau—a tin beautebox by Canco from the 1920s emblazoned with a gold and multicolored image of Rudolph Valentino in a sheik costume. The background decoration as well as those on the sides are resonant of Art Nouveau abstraction. While I have never written about Valentino, I regularly taught *The Sheik* (George Melford, 1921) in my classes. I am sure I would not have purchased the box had it not been an artifact of one of my beloved movements.

A tin beautebox by Canco from the 1920s decorated with gold and a multicolored image of Rudolph Valentino in a sheik costume

World's Fair Memorabilia

In both my books on Art Deco and Art Nouveau, I discussed in some detail the import of the world's fairs of the era pertaining to each movement. *Designing Women* featured both the Paris Exposition of 1925 and the Golden Gate Exposition of 1939, which were important for Art Deco. *Cinema by Design* highlighted the 1900 Paris Exposition Universelle, which celebrated the Art Nouveau style. In all cases, I wanted to possess some "souvenir" from the fair that would position me closer to the event—despite the fact that, quite obviously, such objects would not be mementoes of my own life experience. So for both the 1925 and 1939 fairs, I acquired decorative exposition plates. I also obtained souvenir scarves for the 1939 and 1900 expositions, which I framed and hung on walls of my home. Furthermore, for the latter exposition, I purchased a souvenir silver-plated napkin ring and a bronze medal adorned with a female face. While in *Designing Women*, I merely touched on the Chicago World's Fair of 1939, associated with American Art Deco, I nonetheless acquired a miniature souvenir trylon and perisphere statuette (see the first figure on p. 04). Clearly, its geometric style was an emblem of the movement.

AFTERWORD

By now it should be clear how my collecting habits have stimulated, invigorated, and augmented my research and how the possessions I amassed have provided myriad examples for me to analyze in my writing and use as illustrations for classes, lectures, and texts. However, I must admit that my collection has ranged far beyond what I have harnessed or justified for academic purposes, proving that it defies practicality and has provided pure pleasure in my "civilian" life. However, I would be dishonest if I were not to admit that it has now become something of a burden as I realize that downsizing is in order at this stage of my life. As some theorists have noted, though a collector may adore her possessions, they are usually not cherished by her heirs, and passing them down is often not an option. Finding a new home for my treasures will be challenging (if at all possible), and parting with them will be heart wrenching, years of pleasure ceding to pain.

NOTES

1   André Bazin, "Theater and Cinema, Part Two," in *What Is Cinema?*, trans. Hugh Gray, vol. 1 (Berkeley: University of California Press, 1967), 106.

2   Siegfried Kracauer, *Theory of Film: The Redemption of Physical Reality* (London: Oxford University Press, 1960).

3   Abram Room, "Moi kinoubezhdeniia" [My cinema convictions], *Sovetskii ekran* [Soviet screen] 8 (1926): 5.

4   Francis Ponge, *The Voice of Things*, trans and ed. Beth Archer (New York: Herder & Herder, 1972), 93.

5   There was a hiatus in production from 1973 to 1985.

6   David Frisby and Mike Featherstone, eds., *Simmel on Culture: Selected Writings* (London: Sage, 1997), 206.

7   Lucy Fischer, "The Image of Woman as Image: The Optical Politics of *Dames*," *Film Quarterly* 30, no. 1 (1976): 2–11.

8   The lecture was delivered by Russell Merritt, n.d.

9   Lucy Fischer, *Designing Women: Cinema, Art Deco, and the Female Form* (New York: Columbia University Press, 2003).

10 Donald Albrecht, "The Art of RKO," *Architectural Digest*, July 1, 2009, www.architecturaldigest.com/story/vintage-set-design-article.

11 See the introduction to this volume, p. 00.

12 Lucy Fischer, *Cinema by Design: Art Nouveau, Modernism, and Film History* (New York: Columbia University Press, 2017).

13 Lucy Fischer, "'It Comes to Life': Art Deco and Cinema—Yesterday and Today," in *The Routledge Companion to Art Deco: Fashioning Art Deco*, ed. Bridget Elliott and Michael Windover (New York: Ashgate, 2019), 354–67.

3

MY RECORD COLLECTION
AND THE MAKING OF A DISCIPLINE

Krin Gabbard

I SUPPOSE IT BEGAN WITH the Columbia Record Club. I talked my parents into joining sometime in 1959 or 1960 when I would have been eleven or twelve. It could not have been earlier because *Johnny Mathis's Greatest Hits* was released in 1958 and had immediately become irresistibly popular. Seldom do I meet someone of my generation who grew up in a middle-class household that did *not* include a copy of that LP.[1] My parents bought the Mathis record and three others for a penny with the promise that they would buy four more LPs at full price during the next twelve months. And Columbia had a stealthily effective business plan: every month they sent out a glossy brochure promoting the featured records for the next month. If you did not return a card saying you wanted nothing that month, you would receive an LP anyway. Of course, many consumers would forget to send in the card, and others simply did not know the rules. We were surely not unusual in receiving numerous records we did not order, but Columbia's strategy worked. It was easier to keep the records than to send them back.

The Columbia Record Club was dreamed up by three young executives who took the idea to Goddard Lieberson, who had become president of Columbia Records in 1956. One of these innovators was George Avakian, a man who looms large in jazz history, especially for obsessive collectors of jazz records like me.[2] In 1939, when he was still in college, Avakian invented the concept of the "album" by packaging several 78s within the same binding.[3] He also had the idea for reissuing jazz recordings, making Columbia the first company to rerelease older records, often in albums. Before Avakian, if a record sold well in its day, more copies would be pressed. But as their popularity dwindled, audiences and musicians would leave these single 78s behind and move on. In the 1940s, just as the jazz canon was beginning to take shape, Avakian chose what he believed to be the most significant recordings from the 1920s by artists such as Louis Armstrong and Bix Beiderbecke and made them available in new pressings for the growing population of jazz aficionados. Later, in the 1950s and 1960s, Avakian would produce a stunning series of jazz LPs at Columbia featuring Armstrong, Duke Ellington, Miles Davis, Sonny Rollins, Dave Brubeck, and many others. In all, he produced more than sixty LP records. I think I have them all.

When Avakian and his colleagues had the idea for the Columbia Record Club, there were few choices for direct mail purchase. Ever since the late nineteenth century, Americans could order out of the Montgomery Ward and Sears Roebuck catalogs. The Book of the Month Club was founded in 1926, but that was the extent of specialized large-scale direct-mail sales. Not only did Columbia find a lucrative opportunity in a barely exploited arena, but it also capitalized on multiple trends in the 1950s, most notably a new concept of affluence that included a private home filled with good music chosen specifically by the homeowner and heard in "hi fi" and "stereo."

Mostly my parents bought musical comedy albums from the Columbia Record Club. To this day, I can sing every word to every song from the original cast recordings of *My Fair Lady, Flower Drum Song, South Pacific, Gypsy*, and even *Subways Are for Sleeping*, a Broadway show that flopped but not before Columbia began marketing the original cast album. We surely acquired that one because someone forgot to send

George Avakian, circa 1950

back the card. My brother requested LPs by the New Christy Minstrels and other pop groups that capitalized on the folk music craze of the era, and occasionally we would acquire something jazzy by Ella Fitzgerald or Miles Davis. I vividly recall a compilation LP of jazz from the Columbia archives called *$64,000 Jazz*, which had been specially prepared for release in the event that a contestant on the hit show *The $64,000 Question* chose to be quizzed about jazz.

I had insisted that my parents join the Columbia Record Club, and I was fine with my household's eclectic tastes as I carefully watched the LPs pile up alongside the record player in the living room. I began collecting jazz only after I got to know Alan Coutant, a senior in my high school when I was a sophomore. His father was one of the more affluent farmers in the east-central region of Illinois, where I grew up. Then, as now, the soil was dark black and abundantly fertile. Owning a lot of it could make you rich. Alan's father drove a Chrysler New Yorker, an appropriately named automobile for a family that produced a son with a highly urbanized musical aesthetic.

Alan Coutant played the alto saxophone with dazzling authority. He never told me what artists he had been listening to, but it hardly mattered because I would not have recognized names like Sonny Stitt,

Lee Konitz, and Paul Desmond. At this time, the one and only radio program in east-central Illinois that featured jazz ran on Sunday afternoons for two hours, but the disc jockey preferred the swing bands and the old white Dixielanders. Somehow, Alan had absorbed modern jazz with no help from the radio. Alan and I played in the high school band at 8:00 am during the school year. First thing every weekday morning I could hear Alan warming up by improvising high-flying jazz lines at breakneck speed. I was hooked.

With a subscription to *Down Beat* (a magazine dedicated to jazz and blues originating in Chicago in 1934) and a copy of the Schwann catalog, I began to educate myself about jazz. I had a newspaper delivery route and a sometime-gig mowing lawns, so I was able to acquire my own records over and above what I might naggingly insist that my parents purchase from the Columbia Record Club. At first, I bought records by Stan Kenton, Shelley Manne, Art Pepper, and various other hip white musicians recommended by the jazz enthusiast at a local record store.

As my autodidacticism continued, however, I realized how central African Americans had been to jazz history, and so I moved on to Miles Davis, Dizzy Gillespie, Thelonious Monk, and Charlie Parker. When I went off to college in 1966, I brought along several dozen jazz records. But that was the moment when my music had decidedly ceased to be a signifier of hipness and youthful rebellion. The occupants of my dormitory listened to Dylan and the Beatles, and if they were *very* hip, they listened to Frank Zappa. As a teenager, I had resisted the allure of this music. Not so my college cohort. I failed to convince any of them that jazz was worth a listen. A couple of the fellows on my floor who played folk guitar listened briefly to my LPs of great jazz guitarists like Jim Hall and Grant Green before wandering off with a shrug. Years later, after I had begun teaching in college, a student from Japan told me that, for her, jazz was too *shibui*—dark, elegant, subtle, and unobtrusive. I get it. But in 1966, my friends simply thought that I was crazy to be listening to this marginal music.

Looking back, I think a large part of the disdain for jazz that I encountered among my college friends had to do with race. By contrast, my parents were scrupulously liberal about this kind of thing. When my father ran the theater program at the little university where he taught, he hired the first Jewish faculty member at the school. A few years later he hired the first African American faculty member. She was a single young woman who designed elegant costumes for the university's dramatic productions and who loved to play golf. When the white patriarchs at the local country club would not allow her to join, my parents never went there again. I suppose that my passion for jazz has some relationship to my household's openness to what most white Americans thought of as the other.

My collecting began in earnest when, as a graduate student, I earned the princely sum of $1,100 a year as a teaching assistant. In 1970, I paid $33 a month for a bedroom, kitchen, and bath that I shared with two others. Six or seven dollars a month was all I needed for gasoline to keep my Volkswagen Beetle running. Other than food, my only other regular expense was a subscription to the *New Yorker*. And so I could afford regular trips to record stores where I began exploring jazz history. If I walked out of a record store with only two LPs under my arm, I felt that I had shown admirable restraint. Before long I was carefully consulting auction lists that circulated among collectors and invited bids on used, often rare LPs. These auction lists became increasingly important as I began to collect a number of artists to completion.[4]

The first jazz musician I began collecting as a completist was Duke Ellington. I quickly realized what a quixotic pursuit I had undertaken. During his fifty years as a bandleader, Ellington recorded prolifically, and any number of people recorded his concerts, which would eventually appear on bootleg LPs. To this day, it seems that previously unavailable music by Duke becomes available on CD every month or so. Any serious Ellington collection is inevitably incomplete, but that did not stop me from trying. It was less of a challenge but still difficult to keep up with my other favored artists, whose discographies were also constantly expanding. On a very basic level, I preferred dead artists because they were less likely to be constantly producing new music.

I collected discographies as well. Many of them were self-published and primitively bound, but they were reliable if you were devoted to acquiring every single item an artist had recorded. With some degree of shame, I admit that I took as much pleasure in checking off recently acquired recordings in my discographies as I did in listening to the music. I am not ashamed, however, that my tastes were eclectic and that they came close to embracing the entire history of jazz. I collected Jelly Roll Morton's 1920s recordings just as assiduously as I collected Herbie Nichols's work from the 1950s and Woody Shaw's from the 1980s.

As the LPs piled up on my shelves, I took time to read up on jazz when I wasn't working on a master's degree in classics and a PhD in comparative literature. In those days, almost everyone who wrote about jazz was basically a fan like me and not at all academic. It certainly never occurred to me in the 1970s that I might someday become a "jazz scholar." In fact, at that time, the term was an oxymoron. Even those who were doing what *might* be called jazz scholarship were mostly invested in uncritically praising the accomplishments of their preferred artists. There were, of course, a handful of African American writers, most notably Ralph Ellison, Albert Murray, and Amiri Baraka, who put jazz into a much larger context by centering race. To this day, their writings hold a degree of explanatory power that goes well beyond what is usually said about jazz. White writers were often reluctant to wade into the troubled waters of racial discourse. Or as Toni Morrison writes, "The habit of ignoring race is understood to be a graceful, even generous, liberal gesture."[5]

My comparative literature dissertation was on fifth-century Greek tragedy and sculpture and fifteenth-century Italian poetry and painting. When I took my first teaching job in 1977, I taught four students in second-year Greek, eight in first-year Latin, and about ten in a seminar devoted to seventeenth-century French tragedian Jean Racine. I immediately realized that if I was going to survive in the world of higher education, I needed to reach a larger population of students. I quickly changed my job description to film scholar. This was not a radical transformation for me, even though I had taken no film courses in college or graduate school. I knew a thing or two about movies because my parents were obsessed with them and passed on their enthusiasm at least in part by taking my brother and me out to the movies every

Friday night. The one and only movie theater in our little town was briefly owned by a fellow who set aside Tuesday nights to show "art films" when I was in high school. I saw Federico Fellini's *La Strada* (1954), Akira Kurosawa's *Rashomon* (1950) and Ingmar Bergman's *The Virgin Spring* (1960), among others. The screenings were so poorly attended that it ended after less than a year, but the films had a powerful effect on me. And fortunately, when I made the decision to teach cinema studies, it was not difficult to educate oneself in the discipline because serious, theoretically sophisticated film scholarship was still in its infancy. Prior to the 1970s, most writing about film was as journalistic and nonscholarly as the writing about jazz.

Although I was now trying to keep up with the new writing in cinema studies, I was still a professor of comparative literature, and I was doing my best to keep up there as well. High theory was having its moment in the 1980s. For better or worse, scholarly writing in literary and cinema studies was of little value if methods were not acknowledged and conclusions not problematized. Race, gender, nationality, and ideology crowded out the New Criticism's practice of reading for theme, metaphor, and formal structure. Meanwhile, jazz writing continued to be almost entirely journalistic. With few exceptions, the handful of academics who wrote on artists like Charlie Parker and Duke Ellington treated them just as their musicological colleagues treated Brahms and Debussy—with the kind of formalist analysis that literary scholars had abandoned years earlier.

And so shortly after I was tenured in 1987, I began applying the new strains of critical theory to jazz. I also seized the opportunity to bring jazz to the Modern Language Association (MLA), the premier organization for students and professors in literary studies. By a fortuitous coincidence, the MLA held its annual conference in New Orleans in December 1988. To my knowledge, there had never been a panel on jazz at any previous meeting of the MLA. I therefore proposed a panel called "Storyville Stories," attempting to convince the arbiters at the MLA that the time had come for serious talk about jazz and literature and that New Orleans was the ideal place for it. To my surprise, my proposal was accepted. I was also surprised when more than twenty people responded to my call for papers, several of whom were not professors of literary studies but were willing to pay dues to the MLA if it meant speaking about jazz at an important conference.

"Storyville Stories" ultimately consisted of four presentations, two of them by history professors who spoke about the practice of jazz autobiography. A professor of English gave a paper on Eudora Welty's story "Powerhouse," and a literary theorist cataloged a number of jazz "tropes," explaining how they could be applied to the writing of a prose. The panel was well attended, and several colleagues urged me to put together another MLA session on jazz, which I did. At the 1990 conference in New York, I chaired a panel called "Representing Jazz."

Frederick Garber was a professor of comparative literature at SUNY Binghamton when I was in the comparative literature department at SUNY Stony Brook. Mostly he wrote about romantic poetry, but like me, he was fascinated by jazz and how it was portrayed in movies. I was happy to include his paper on Michael Curtiz's 1950 *Young Man with a Horn* when he asked to be included on the "Representing Jazz" panel. It was also Professor Garber who encouraged me to put together an anthology of scholarly writing on jazz. He urged me to call it *Representing Jazz*. Because so many people had sent in proposals for the "Storyville Stories" panel, I was networked into a group of people who could contribute to the anthology, several of whom knew people who might also wish to participate. And every now and then a colleague would happen to have written something about jazz. I had known Jed Rasula in graduate school, long before he became a distinguished professor of English at the University of Georgia. In about 1990, I ran into him at a comparative literature conference. I read with great interest his unpublished essay critiquing the practice of building jazz histories around recordings.

Soon, *Representing Jazz* had become a project big enough for two books. By another fortuitous coincidence, the twenty-four essays I had collected fit neatly into two stacks, one with papers about jazz in literature, cinema, dance, and painting and a second with essays like Rasula's that were primarily theoretical. I now had the makings of a second anthology, which I called *Jazz among the Discourses*. Both were published in 1995 by Duke University Press.

The initial reception of the two anthologies was mixed. Jazz more or less belonged to music departments at that time, but only one of the contributors to the two anthologies was a musicologist. The rest were professors or students of literature, history, and philosophy who brought a more interdisciplinary perspective to the music. One musicologist who reviewed the books said that theory hung over the two anthologies "like a blimp." (I later told her that she should have said "like a star ship.") A handful of journalists also reviewed the books, at least one of whom accused the contributors and me of "not loving the music enough." The first indication that the anthologies were having an effect came when I ran into Robin D. G. Kelley, who was then teaching history at New York University and would eventually write a brilliant and definitive biography of Thelonious Monk. When Kelley congratulated me on the publication of the books, I thanked him, but I also said that so far as I could tell, only a handful of people had bought them. He replied, "I know them all."

One of my two contributions to the anthologies was a series of observations on canons in jazz history. In *Jazz among the Discourses*, I argued what many in literary studies had been saying for a while, that canon formation was a discourse of power. What made jazz unusual was that so many of its practitioners were radically disempowered. Most of the article was devoted primarily to describing how a jazz canon comes into being, for example, how a critic such as Martin Williams, who studied the New Criticism when he was a graduate student in English Departments in the 1950s, could make the case for Ornette Coleman in much the same way that T. S. Eliot once made the case for Virgil. But a recording can also be canonized when other artists consistently reference it in their recordings. I went through my collection tracking down the many references to Louis Armstrong's remarkable a cappella cadenza at the beginning of "West End Blues" (1928). I found, for example, a 1930 recording by Zach Whyte's Chocolate Beau Brummels, in which two trumpets reproduce the cadenza in unison while a drummer keeps time.

My contribution to *Representing Jazz* was an excerpt from my book, *Jammin' at the Margins: Jazz and the American Cinema*, which would be published in 1996 by the University of Chicago Press. Here, my interests in jazz and film came together. In that book, I was concerned with a number of myths that seemed to determine how jazz and jazz musicians were depicted by filmmakers. In the chapter that appeared in *Representing Jazz*, I wrote about the Black men who risked harsh punishment if they expressed their masculine aspirations but who nevertheless chose to outdo white trumpeters by playing louder, higher, and faster and with greater skill. Instead of being lynched, these African American men were applauded, and many white male artists (and many female artists) imitated their style. With my long history of listening to recorded jazz, I could identify stylistic tendencies in the work of several trumpeters and associate them with various versions of masculinity. As a cinema scholar, I cataloged scenes from a number of films, including *Young Man with a Horn*, that feature male trumpet players undergoing personal crises that impede their ability to hit a high note. At a climactic moment, they "can't get it up." Only in the movies can a trumpet signify impotence. Borrowing a term from Henry Louis Gates Jr., I called the essay "Signifyin(g) the Phallus." To this day, if I meet someone who is familiar with my writings, it is usually because of that essay. For better or worse, I am the trumpets-and-penises guy.

My record collection has always been essential to my writing about jazz. I am often somewhere between my yellow legal pads and my record player when I am writing. Just as importantly, the liner notes that come with the records have extremely useful information that is available nowhere else. A good example is the booklet by Stanley Dance included with a three-disc set called *The Ellington Era 1927–1940*, which I purchased early in my days as an Ellington completist. Dance, who would later edit Ellington's autobiography, quoted Duke on the meaning of one of his most popular compositions, "Black and Tan Fantasy." According to Ellington, a Black and Tan was a speakeasy "where people of all races and colors mixed together for the purpose of fulfilling their social aspirations."[6] So when I wrote an essay about the large body of films about jazz musicians that include highly fictionalized relationships between whites and Blacks, I called it "Black and Tan Fantasies."

In 1983, Michael Cuscuna and Charlie Lourie founded Mosaic Records and began producing boxed sets of jazz recordings aimed at serious collectors. Like the Columbia Record Club, it was entirely a mail-order business, so my earlier collecting method was repeated. Mosaic issued handsomely packaged collections with austere black-and-white (*shibui?*) covers. Because Cuscuna and Lourie were record company royalty, they had access to vaults where previously unavailable material was stored. I was overjoyed to acquire their boxed sets because they almost always bore titles like *The Complete Jimmie Lunceford Decca Sessions* or *The Complete Hank Mobley Blue Note Sessions, 1963–70*. The key word here is, of course, "complete." Once a box arrived, I could put comfortably grouped sets of check marks in the appropriate discography. All of the music was presented in beautiful transfers, first on LPs and a few years later on CDs. Even better, the liner notes inside every box were thorough and even scholarly. Mark Tucker, a music professor at Columbia University, who wrote the definitive *Ellington: The Early Years* (1997), wrote the essay for *Duke Ellington: The Complete Reprise Studio Recordings*. I must have purchased more than one hundred Mosaic boxes during the first thirty-seven years of their existence, and I cherish them to this day. All that music, thoroughly annotated, and presented, yes, *complete*.

At one point, I even made my collecting a part of my writing about jazz. A handful of thoughtful writers, most of them women, have made important contributions to the discipline of literary studies by foregrounding their presence within their texts. Unlike canonizing white males who write unselfconsciously from a godlike perspective, female critics were speaking honestly about why they were interested in certain material and how their own lived experienced gave meaning to what they were reading. For a long time, I had been aware of, shall we say, the idiosyncrasies of record collectors, not least my own. But I did not adopt the female critics' confessional mode and dwell seriously on the matter until I received a call from Murray Pomerance, a highly active compiler of writings in cinema studies. Murray told me to think of something I had considered writing but did not because I assumed no one would publish it. He continued, "Whatever it is, I will publish it."

I ended up calling my article for Murray's anthology "Revenge of the Nerds: Black Jazz Artists and Their White Shadows."[7] I concentrated primarily on a handful of films with a cast of characters that included jazz record collectors and serious fans of the music. Many of these white characters looked up to Black jazz musicians for their talent, their grace, and/or their manliness. A good example of the type is Francis (François Cluzet) in Bertrand Tavernier's *Round Midnight* (1986). Francis lives in Paris and is fascinated by the American ex-patriot saxophonist Dale Turner, who is played by the real-life American saxist Dexter Gordon. (I used to collect Dexter's records as a completist.) Not only does Francis have all of Dale's records; he collects Dale himself, inviting him to live in the same apartment with Francis and his daughter. At one point, Francis tells his ex-wife that he is devoted to Dale because "he inspires me." When the ex-wife asks, "Did I ever inspire you?" Francis stares back at her blankly.

Writing about films that feature collectors, I also drew on the writings of theorists such as Susan Stewart to explain the gendered positions of collectors. As Stewart argues, women are likely to have an emotional connection to what they collect. They can point to an item and tell you where it came from and why it is important to them. Men, by contrast, collect *serially*. If there are five books or five LPs or five salt-shakers in a set, a male collector will make sure he has them all.[8] I know no serious jazz collector who has volume 1 and volume 3 of something but not volume 2. And my male collector friends are very unlikely to be able to tell you where they found each one. Although men who collect in this fashion are usually declared to be anal retentive, I prefer Jacques Lacan's theories about bodies in the Symbolic Order.[9] The man whose collection is complete has no gaps and thus no anxiety about what is not there. Essentially, by seeking plenitude, the serial collector is warding off castration. Not surprisingly, during the many years that I presented these ideas to college students, very few women told me that they collected "like men." Even fewer male students admitted to collecting like women, assuming that some actually did.

Perhaps the most notorious collector of Black music in cinema history is Shrevie (Daniel Stern) in Barry Levinson's *Diner* (1982). In one memorable scene, Shrevie harshly scolds his wife for misfiling his records and for not knowing who Charlie Parker is. Male collectors of jazz, like Shrevie in *Diner* and Francis in *Round Midnight*, can be accused of more than just castration anxiety. Francis exhibits unresolved homoerotic longings in his fixation on the music and the body of Dale Turner, and Shrevie prefers the company of male friends who know more about jazz and pop than his wife does. Serious jazz collectors can also be charged with slumming, colonizing, voyeurism, and even a "permissible" form of racism in which African Americans are considered monolithically to be more musical, more spiritual, and more "authentic." Writing as a good postmodernist, I spared no one, including myself, from radical problematization. But if you had asked me in those days what I really thought, I would have told you that the music itself was worth owning and that it had only a casual relationship to the awkward blocks of vinyl on my sagging shelves.

By the beginnings of the twenty-first century, my jazz books were being read widely. I was regularly invited to speak at various universities with interdisciplinary jazz programs, especially in the United Kingdom. I have also been invited to speak in Switzerland, South Korea, Ireland, Singapore, Hungary, Australia, Portugal, and the Netherlands as well as several venues in the United States. On my travels I met new groups of jazz scholars, many of them substantially younger than me. On more than one occasion, a young colleague would refer to me as the "Father of the New Jazz Studies." Although I still think of myself as a film scholar, I am much better known for my writings on jazz. My last book was an "interpretive biography" of jazz bassist and composer Charles Mingus.

When I was teaching at Stony Brook, I had few opportunities to bring jazz into my teaching. Mostly I taught literature and cinema studies throughout my thirty-three years at that university. But after I retired in 2014, I was invited to teach an occasional course in the jazz studies program at Columbia University. I took great pleasure in teaching "Jazz and American Culture" on more than one occasion, always to classes filled with brilliant students, a few of whom were connoisseurs but most of whom were delighted to encounter for the first time the stories of James Baldwin, the autobiography of Sidney Bechet, and the films of John Cassavetes.

My collecting practices changed around 2010 when I began to run out of room in the New York apartment where my wife and I had been living since 1991. More disturbingly, one set of shelves filled with LPs began to lean forward precipitously. I decided that it was time to weed my collection and put most of the LPs into storage. I had been replacing my most beloved LPs with CDs for many years, and I fully realized that replacing everything was impossible. Nevertheless, I ended up putting thirty-one linear feet of boxes filled with LPs into a storage unit in a large facility a few blocks from where I lived. Because I chose a less expensive location within the facility, my LPs became almost totally inaccessible. I continued to buy CDs, often as replacements, but perhaps because I was now in my sixties, I lost my zeal for completism.

Every year that my LPs were in storage, the company that ran the facility raised their fees. By 2018, I was paying more than $80 a month. As a retiree on a fixed income, I made the difficult decision to empty my storage unit and to give my entire collection of LPs to one of the dealers whose auction lists were once so important to me. He took them all and slowly sold them to other collectors. For the next several months I received his checks, some of them in the four-figure register. I began to believe that my LPs were in good hands.

Jazz collectors live very different lives in the twenty-first century. With almost every piece of music now available for free on the internet, it is no longer necessary to own all those LPs and CDs. But I understand why someone would want to own them anyway. It's what collectors do. One of my friends collects Louis Armstrong on 78 rpm shellac, a medium that disappeared in the 1950s. He never listens to them, but he has them all. He surely takes as much pleasure in his collection as any numismatist or philatelist who has filled every empty space in an album. And then there is the very real absence of information if you listen to Spotify or Pandora. If you ask to hear Duke Ellington's recording of "Creole Love Call," for example, you will hear one of the hundreds of recordings he made of that tune but without any information about where, when, and who. Of course, if you have access to a good jazz discography, and there are several online, you can usually figure out the provenance of a recording as well as the names of the side people. But it is just not the same as owning the record.

A portion of the author's LP collection in the hallway of his apartment prior to being shipped off to a dealer, circa 2018

My life as a collector came full circle in the 1990s when I was speaking at a conference devoted to Louis Armstrong. Another speaker was none other than George Avakian, by then an elegantly dressed retired gentleman with a perfectly trimmed goatee. The man who several decades earlier had become a foundational figure in my own collecting history was now my friend. Before his death in 2017, we shared many a cup of coffee and many a glass of wine earnestly debating the finer points of jazz history. He even told me that when he and his two colleagues proposed the idea for the Columbia Record Club to Goddard Lieberson, he thought it was a bad idea but told them to go ahead anyway with their cockamamie scheme.

Eric Dolphy's LP, *Out to Lunch*, released in 1964

The author with Paula, Irene, and a few LPs in 1992

I still buy jazz now and then but always on CD. Even though I still believe that LPs sound better, I prefer the CD player to the clumsy apparatus designed for LPs. And I do not buy from auction lists as I did during my days as a completist. Mostly I buy the music of artists with whom I have a personal connection. For example, I will buy anything new by Charles Mingus, to whom I devoted several years of my life writing his biography. And when I was first falling in love with a young woman with refined tastes in music, I put on Eric Dolphy's *Out to Lunch* for her. When it was over, Paula said, "Do you have any more like that?" Reader, I married her. To this day, I will buy any new release by Eric. I now collect like a woman.

NOTES

1 Throughout this essay, I will be referring to "LPs," the dominant form of recorded sound from the early 1950s until the 1990s, when they were

effectively replaced by compact discs. For those who are too young to have experienced them, the old twelve-inch, long-playing (LP) records were made from vinyl and had room for about twenty-five minutes of music on each side. They had to be manually flipped over if you wanted to hear what was on the other side.

2   Sadly, George Avakian (1919–2017) did not write his memoirs. His interviews, however, can be found in Michael Jarrett, *Pressed for All Time: Producing the Great Jazz Albums* (Chapel Hill: University of North Carolina Press, 2016); Marc Myers, "Interview with George Avakian," Jazz Wax, March 15, 2010, www.jazzwax.com/2010/03/interview-george-avakian-part-1.html; and Monk Rowe, "Interview with George Avakian," Filius Jazz Archive at Hamilton College, April 21, 1998, YouTube, www.youtube.com/watch?v=LI5XKcirT60. I thank Susan Schmidt Horning for giving me a transcription of her interview with Avakian.

3   "78s" were ten-inch records with about three minutes of music on each side. They were made from shellac and easily broken. They dominated the market until the arrival of LPs, which had better fidelity, more music on each side, and much less fragility.

4   Once I had established myself as "an advanced collector," I began receiving auction lists in the mail. In the 1990s, of course, dealers who had previously mailed out these lists began selling their LPs on websites like eBay.

5   Toni Morrison, *Playing in the Dark: Whiteness and the Literary Imagination* (Cambridge, MA: Harvard University Press, 1992), 9–10.

6   Stanley Dance, Liner notes to *The Ellington Era 1927–1940*, Columbia Records, 1967.

7   See Krin Gabbard, "Hipsters and Nerds: Black Jazz Artists and Their White Shadows," in *Ladies and Gentlemen, Boys and Girls: Gender in Film at the End of the Twentieth Century*, ed. Murray Pomerance (Albany: State University of New York Press, 2001), 223–48. A longer version of the article appears in Krin Gabbard, "Revenge of the Nerds: Representing the White Male Collector of Black Music," in *Black Magic: White Hollywood and African American Culture* (New Brunswick, NJ: Rutgers University Press, 2008), 199–232. (2004).

8   Susan Stewart, *On Longing, Narratives of the Miniature, the Gigantic, the Souvenir, the Collection* (Durham, NC: Duke University Press, 1993).

9   Jacques Lacan, *The Four Fundamental Concepts of Psycho-analysis* (London: Hogarth, 1977).

4

ANIMATE OBJECTS

Joanne Bernardi

> Collecting as a process works in the shadowland,
> making its meaning on the edge where the practices of
> the past, the politics of present power, and the poetic
> capacity of each human being blur together.
>
> Susan M. Pearce[1]

MANY PEOPLE ROUTINELY TAKE STOCK of their belongings and fastidiously purge things that no longer serve a purpose. I am not one of these people. For as long as I can remember, I have always kept otherwise purposeless objects because they have a special presence for me as markers of moments, places, people, or interactions. Placeholders for the memories that form the fabric of my life, they reverberate with meaning. I am intrigued by how that meaning shifts or becomes magnified when I arrange these "souvenirs" of my life to create associations, like family photographs on a fireplace mantel. As with Scrabble tiles, the potential for connections increases exponentially with each new configuration. I first understood how even trivial objects can generate meaning or harbor memories that can be reexperienced when I was eighteen and under orders to fit my belongings into just two boxes. My family was moving back to the United States after residing overseas for most of my formative years. I couldn't justify packing many of my most treasured mementoes of this experience—plastic toys from hollow chocolate Easter eggs, odd labels, postcards, a disemboweled wristwatch, painted

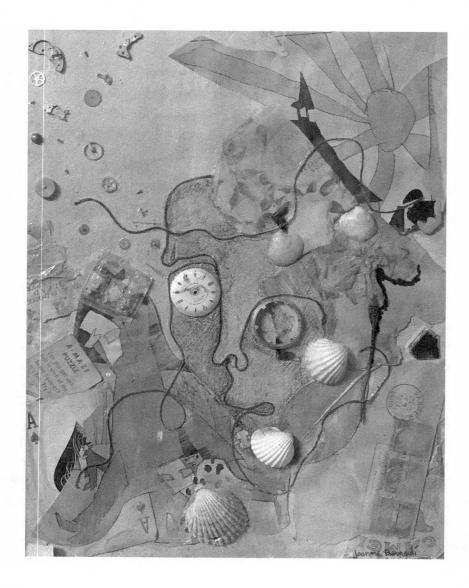

chicken wishbones (a mercifully brief hobby)—so I bought two blank canvases and made them into collages. I didn't legitimize these objects by transforming them into "art." Their intrinsic value as human-made and used objects made this process of meaningful assemblage possible. My mother had the collages framed and I met my two-box quota.

The author's two collages made to salvage treasured memories

Today, one collage is with my brother (it was his watch that I dissected), but I can still summon a whirlwind of memories from my expatriate childhood when I see its partner on my living room wall.

For a long time, the power of objects to resonate with meaning made me wary of becoming "a collector," someone who deliberately acquires things in a more strategic way. I did not think I had the time, money, or temperament that a more dedicated pursuit of desirable objects would entail. I continued to become attached to things that held personal significance for me, but I do not recall being motivated to keep things because of their broader practical, cultural, sociohistorical, or economic value. This attitude changed twenty years ago when I became a collector through my work as a scholar and teacher of film and media studies and Japanese culture. In 2000, I began searching online auctions for Japan-related ephemera from the first decades of the twentieth century to use as a personal cache of research and teaching resources. The impulse to seek out tangible traces of this period was a natural extension of research I had just completed on Japanese cinema from the 1900s through the early 1920s, a period of filmmaking seldom discussed without disclaiming its dearth of extant, accessible film prints.[2] I was curious to discover whether objects representing or reflecting lived experience and the landscape of Japan at this time were readily available online. If so, what types of objects would I find and what could they tell me about this transformative, modernizing moment in Japan's past that is so elusive today in moving images?

I am not sure when I realized that by creating parameters and a unique taxonomy for the objects I acquired, I had become a collector. My experience corroborates Mieke Bal's observation that "whereas it is virtually impossible to define collecting, and narratively speaking, to mark where that activity begins, a collecting attitude is unmistakable and distinct."[3] By 2013, I was on the fifth iteration of a dedicated course, Tourist Japan, which I had designed to complement my collecting and related research. At this point, the collection itself had reached sufficient critical mass to generate a large-scale collaborative digital humanities project, Re-envisioning Japan: Japan as Destination in 20th Century Visual and Material Culture (REJ), with an open-access, multimedia digital archive designed to dynamically display the collection online.

REJ is an open-ended project: the heterogeneous collection and digital archive are both works in progress. In 2017, we launched a second iteration of the REJ digital archive that better meets the challenges of displaying the collection's wide range of media formats, from bibliographical material, pamphlets and brochures, and other print ephemera (stereographs, photographs, albums, maps, and magazines) to three-dimensional objects such as souvenirs, glass lantern slides, and films. REJ investigates changing representations of Japan and its place in the world—how Japan defined itself and was defined by others—as documented by material objects from the late nineteenth century to 1970 in the general categories of travel, education, and entertainment. Collecting, curating, and using these objects in the classroom while developing this project has encouraged me to push beyond disciplinary boundaries to think critically about these inherently interactive tasks and to take full advantage of material culture's unique capacity to recover marginalized histories or create new frameworks for familiar narratives. Working on this project has given me a keener sense of collecting and curating as social and political acts: methods of communication that can influence how we make sense of the past and how our past relates to our world today. In sum, by making me a collector, REJ radically altered how I research, teach, and think about moving image media and Japanese culture.

A BRIEF COLLECTING BACKSTORY

It is difficult to arrive at a single definition for the human impulse to collect material culture, defined by James Deetz as "that sector of our physical environment that we modify through culturally determined behavior."[4] As REJ evolved, I became more adept at appreciating how objects signify differently depending on the conceptual frameworks I use for them and how I perceive their relationships to each other as well as to myself, a basic premise in material culture studies. Curating the REJ digital archive and working collaboratively on building the collection with my students and others repeatedly underscores the dramatic extent to which the meaning of objects is an unmoored entity, changing over time and according to context, subject to the biases and (to borrow from Susan M. Pearce, quoted in the epigraph) the "poetic capacity of each human being."[5]

Similarly, my title for this essay, "Animate Objects," can be understood on different levels corresponding to stages in building and working with the REJ collection. In the first presentations I gave on REJ about fifteen years ago, I used the terms *to animate, animating*, or *animated* quite literally to convey the sense that I was "bringing to life" both the objects and the subject matter at hand by strategically juxtaposing and framing tangible material culture and abstract ideas, concepts, and narratives, a kind of curation in itself. In time, *animate* took on an expanded range of meanings that encompassed my deeper understanding of objects as simultaneously "ensouled" (bearing traces of the human touch) and as springboards for activating the dynamic and complex processes through which objects make meaning as we appreciate and seek to interpret them as connections to our personal and collective past. My reluctance to think of myself as a collector until after REJ was well underway kept me from noticing possible connections between my personal fascination with (and attachment to) objects since childhood and the purposeful collecting central to my work today.

Childhood Collections

When I was around eleven or twelve my parents encouraged me to collect stamps and dolls in national dress from around the world as hobbies. I had inherited my eldest brother's stamp collection shortly after we moved to Europe, where I was able to substantially develop it further. By the time I received the collection, some of the older stamps were from countries that no longer existed or, as in the case of "Siam" (Thailand for a short time in the late 1940s), had long since changed names. I vividly recall enjoying the challenge of tracing these shifts in the configuration of the world, learning the names of different countries in their native languages, and discovering the unique cultural and geographical characteristics, prominent figures, and contemporary or historical events as portrayed by stamps. In retrospect, collecting dolls from different countries, with each doll dressed in characteristic "native costumes," similarly became an opportunity to learn about the world through objects. My first "international doll" was a souvenir from the Japanese pavilion of the 1964 New York World's Fair, a memorable and transformative event. Both of these hobbies underscore the extent to which actual or vicarious travel, a central motif in the REJ collection, strongly influenced my childhood interests.

Collecting Mentors

Just as family members encouraged my childhood collecting, friends and mentors helped me appreciate collecting as a critical framework and personal collections as resources during my graduate studies and professional career. A year studying abroad in Japan as a film student in college influenced my decision to choose East Asian studies as my home base for graduate work. My department focused on East Asian languages, literatures, history, religion, and thought. My plan to specialize in Japanese cinema was welcomed, but I worried about my objectives being marginalized or even whether I would find Japanese cinema resources in the library. A Japanese neighbor and family friend (a librarian familiar with the university's Japanese collections) allayed my fears. She said that if I found institutional collections lacking, I should just create a collection of my own to meet my needs. This insight was critical when I began research on silent Japanese cinema in the early 1980s and found that resources and archival access were limited.

While in Japan for doctoral research, I became indebted to private collectors with the foresight, knowledge, and experience to save or collect magazines, journals, books, pamphlets, trade publications, screenplays, souvenirs, postcards, advertisements, photographs, and other ancillary, mostly ephemeral print material essential to my work. They generously welcomed me into their homes, shared their knowledge of their collections, and taught me that private collections are key factors enabling research outside of well-established disciplines and topics of study.

In the late 1990s, a friend specializing in American silent cinema started a book project based on print ephemera she had purchased online, and this inspired me to explore online auctions myself. I first sought out film programs for classic (late 1970s to early 1980s) Japanese anime features that I routinely teach. Often large-format elaborately designed publications with glossy color photographs, plot synopses, film production notes, interviews with members of the cast and crew, and other types of commentary, these souvenir programs are commonly sold in film theater lobbies in Japan. I bring such programs to class when I can because I always find something about their layout or contents relevant to discussions, and it is gratifying to share this detail of the Japanese theater-going experience with my students.

Researching *Osaka Elegy* and 1930s Osaka

In 2005, I first effectively marshaled my emerging collection for my research while writing an essay on Kenji Mizoguchi's 1936 film *Osaka Elegy* (*Naniwa ereji*),[6] the first of Mizoguchi's many collaborations with screenwriter Yoshikata Yoda. The film depicts the downward spiral of Ayako (Isuzu Yamada), a young, modern working woman whose self-assertiveness and agency are undone by patriarchal social and cultural forces beyond her control. The specificity of Osaka's neighborhoods, architecture, and locations, all identified in Yoda's screenplay, make the city palpably recognizable. Both the script and film open, for example, with the bright neon lights illuminating Dōtonbori, the city's entertainment center, and end with Ayako alone at night on Ebisu Bridge, an extension of the Shinsaibashi shopping district just north of Dōtonbori's theaters, variety halls, restaurants, and bars.

I had been teaching *Osaka Elegy* for years, but when I watched the film and read the script again thinking about how to frame my essay, my collecting experience now gave me a keener sense of how and why the filmmakers skillfully wove Osaka's sights and sounds (Dōtonbori's neon lights and jazz tunes, the ultramodern Daimaru department store, the Osaka Iron Works and shipyard, etc.) throughout a drama rife with gender and class disparities and the zeitgeist of a politically precarious, modernizing Japan.

My guidebooks, maps (including a 1936 map of Osaka), travel guides, postcards, and photogravures brought alive a landscape and period that I had previously seen as a backdrop.

RE-ENVISIONING JAPAN

Over the past twenty years, REJ has evolved organically from individual research to an interdisciplinary faculty-library-student collaboration accommodating both research and teaching objectives.[7] The inclusion of small-gauge films in the collection and the possibility to stream many of these online in the context of other objects are features that make the project unique. As a hybrid project grounded in a unique relationship between the physical world (the REJ collection) and digital space (the REJ digital archive), REJ is recuperative (saving things otherwise lost to time), interpretive (organizing them in meaningful ways in critically mediated space), and generative (providing paths that allow others to discover and make use of them to generate new knowledge). The collection mainly comprises common-use, ephemeral objects dating from the late nineteenth century through the 1970s. Such objects are less likely to be prioritized by collecting institutions for detailed metadata, cataloging, and curation. This is also true for the films in the collection, which primarily fall under the category of orphan works.[8] By focusing on travel, education, and entertainment—closely related social activities contingent on the circulation, exchange, and interpretation of things through space and across time—REJ redefines such ephemeral objects as important to preserve because they can help us rethink received dominant narratives and assumptions about Japan and its place in the world during each object's time.

REJ and Researching and Teaching Japanese Film

My research on Japanese silent cinema was the most influential factor motivating me to start a collection of my own to draw on for both research and teaching. Pursuing traces of films that were important in their time but have long since disappeared left me preoccupied with the relationship between material loss and the history-making process. I initially sought photographic images of early-twentieth-century Japan that might bring me closer to the period that had long been the focus of my silent cinema research. I was immediately drawn to vintage postcards as visual records of place, especially the urban landscapes that might have been captured on film. There is in fact a close correlation between postcards and early cinema, especially travel films, as popular forms of media, evidence of place, and embodiments of image and movement.[9] The first postcards I collected helped determine REJ's subsequent focus on the three broadly defined categories of travel and tourism, education, and entertainment, and they comprise the largest media format represented in the collection.

While collecting postcards, I became increasingly invested in other representational practices that promoted Japan as a tourist destination, and objects generated by travel, education, and leisure that I interpreted as forging global connections. By 2002, my collecting led to an eponymous course, Tourist Japan, that has become a kind of sandbox for my research. This course is cross-listed with Film and Media Studies and includes weekly required screenings that complement readings on subjects that include the travel film (e.g., *Beautiful Japan*, Benjamin Brodsky, 1918).

Tourist Japan is a problem- and object-based course providing students with an opportunity to work directly with the objects in the REJ collection and digital archive and contribute to the project. Like the REJ project itself, Tourist Japan has now become a collaborative effort that bridges academic inquiry with curatorial practice. This was facilitated by REJ's migration from WordPress to Omeka in 2017.

During the first two to three weeks of class, students work with colleagues in the River Campus Libraries Department of Rare Books, Special Collections and Preservation to learn best practices in working with special collections and creating metadata, and there are two field trips to local cultural institutions. At George Eastman Museum, students can view early photographic images of Japan, and at the Memorial Art Gallery they ponder over tea box labels of unknown provenance illustrated in the Japanese style but believed to be locally made.

I introduce students to the heterogeneous nature of the REJ collection during the first week of class by asking them to browse through the archive and write a brief response on one film and one object in another format. I also show them "The World's Fair in a Nutshell," an "Object Encounter" that I devised with REJ collaborators as a prototype curatorial feature in Omeka for showcasing individual objects. These Object

Encounters are visual explorations of an object with a minimum of narrative intervention. They are inspired by Jules David Prown's step-by-step process of material culture analysis that advances through successive stages of description, deduction, speculation, and interpretation.[10]

After the first week of class, I scaffold hands-on classroom exercises into the course to provide students with tools they will need to make their own Object Encounter, the final project for the course. Especially through the process of building their own Object Encounter, students learn firsthand that the questions we ask of an object determine its levels of meaning. The exercises leading up to the completion of this final project include a metadata workshop (groups of students work with objects from three different media formats) and a trial run creating metadata in a dedicated Omeka sandbox site. We also practice Prownian analysis in class with a variety of objects from the collection, but I always start with an object that is unrelated to REJ or Japan but is challenging to identify. This is an obsolete kitchen utensil that students immediately think they can recognize because it resembles a familiar but different common-use object. "Twenty Questions to Ask an Object," a modified version of the classic game devised by the Material Culture Caucus of the American Studies Association, is another useful classroom exercise that helps students think about the narratives embodied by various collection objects.[11] Finally, students make a permanent contribution to REJ by creating or modifying metadata in the digital archive and posting their final Object Encounter to the site.

Tourist Japan students have always worked directly with the objects in the REJ collection as an alternative approach to understanding twentieth-century Japan through patterns of production and use, human interaction and cross-cultural exchange. By introducing the digital archive as a pedagogical tool, I transformed the course into a heuristic digital humanities lab where students could interact with the archive and learn the skills involved in cataloging and curation while haptically studying the objects in hand.

A HETEROGENEOUS COLLECTION

The REJ collection's approximately five thousand postcards and three thousand objects in other media formats are of mixed origin, but they were mostly made for Japanese- or English-language audiences. As such, they denote points of contact between Japan and the United States and, to a lesser extent, the United Kingdom. Only a portion of these objects have been digitized and made accessible online. Space precludes describing the full range of the collection, but I introduce three key formats: postcards, sheet music, and moving images. More broadly, other notable types of objects include shopping guides and advertising ephemera (e.g., matchbox labels and trade cards, often tie-ins with stage or screen productions). There are also souvenirs and brochures from international expositions, exhibitions, and world's fairs in which Japan participated. The collection includes several genres of literature, including magazines, memoirs, travel books, and children's literature as well as bibliographic and print ephemera related to general culture, history, and language. In addition to photographs and stereographs that I have acquired, the digital archive hosts a significant collection of lantern slides belonging to Rochester's Visual Studies Workshop. Remaining categories include missionary and social work ephemera, World War II propaganda (from both United States and Japan), and objects related to Japan's Allied Occupation period. The largest core thematic category, tourism and travel, includes general and site-specific guidebooks, maps, travel and hotel brochures, pamphlets, and ephemera related to both international and domestic travel.

Postcards

The postcard subgenres in the collection include those with views of cities and sites, especially urban entertainment centers (e.g., Tokyo's Asakusa district and Shinkyōgoku in Kyoto) and locations considered emblematic of Japan. There are also postcards with notable personal messages that are unique, surviving traces of relationships, often between Japanese pen pals and their English-language counterparts. Another postcard category provides a glimpse of Japan's rising profile in the international world

Undated postcards (ca. 1900) of Japan transported to the United States, with similar torii gates at Revere Beach in Revere, Massachusetts, and Ontario Beach Park in Rochester, New York (REJ collection)

order. For example, the Japanese flag or symbols of Japan (e.g., the chrysanthemum or a woman in kimono) are included in such series as "Our Allies" and "Flags of All Nations," and many postcards document Japan's presence at world's fairs and other international exhibitions. I am constantly intrigued by how many postcards depict Japanese gardens located outside of Japan, often in out-of-the-way towns or personal residences. I have even discovered cards depicting an imaginary Japan, such as various "Japanese villages" in the United States and Europe. Notable examples include postcards of an attraction at the Wonderland Amusement Park, Revere Beach, Massachusetts, described in one caption as a "15 Minute Trip through Flowery Japan" complete with its own "Mt. Geisha." Other subgenres include advertising postcards; postcards featuring children; colonial subjects; the imperial family; Japanese acrobatic teams, vaudeville and stage actors, and movie stars; women in a variety of dress, occupations, and settings; commemorative postcards; illustrated postcards; Japanese postcards with military and patriotic themes; and US World War II anti-Japanese propaganda. Many postcards are directly related to transportation and travel, such as those issued by the various iterations of Japan's government-run tourism and travel agencies and Japan's major shipping lines, airlines, and hotels.

Sheet Music and Films

The audio and video files that we created for the sheet music and films in the REJ collection and their interactive mode of presentation greatly enhance the archive's multimedia dimension. The two hundred pieces of "Japanesque" or Japan-inspired sheet music in the collection range from selections from Gilbert and Sullivan's 1885 *Mikado* and Tin Pan Alley tunes to World War II anti-Japanese propaganda. Forty-six of these songs were recorded by a team of graduate students at the Eastman School of Music working under the direction of a colleague, and they can be streamed online.

I deliberately avoided collecting films until five years into the project, but because moving images defined the twentieth century in an unprecedented way, they were too germane to ignore. A tip from a fellow collector I met online precipitated this change in my collecting. He drew my attention to a film can with an intriguing Sakura Film Company label and the words "Board of Tourist Industry, Japanese Government Railways, Tokyo Japan" printed in English. We both assumed the can was empty (it was cheap), but when it arrived on my doorstep, I was startled to find a reel inside. The print was visibly warped and gave off the pungent odor of decomposing acetate stock, indications that it might be too shrunken to project. I took it to colleagues in the George Eastman Museum's Moving Image Department who helped me view it on a flatbed. I had inadvertently purchased the second reel of *Women in Japan* (*Nippon no josei*, 1941), subtitled in English. An old business card enclosed in the can suggested the film traveled the educational film circuit in the United States. This wartime print's edge code revealed that it was made on Kodak film stock manufactured in Germany. The amount of information that I gleaned from an incomplete reel of film in its original can—information I would not have learned from a VHS or DVD copy—convinced me that I could no longer ignore acquiring films.

I attended the L. Jeffrey Selznick Certificate Program in Film Preservation at George Eastman Museum while on leave during the 2007–8 academic year to learn how to handle and inspect film prints in different stages of degradation and to research provenance and copyright status so films I collected could be digitized and accessed online. As I selectively acquired small-gauge (16 mm, Regular or Standard 8 mm, and Super 8 mm) films, I became more conscious of photochemical film as a mutable, organic object with a finite life cycle, much like everything else in the collection. This experience led to a course I designed and taught in 2009 called Film as Object, drawing from core topics in the Selznick Program. I continue to regularly teach this course on film materiality, preservation, and archiving in collaboration with George Eastman Museum's Moving Image Department.[12]

The approximately two hundred small-gauge films in the collection include amateur and educational films, stock footage, TV commercials, documentaries, travelogues, and films marketed for home entertainment. Many of these are digitized and available for streaming, allowing users to consider them in the context of other objects.[13]

There are critical intersections between small-gauge films, tourism, and education throughout the twentieth century. From the late 1920s through the 1930s, the growing popularity of amateur travel films and travelogues reflected the rise of popular tourism. After World War II through the 1980s, educational and promotional films about Japanese culture, contemporary society, and the nation's industrial and economic resurgence were plentiful, often sponsored by the Japan National Tourist Organization and the Japan External Trade Organization. Both before and after the war, foreign tourists could purchase mass-produced small-gauge films as souvenirs of their trip. They could choose from a number of topical subjects that included popular cities and sites, seasonal festivals or natural scenery, or unique aspects of traditional or contemporary culture. The amateur films in the REJ collection date from the 1930s through the 1980s.

In presenting the films online, I made the curatorial decision to leave leader at the heads and tails of each reel in order to emphasize the physicality of film as a material object. Another feature enhancing this sense of film as an object is the custom-built Video Player that allows users to change playback speeds by manipulating the frame rate in the Viewer Window's upper right-hand corner. This is especially useful for footage originally shot at slower speeds and later duplicated at today's standard rate of twenty-four frames per second. This is the case, for

An undated pamphlet advertising English subtitled Sakuragraph 16 mm souvenir films alongside footage from Sakuragraph's "Kamakura" (REJ collection)

example, for the oldest images in the collection that appear to have been shot sometime around 1905–10 but were acquired as a reel of stock footage dating from the 1960s.

Adding these films to REJ has been a labor-intensive but rewarding process. The collection is full of surprises. For example, the composer Tōru Takemitsu, known for his New Wave film soundtracks composed in the 1960s and 1970s, also scored a film in 1961 for the Japan External Trade Organization about water as an energy source. Bing Crosby narrates *Kyoto*

Saturday Afternoon (1952), a film about a day in the life of a foreign mis-sionary couple. In *Lantern Serenade* (1961), commissioned by the Philadel-phia Dairy Council and featuring puppets by the well-known puppeteers Frank and Elizabeth Haines, an American governess admonishes the Jap-anese emperor's sons that although "fish is delicious and rice is nice," they should "drink milk four times a day" to grow up big and strong.

Finding such unexpected connections has been more rewarding than I imagined when I first typed "Japan" in an online auction search box. Collecting lets me explore the past firsthand and discover traces of how people lived, what they believed and valued, and why. Whether the smallest detail of a single object, or larger contexts created through associations, both evince trends, influences, and intersections bringing our collective past into sharper focus.

It does not matter whether every object in my collection or each discovery I make finds its way into my work. As an open access resource, the REJ digital archive has already become useful to others, and there are plans for permanent stewardship of the physical collection. I continue to collect because of the endless questions objects raise: Who made them, saved them, and why? How were they used? What do they tell us about their past and their purpose, now perhaps lost? What do their "voices" tell me about the present and the future, about my work, my relationship to it, and myself?

NOTES

1   Susan M. Pearce, *Collecting in Contemporary Practice* (London: Altamira, 1998), 1.

2   I had just published *Writing in Light: The Silent Scenario and the Japanese Pure Film Movement* (Detroit: Wayne State University Press, 2001). In completing this book, I needed to rely on ancillary primary sources, espe-cially published scenarios, trade publications, and fan magazines in order to compensate for the lack of extant film prints. The experience height-ened my appreciation of the critical context ephemeral material provides.

3   Mieke Bal, "Telling Objects: A Narrative Perspective on Collecting," in *The Cultures of Collecting*, ed. John Elsner and Roger Cardinal (Cam-bridge, MA: Harvard University Press, 1994), 97–115, 99.

4 James Deetz, *In Small Things Forgotten: The Archaeology of Early American Life* (New York: Doubleday, 1977), 24.

5 Catherine Whalen uses the evocative term "unmoored" in a similar context in Whalen, "Collecting as Historical Practice and the Conundrum of the Unmoored Object," *The Oxford Handbook of History and Material Culture*, ed. Ivan Gaskell and Sarah Anne Carter (New York: Oxford University Press, 2020): 593–618.

6 Joanne Bernardi, "Osaka Elegy (1936): Revisiting 1930s Mizoguchi," in *Film Analysis: A Norton Reader*, ed. Jeffrey Geiger and R. L. Rutsky, 2nd ed. (New York: Norton, 2013): 240–61. The first edition was published in 2005.

7 For more details on REJ's origins and early stages as a collaborative project, see Joanne Bernardi and Nora Dimmock, "Creative Curating: The Digital Archive as Argument," in *Making Things and Drawing Boundaries: Experiments in the Digital Humanities*, ed. Jentery Sayers (Minneapolis: University of Minnesota Press, 2017), 187–97. Manifold Project digital edition, July 2019, dhdebates.gc.cuny.edu.

8 The term *orphan work* denotes ephemeral works that fall outside the purview and custodianship of identifiable rights-holders.

9 See, for example, Tom Gunning, "The Whole World within Reach: Travel Images without Borders," in *Virtual Voyages: Cinema and Travel*, ed. Jeffrey Ruoff (Durham, NC: Duke University Press, 2006), 25–41.

10 See Jules David Prown, "Mind in Matter: An Introduction to Material Culture Theory and Method," *Winterthur Portfolio* 17, no. 1 (1982): 1–19; and Kenneth Haltman, "Introduction," in *American Artifacts: Essays in Material Culture*, ed. Jules David Prown and Kenneth Haltman (East Lansing: Michigan State University Press, 2000).

11 I am indebted to Professor Catherine Whalen, Bard Graduate Center in New York City, for introducing the "obsolete kitchen utensil" exercise (the object is unnamed in order to continue the tradition) during a 2013 NEH Summer Institute on material culture convened at the center under the directorship of David Jaffee. For the "Twenty Questions to Ask an Object" exercise, see "Twenty Years, Twenty Questions to Ask an Object," YouTube, December 13, 2014, youtu.be/mPSeQF3OF1Q; for the related handout, see Patrick Cox, H-Net Editor, and H-Net Staff Editor, "Twenty Questions to Ask an Object: Handout," January 19, 2015, networks.h-net.org/twenty-questions-ask-object-handout.

12 Weekly topics include an introduction to the primary materials used in handling film, nitrate film and nitrate film conservation, film identification, using nonfilm (photos, stills, and paper) collections, film curatorship

and the history of film archiving, digital preservation, color and sound technology, film exhibition, and archival projection.

13   Joanne Bernardi, Re-envisioning Japan: Japan as Destination in 20th Century Visual and Material Culture (University of Rochester Digital Scholarship Lab, River Campus Libraries, Rochester, NY). First Word-Press iteration (2013–2016); current Omeka iteration (2017–present), rej.lib.rochester.edu.

5

GODZILLA ON THE SHELF

Spectacle and the Gigantic in Miniature

Mark Best

I COULD EASILY HAVE GROWN up watching *Godzilla* movies late at night or on Saturday afternoons but instead had the general awareness of Godzilla as a global pop culture icon and little more. So when I "discovered" *Godzilla* and other giant monster films many years later as an adult who works and teaches film studies and also collects toys, paying more academic attention to both *kaiju* (giant monster) films and their licensed toys was perhaps inevitable. At first, I was reluctant to head down the slippery slope of monster toys but eventually acquired a vinyl figure of the giant flying, fire-breathing, saber-toothed turtle Gamera, specifically from *Gamera: Guardian of the Universe* (Shūsuke Kaneko, 1995), the film responsible for my "conversion" to *kaiju* fandom. What I have found since is not only a stunning variety of fun toys in many styles but also a rich body of paratextual material with complex relationships to the narrative and spectacle of the films on which they are based.

Teruhisa Kitahara, a super-collector of vintage Japanese tin robots and other toys, observes that "many people indulge in a passion for collecting because in this way they can continually expand and enlarge the world which they themselves have discovered."[1] This is doubly true for collecting toys based on film and television franchises. After all, the toys are ostensibly created for children to expand on the diegetic world and action of a film or TV show through play. Every action figure based on a Marvel or *Star Wars* film promises the creation of new narratives, even if those narratives ultimately have nothing to do with the original text. The adult toy collector, however, faces the stereotypical dilemma of either "playing" with the action figure or "keeping it on the card"—or perhaps purchases two, one to keep and one to play with. As film- and television-based toys aimed specifically at collectors have increased in quantity and cost over the past few decades, so have figural details and elaborate packaging intended to appeal to the collector.[2] The result is a tension between play and "dis-play," an undoing of play if you will, where display becomes a sort of play for the collector.[3]

When I first began collecting Godzilla and other giant monster toys, my focus was on the variety of highly detailed vinyl figures produced primarily by Bandai since the early 1980s.[4] Because of the number of monsters and monster suit redesigns in the *Godzilla* series, Bandai has been able to make vinyl dolls based on both the *Godzilla* films released in the decades prior to the company's entry into monster film merchandise in 1983 and those released since. Godzilla figures in different sizes and scales, other monsters from Toho films, and other monster film and television franchises,[5] as well as products from other Japanese toy companies, has resulted in a *lot* of toys, which is why I was initially reluctant to purchase any monster toys at all.

At the same time my collection began, I was the chair of the "Toys and Games" area of the Midwest Popular Culture Association conference. I had previously presented there on other toys unrelated to film or television franchises but that demonstrate the tension between play and display. Consequently, as my Godzilla collection grew, I began to pay attention to one particular type of toy that foregrounds this tension and, more importantly for me eventually, comments on the specific pleasures offered by the films themselves: the diorama. Therefore, my first foray into the academic exploration of *kaiju* films in general, a conference presentation on these dioramas, was focused on the toys in my collection and the history behind them.

Despite being a commercial success, the first *Godzilla* film (*Gojira*, Ishirō Honda, 1954; "Americanized" and released in the United States as *Godzilla, King of the Monsters!* in 1956) inspired no toys or other spin-off products. Perhaps this was due to the film's portrayal of the monster as bringing bleak and relentless nuclear destruction, a representation of the abject far from the beloved cultural icon he would become, both in Japan and the United States. Indeed, in the first ten years after the film's release, only two licensed toys were manufactured—an air rifle in Japan, coinciding with the first *Godzilla* sequel, *Godzilla Raids Again* (Ishirō Honda, 1956), and a board game, released by Ideal in the United States to accompany a *King Kong* board game. Only in the mid-1960s, when the *Godzilla* film series had begun targeting a younger audience, did Godzilla toys really begin to take off. The first widely popular Godzilla toy was a model kit manufactured by Aurora in the United States in 1964. Its ongoing production would last through the height of Godzilla's success in America, remaining on store shelves until the mid-1970s, when the film series itself temporarily petered out. In 1966 in Japan, two years after the release of the America model kit, the Japanese company Marusan produced the first Godzilla vinyl figure, as well as those of several other monsters from *Godzilla* movies.[6]

The success of Aurora's Godzilla model kit in the 1960s and 1970s was predicated not only upon the popularity of Godzilla at the time but, more significantly, upon the general popularity of plastic model kit building. Plastic model kits took off in the United States in the early 1950s thanks to the dramatic increase in middle-class income and free time in the postwar era. The do-it-yourself hobby industry, including paint-by-numbers kits, model railroads and rockets, and many other arts and crafts, filled the void created by leisure hours. These hobbies occupied an unsteady cultural space, superior to idle hands doing the devil's work, on the one hand, but inferior to "true" art, on the other, against which they were defined as kitsch at best. Karal Ann Marling has described the popularity of plastic model kits in this larger context:

There was a wide margin for error. Satisfaction was virtually guaranteed. . . . Suddenly, men everywhere seemed intent on recreating in miniature their days of glory in the service or some bygone, golden era of chuffing locomotives and Tin Lizzies, back before the advent of traffic jams and last-minute dashes to catch the morning's last commuter local to the city. . . . Lou Glaser, the inventor [of Revell model kits], believed they appealed to the child in the man: models were, after all, toys for grownups. Because they were easy to make but looked so complicated when finished, they also generated a disproportionate and addictive upsurge of pride in achievement.[7]

Despite being mass produced, relatively easy, and aimed primarily at kids, the first Godzilla model kit in 1964 somewhat foregrounded its intention to be assembled with some degree of ability. Originally cast in a bright fuchsia, a far cry from the dark grayish green of the actual screen monster (and later editions of the kit), the model would require some application of skill, as well as paint, to begin to resemble the "real" Godzilla. Indeed, as an accurate figural representation of Godzilla, the kit is a failure. Despite the changes made to Godzilla's physical appearance from film to film, sometimes minimal, sometimes drastic, resulting in as many Godzillas as there have been *Godzilla* movies, the monster of the Aurora kit resembles none of them, except in a more general, iconic way.

I am especially interested in a feature that sets the 1964 Aurora Godzilla model apart from the vast majority of cars, airplanes, battleships, and other vehicles dominating the plastic model kit hobby at the time. Along with a handful of other monster, dinosaur, and figural kits made by Aurora and other manufacturers, the Godzilla model is a diorama: instead of standing alone, the monster stands on a base representing an urban landscape in the process of being destroyed by the monster. And once assembled, the primary purpose of this figure is to be placed on a shelf and admired, not just as a demonstration of the owner's model-building skills but also as a frozen diegetic moment from a (in this case, nonexistent) *Godzilla* movie.

Since the Aurora kit of the 1960s, the diorama has become a category of Godzilla toy in itself, whether in model kit form or prepainted and easily assembled. Unlike stand-alone figures, dioramas represent fantasies of the monster's presence in the larger world or the world of a specific film. Godzilla dioramas often depict moments of maximum spectacle from the films: the monster's first appearance, a moment of great devastation, a spectacular moment of battle with another monster. In the early 2000s, Bandai released a long series of miniature dioramas based on the work of Yūji Sakai, a sculptor of Godzilla and other monster figures often reproduced as toys or model kits. Each figure in the series features Godzilla in a specific moment from each *Godzilla* film up to that time. Meticulously detailed and painted, the figures emphasize the differences among various Godzilla suits over the decades, and the landscapes range from barren rubble to complex urban settings, depending on the film, all in precise scale. Sometimes consisting of only three or four pieces to assemble, these dioramas are also much smaller than the Aurora model kit and most other Godzilla toys in general.

For example, one diorama depicts Godzilla menacing a sprawling Diet Building from the original 1954 film, the figures painted in shades of gray because the film was in black and white. In the figure for *Godzilla vs. King Ghidorah* (Kazuki Ōmori, 1991), Godzilla is dwarfed by Tokyo Tower, its digital clock reading 7:00, just like in the film. My favorite of these dioramas is for *Godzilla vs. Destoroyah* (Takao Ōkawara, 1995). About to go into radioactive meltdown—emphasized by body parts of orange translucent plastic—Godzilla casually walks through the Wan Chai district of Hong Kong. The Central Plaza building stands ahead, as tall as Godzilla, while the monster's right hand begins to knock the top off a nearby high-rise. Windows in the surrounding hotels and office buildings are painted individually, and streetlights cast pools of light on a bypass below. The figure is only three inches tall (and each eighth-inch streetlight is tipped with the same clear orange plastic as Godzilla's burning parts).

In contrast to the Aurora model kit or, say, larger model kits sculpted by Sakai and other artists, this representation of Godzilla about to devastate parts of Hong Kong consists of eleven pieces designed to fit

Godzilla in Hong Kong from *Godzilla vs. Destoroyah* (Takao Ōkawara, 1995), Yūji Sakai, Real Product Stage Godzilla Complete Works 1, Bandai, 2004

perfectly together, involving no skill and perhaps a minute or two of labor. Its purpose is to be looked at, appreciated for its level of detail in miniature (the product of Yūji Sakai, on the one hand, and workers in a Chinese toy factory, on the other) and for the moment of (imminent) spectacle that it depicts. However, such dioramas can also take a given film's spectacle further than the film itself. Another Yūji Sakai diorama, also based on *Godzilla vs. King Ghidorah*, represents Godzilla gripping the nose of a Russian nuclear submarine. The monster's tail and the length of the submarine extend beyond the small base, signifying by synecdoche the broader ocean and seabed. This precise moment is not actually seen in the film itself. In the film, we see shots of the submarine, distressed crewmen, and the blurry form of Godzilla, intercut with one another, culminating in a generic undersea explosion. The diorama shows us what the film's limited underwater special effects can only suggest.

Georgia canned coffee premiums for *Godzilla: Tokyo S.O.S.* (Masaaki Tezuka, 2003). Godzilla and Russian submarine from *Godzilla vs. King Ghidorah* (Kazuki Ōmori, 1991), Yūji Sakai, Godzilla Appearance 2, Bandai, 2002

Implicit in these figures is the idea of the toy as art, despite being mass-produced toys or figurines. Indeed, beautifully staged photographs of Yūji Sakai's Godzilla sculptures (which are much larger than the Bandai dioramas, of course) have been collected and published in book form, offering the fan or collector another way of appreciating Sakai's skill beyond the miniature on the shelf. Another set of toy dioramas in my collection, produced by the Japanese company Megahouse, also in the 2000s, promotes the miniature's status as art even more explicitly. The series is called the "Art Works Collection featuring Yūji Kaida," an artist and illustrator known for his paintings of elaborate scenes of intense spectacle—again, first appearances, battles, destruction, and so on—used for posters, magazine and comic book covers, and the like. Most of these dioramas are fairly straightforward in their representations of Kaida's paintings, such as a miniature representation (of the artist's own representation) of the climactic moment in *Gamera: Guardian of the Universe*, when the heroic giant turtle absorbs the flames from massive explosions into its body. Like Sakai's burning Godzilla marching through Hong Kong, and with a similar level of detail, the diorama uses translucent orange plastic for explosions behind Gamera, trails of flame circling the monster, and parts of the monster itself. A few industrial buildings stand low in the foreground, emphasizing the size of the monster and the explosions, just like both Kaida's painting and the scene it is based on.

However, Kaida often uses exaggerated perspective in his paintings to further emphasize the spectacle from the films or television shows his works are based on, and some of the miniature adaptations attempt to reproduce this perspective with mixed results. In another Kaida painting based on *Gamera: Guardian of the Universe*, the giant turtle dominates the bottom two-thirds of the scene, while behind and above him the evil flying lizard Gyaos roosts on a broken Tokyo Tower. The size of the monsters is emphasized by impossibly small burning buildings in front of Gamera's feet, all viewed by the spectator from across a river or bay, which reflects the flames. The image has the aesthetics of a movie poster, emphasizing key features of the film and the promise of the spectacle of destruction, without concern for scale. The miniature diorama based on this painting uses forced perspective to squeeze this spectacle into a few inches of three-dimensional space. All the elements of the painting are present, including the tiny burning buildings (more translucent orange plastic) in the foreground, but now Tokyo Tower looms impossibly huge above the cityscape with a tiny Gyaos perched atop it. Consequently, the diorama best reproduces the visual impact of the painting if the viewer holds it a few inches in front of one eye—thus far less impressive sitting on the collector's shelf, despite the remarkable details.

Other dioramas from the series use similar forced perspective and require similar viewing to achieve something close to the visual effect of the paintings they are based on. However, speaking for myself at least, the pleasure in these toys is based less on how well they reproduce the original images and more on the fact that they attempt to do

Dioramas based on Yūji Kaida paintings of *Gamera: Guardian of the Universe* (Shūsuke Kaneko, 1995), Art Works Collection featuring Yūji Kaida, Megahouse, 2006

so at all—that is, that they even exist—at least *evoking* the spectacle of the paintings, which in turn reproduces (or more often enhances) the spectacle of the films.

While all these examples of toy dioramas are based on preexisting films, another set of miniature scenes in my collection uses different strategies to emphasize the spectacle of destruction, in this case for promoting and marketing the film *Godzilla: Tokyo S.O.S.* (Masaaki Tezuka, 2003). Packaged with Georgia canned coffee, these tiny dioramas, sometimes with more pieces than the Sakai or Kaida dioramas just described, feature the giant monsters from the film menacing major Tokyo landmarks: Godzilla topples Tokyo Tower, Mecha Godzilla batters the Takashimaya Department Store or stands next to the Mori Tower in Roppongi Hills, a Mothra larva crawls onto the Tokyo Metropolitan Government Building.

Standing 1½ to 3 inches tall, with Godzilla himself about 1½ inches, these tiny scenes lack the detail that even slightly larger figures allow. Simple lines of paint suggest signage on the Takashimaya Department Store, in contrast to the individually painted windows of Sakai's Godzilla in Hong Kong. Correct scale is irrelevant. In one figure, Godzilla is accurately dwarfed by Tokyo Tower, while in another he stomps one foot onto the roof of the Tokyo Dome, a stadium that could easily contain the King of the Monsters in the film. Rather, the primary goal of these figures is to associate large, iconic Tokyo buildings, specifically ones associated with official institutions and consumption, with iconic Toho monsters.[8] In fact, these promotional toys promise moments of spectacle that never actually occur in the film itself. While the film features lots of generic urban destruction, and the Diet Building (which is not featured in these dioramas) and Tokyo Tower are both destroyed in major special effects set pieces, most of the buildings in these promotional toys are never seen on the screen at all.

By freezing, containing, and miniaturizing such moments of giant monster movie spectacle, whether diegetic or invented, these toys have been illuminating to me of how the *kaiju* genre's filmic pleasures may work for the viewer. As a mode of representing the giant monster, the diorama involves several apparent paradoxes. Susan Stewart has argued that the miniature, as encountered in the dollhouse, the toy railroad, and the like, represents interiority, domesticity, the private, "a mental world of proportion, control, and balance."[9] However, the Godzilla diorama does not portray a scaled-down (and thereby defamiliarized) version of the adult world. Rather, it represents the opposite of the miniature, the gigantic, which Stewart associates with "infinity, exteriority, the public, and the overly natural"—with "disorder and disproportion."[10] The Godzilla diorama embodies a tension between these opposing trajectories, simultaneously evoking and containing the disorder of the gigantic, while both using and challenging the order of the miniature.

The same could be said of many toys in Japanese popular culture, where most toy robots signify giant robots and superheroes like Ultraman stand as tall as the giant monsters they fight. However, in contrast

Three-inch-tall Godzilla and Hong Kong with ⅛-inch-tall streetlights versus 1½-inch-tall Godzilla and ¼-inch-tall Tokyo Dome

to the technological and social order represented by the robot or the hero, these Godzilla dioramas celebrate the destruction of that order. The spectacle of destruction is the greatest pleasure of giant monster movies, of course, as most famously argued by Susan Sontag in "The Imagination of Disaster" in 1965 and explored by a number of scholars since.[11] Regardless of whether the monster is a straightforward metaphor for the horrors of nuclear holocaust, as in the 1954 film *Gojira*, or is a superhero defending humanity from other monsters, as in many of the *Godzilla* films of the 1960s and '70s, or is a force of nature analogous to a typhoon or earthquake, as in more recent Godzilla films such as *Shin Godzilla* (Hideaki Anno and Shinji Higuchi, 2016), an essential convention of the genre is the destruction of urban landscapes. Whether we choose to view a Japanese monster movie seriously, as the original 1954 film demands, or from a camp aesthetic, laughing at actors in rubber suits, the spectacle of destruction is essential to our enjoyment.

In his short essay on toys in *Mythologies*, Roland Barthes protests children's toys that reproduce the adult world in miniature and thereby socialize children into the bourgeois values of that adult world.[12] Godzilla toys offer the opportunity for a child to fantasize about destroying that world, or the collector to display that destruction in miniature, especially in the diorama form. As noted above, the tiny Georgia Coffee dioramas promoting *Godzilla: Tokyo S.O.S.* depict the monsters threatening monumental symbols of official authority and social order in Japanese culture more so than the film itself.

Stewart argues that the miniature tableaux of the historical diorama functions to "bring historical events 'to life,' to immediacy, and thereby to erase their history, to lose us within their presentness."[13] Whether depicting the monster's initial appearance or the monster's destruction of a skyscraper or monument, the Godzilla diorama suspends the most transient and liminal of moments, the moment between completeness and absence. I would suggest this may also be the moment of the viewer's greatest and most radical pleasure, the moment revealing Godzilla to be the enemy of hegemony, the fantasy of knocking down the institutions that function to structure our relationships to authority, structures that are gigantic themselves.[14]

Inevitably, this moment and pleasure will be displaced, shifting to the reconfirmation of the status quo. Godzilla and his friends will be vanquished, or just go back to Monster Island, or, in the case of the original Gamera films, fly away while children wave adoringly. But with each film's return to normalcy comes the promise of the monster returning in a sequel to destroy Tokyo yet again. The Godzilla diorama is perhaps more effective in containing the threat of the monstrous and the gigantic even as it attempts to celebrate and preserve it, because of the connotations of craftsmanship and artistry that are attached to the diorama. The successful representation of destruction is predicated upon the skill of a builder. Ultimately, the Godzilla diorama reasserts the order it challenges. As Marling succinctly puts it, in her discussion of the American plastic model hobby during the Cold War, "Industry analysts suggested that hobbyists were people who craved realism, precision, and certainty in lives lived in the shadow of nuclear terror."[15] As

Godzilla and what his capacity for destruction represent have changed over the past six decades, the diorama's ability to simultaneously evoke and contain those meanings has remained the same.

The artistry of the Godzilla diorama references another relationship of scale between the viewer and the monster, namely the miniature landscapes of the monster movie set and the suitmation actor in the monster's costume.[16] The skill of the hobbyist or model kit artist is analogous to that of the cinema craftsmen, set designers, monster suit makers, and model makers who create the temporary urban settings—the miniature buildings, trains, and monuments—that the man in the suit will proceed to trample. Or these skills directly overlap: the sculptor Yūji Sakai has also designed and modeled monsters for several Godzilla films, not surprisingly, in addition to creating toys. Giant monster films are the product of many artisans, and like the moment of destruction preserved in plastic or vinyl, the success of each film's spectacle of destruction itself signifies "proportion, order, and balance" in the cinematic craftsmanship preserved on film.

Born out of my collecting, my growing awareness of this craftsmanship and spectacle led to greater academic interest in the films themselves, specifically my ongoing research on the history of the *Gamera* film series and development of a course on giant monster movies. Both projects explore questions of genre, representation, and pleasure extensively, and, in the case of my Gamera book especially, examine production history in detail. The original *Gamera* films, released from 1965 to 1971, offer a case study of the challenges of producing convincing miniature-based spectacle against limited budgets.

One of my favorite examples of the negotiation of budget restrictions, miniature special effects craftsmanship, and other unexpected constraints is the 1970 film *Gamera vs. Jiger*. The film was intended to promote the Japan World Exposition of 1970—Expo '70—a world's fair held in Osaka, Japan. Expo '70 was an ideal setting for a *Gamera* film, its brightly colored, experimental architecture perfect for monster mayhem, and its Expoland amusement park offering real children something like the sci-fi adventures their cinematic counterparts had enjoyed with Gamera in previous films. Most of the human action in the film is set in and around Expo '70, and the film includes a short, documentary-style description of the fair that also connects it to the film's monster plot.

However, while the focus on Expo '70 gave the film's director Noriaki Yuasa a somewhat higher budget compared to the previous films in the series, he was also forbidden by the Expo '70 staff to show the destruction of any Expo '70 buildings on film. Thus, for example, an impressive special effects set piece features a sick and injured Gamera shambling through a detailed industrial district and collapsing into Osaka Bay, while the closest the film comes to meeting the expectation of Expo '70 destruction is the evil monster Jiger bumping her nose against the fair's Soviet Pavilion. Instead, Gamera saves Expo '70 from any further threats. Osaka itself is not spared from miniature destruction, but an undeveloped area adjacent to the world's fair becomes the site, again in miniature of course, of Gamera's climactic battle with Jiger to protect the fair.

While saving Expo '70 from Jiger becomes a major goal of the film's human heroes—and eventually its monster hero as well—Yuasa cleverly extends the presence of Expo '70 in the film by association. In one early scene, helicopters hoist an ancient statue from a Polynesian island to display at the fair. Later, the film's two boy heroes pilot a pocket submarine labeled "Expo '70" down a comatose Gamera's throat and into his lungs to fight a parasitic baby Jiger. Through the film, Yuasa and his crew use these well-crafted miniatures—generic urban and industrial landscapes, Osaka Tower, the helicopters and submarine—to navigate the expectations of the spectacle of destruction and the limitations of the film's budget and producers.[17] And perhaps not surprisingly, in the mid-aughts the Japanese company Iwakura, which has produced numerous monster miniatures based on unexpected subjects from various *Godzilla* and *Gamera* films, and on other, more obscure special effects and horror films, released a diorama of the Expo '70 pocket submarine and baby Jiger.

I should clarify that I do not only collect miniature monster dioramas. Posable vinyl toys were the first I acquired, like most other fans and collectors, I suspect. Like the dioramas, these figures are characterized by the detail of the sculpting, and they attempt to evoke the spectacle of particular films by replicating the specific monster suit designs found in each film. However, without a dioramic context defining them as frozen moments on display, these toys foreground their capacity for play, and the player (whether child or adult) must provide the larger narrative context, whether it be the destruction of skyscrapers made of building blocks or monsters enjoying a picnic. The specificity of a preserved tableau is replaced by the potential of imaginative play. Of course, the owner of the toy can equally choose to preserve and display the toy instead, thereby foregrounding the meaning signified by the toy's details.

Among these vinyl figures, however, are those which reference Godzilla's cinematic past in an altogether different way. As the *Godzilla* films themselves began including children in their target audience, so Godzilla toys began to be aimed specifically at children, and the style of these toys foregrounded their "toyness." Emphasizing iconic representation over precision, detail, and "realism," these toys featured wild color schemes (of both vinyl and paint applications) and almost crude sculpting.

Today these vintage toys are highly sought after and expensive collector's items. Consequently, they have been reproduced and imitated by multiple companies and have led to a cottage industry of both Japanese and American artists who make their own original monster toys in this retro style. This style signifies these figures' status as "playthings," toys to be played with, even as their limited availability and prices indicate that they are aimed at an audience of adults with money to spend on collectibles. Indeed, instead of invoking the pleasures of the spectacle of destruction fleetingly offered by viewing the film, and ignoring the craftsmanship associated with both the diorama and the film set, these newer toys embody the nostalgia that has inspired them. In 2005, the company Iwakura released a series of miniature vinyl versions of the vintage toys. Carefully reproducing the sculpting and vibrant colors of the originals, the figures came packaged in clear plastic bags with little header cards, perfectly miniaturized for the collector with limited funds and/or space. Standing on a shelf next to highly detailed miniature dioramas in muted colors, or among a host of much larger and realistic Godzilla figures, and bypassing the tensions between craftsmanship and destruction, between order and chaos that I have attempted to suggest, these bright and cheery toys demonstrate the vast capacity for signification that Godzilla and his fellow *kaiju* have acquired over almost seventy years.

NOTES

1   Teruhisa Kitahara and Yukio Shimizu, *Robots, Spaceships & Other Tin Toys: The Teruhisa Kitahara Collection* (Cologne: Taschen, 2011), 8.

2   Toys marketed at adult collectors also include more simplified and stylized toys and packaging based on the now-expensive toys of the past, to appeal to the collector's nostalgia.

3   Somewhat regretfully I should note that the words *play* and *display* do not share roots, and *display* is not *play* with the prefix *dis-* added.

4   While these toys from Bandai could be called "action figures," they tend to be articulated only at the shoulders and hips (or just hips for quadrupedal monsters) or even less, not allowing for much "action." Many collectors refer to them simply as "vinyl dolls." Of course, far more posable and complex monster toys also exist now, but these simply posable figures are the most common.

5   For example, the Gamera series, originally from Daiei Studios and the most successful rival to Toho's Godzilla, and my main interest as a collector and scholar; Ultraman, the television superhero from Tsuburaya Productions who has battled a host of giant monsters since 1966; and many others.

6   Sean Linkenback, *An Unauthorized Guide to Godzilla Collectibles* (Atglen, PA: Schiffer, 1998), 11–13.

7   Karal Ann Marling, *As Seen on TV: The Visual Culture of Everyday Life in the 1950s* (Cambridge, MA: Harvard University Press, 1996), 58–59.

8   For Japanese consumers unfamiliar with Tokyo's architecture, each figure comes with a small paper identifying the landmark.

9   Susan Stewart, *On Longing, Narratives of the Miniature, the Gigantic, the Souvenir, the Collection* (Durham, NC: Duke University Press, 1993), 74.

10   Stewart, 70, 74.

11   Cf. Susan Napier, whose article "Panic Sites: The Japanese Imagination of Disaster from Godzilla to Akira," *Journal of Japanese Studies* 19, no. 2 (1993): 327–51, explicitly evokes Sontag in its title.

12   Roland Barthes, "Toys," *Mythologies*, trans. Annette Lavers (New York: Noonday Press, 1990), 53–55.

13   Stewart, *On Longing*, 60.

14   The film *Shin Godzilla* (Hideaki Anno and Shinji Higuchi, 2016) may be the most explicit example of this, through its intentionally excessive emphasis on the ineffective structures of Japanese bureaucracy attempting to contain the giant monster's rampage. The film can easily be read as a commentary on the government's response to the 2011 Tohoku earthquake and tsunami and the resulting nuclear disaster in Fukushima.

15   Marling, *As Seen on TV*, 59.

16   As the term suggests, *suitmation* refers to the familiar practical effects of older Japanese *kaiju* films involving an actor in a monster suit destroying miniature landscapes and battling other actors in other monster suits.

17   I was able to present on the complex relationship between this film and Expo '70 at the BIMI-Pitt Research Workshop, a collaborative event between the University of Pittsburgh and the Birkbeck Institute for the Moving Image at Birkbeck University, London, in 2017.

6

APE AND ESSENCE

Adam Lowenstein

MY VOYAGE TO THE WORLD of film scholarship began with an intensive residence on the planet of the apes.

I was not aware of it at the time, but my teenage obsession with collecting all things connected to the *Planet of the Apes* film series now feels like my first foray into the sort of research project that would characterize my professional career as an academic film scholar. Back then, I tracked down everything from movie posters and film stills to trading cards and comic books, with soundtrack albums, model kits, action figures, and even a bar of soap (I can still conjure its artificially perfumed scent!) in between. If it had something, anything, to do with *Planet of the Apes*, I had to have it.

Today, I recognize the traces of such obsessive tendencies in my passionate attachment to my subjects of research. When I study the horror film or surrealist cinema, for example, I no longer feel the need to collect the things attached to the films. But I do feel powerfully driven to immerse myself as completely as possible in their cinematic worlds. I still want to dwell in those realms of experience that blur the line between film and life. For me, the collecting impulse survives in my "sensory surround" approach to research and teaching: devoting my energy to extending the cinematic encounter beyond the confines of the screening and into the experiential arenas of history, thought, feeling, and self-reckoning. You might say that as a film scholar and as a spectator (as well as a scholar of film spectatorship), I am always returning to the planet of the apes—or perhaps I never really left.

I was born in 1970, so I was too young to experience *Planet of the Apes* in movie theaters. In five films commencing in 1968 and concluding in 1973, producer Arthur P. Jacobs and his collaborators created a remarkably ambitious and imaginative science fiction universe drawn initially from Pierre Boulle's French novel *Monkey Planet* (1963). I use the term *universe* here deliberately, in that current connotations of the concept are often attached to superhero and fantasy-themed film franchises (such as the Marvel Cinematic Universe built around *The Avengers*) that I believe the *Planet of the Apes* films had a hand in shaping: the stories and characters developed across multiple films and media platforms, the plentiful marketing, and the product tie-ins. But I cannot dwell in the Marvel Cinematic Universe or the Middle-earth of *Lord of the Rings* or the Hogwarts of *Harry Potter* or even the well-crafted reboot of the *Planet of the Apes* film series begun in 2011 the way I lived on that original planet of the apes. Doubtlessly this has a lot to do with my age, then and now, but I think it is also connected to a poignant sense of belatedness, of getting to the planet of the apes out of time rather than on time.

I first encountered *Planet of the Apes* on television. I can still recall in vivid detail that first overwhelming image, even on a tiny black-and-white TV, of a gorilla on horseback, dressed in military garb and toting a rifle poised to fire at fleeing humans during a hunt. I was just five or six years old, and I was hooked at first sight. So scary, so fascinating, so unexpected, so topsy-turvy. I had no idea that this was *Planet of the Apes* (Franklin J. Schaffner, 1968), a film older than I was. But the film's deep imprint on popular culture, with its four sequels and two TV series and countless spin-off artifacts, meant that *Planet of the Apes* was something I could discover even after missing its initial impact.

I did not start collecting *Planet of the Apes* memorabilia in earnest until I was twelve or thirteen years old. The films had acquired a new, more adult allure for me as allegories of racial conflict and the civil rights struggle—precisely the kinds of historical trauma on film I would go on to study in my academic career.[1] This was also the era when the marriage of my parents disintegrated, eventually ending in divorce. By this time, I was a newspaper delivery boy with some money of my own. I used these funds, along with birthday and bar mitzvah gifts, to amass a collection I still own today, stored away in a trunk in my basement. This essay constitutes the opening of that trunk, what Walter Benjamin calls "unpacking my library": exploring the ways in which my *Planet of the Apes* collection has shaped who I am not only as a film scholar but also as a person always struggling to understand the impact of the past on the present. The mystery of how personal history and public history intertwine, how horror and trauma move between registers of internal and external, has its roots for me in my *Planet of the Apes* collection and that collection's relation to my experience of the cinematic itself.

Although they are almost always considered science fiction movies and not horror films, the shock of the horrific was central to my childhood attraction to the *Apes* films. As a number of scholars have noted, there is significant overlap between the horror and science fiction genres.[2] In my own teaching, I tend to distinguish between them as a matter of tone more than anything else. If the dominant tone of science fiction is the thoughtful "What if?," then the dominant tone of horror is the visceral "Oh no!"[3] My own experience with *Planet of the Apes* was always rooted in horror, with that initial terrifying image of the armed gorilla on horseback, even if it bloomed through science fiction's fascinations with subjects such as time travel and alternate evolution.

Today, in a movie culture rampant with digitized animals squeaking and squawking for every dollar a pleading kid can cajole from their parents, many people tend to assume the original *Apes* films must have been targeting young children primarily. This is simply untrue, even if the movies wound up reaching a young audience, especially after the creation of a live-action and then an animated TV show after the movies ceased production.[4] The *Apes* films may not be horror films at first glance, but their ability to stare at the horrific in ourselves through the lens of an other is never less than sobering and often quite haunting.

Their effect on me was deep, profound, and long lasting, especially in terms of my own approach to horror as a genre intimately linked to history, trauma, and otherness.

The *Apes* movies brush up against horror when they play with distinctions between self and other. These films are constantly positing the apes as other to us and therefore frightening for us. But then the films will reverse the lens and demonstrate how the apes suffer at the hands of those who consider them their others—the humans, us. Often it is the humans who are inhumane, and the apes who are humane; or if the apes act inhumanely, they ultimately remind us more of ourselves than our others. And this vertiginous sensation, laced with the uncanny Freudian shock when the horrifyingly unfamiliar metamorphoses into the discomfortingly familiar, often carries the films into the territory of horror. The apes can be as monstrous as the humans and vice versa, so monstrosity confronts us at every turn no matter who we label as "other." It is not merely a trivial detail that one of the screenwriters on the original film was none other than Rod Serling, the guiding light behind *The Twilight Zone*—one of the most uncanny and often terrifying television programs ever produced.

Planet of the Apes gives us our first glimpse of John Chambers's ingenious prosthetic makeup design (long before the computer-generated imagery that made the series reboot possible) in the midst of a frightening hunt sequence where civilized, talking gorillas are the hunters and primitive, mute humans in loincloths are their prey. Taylor (Charlton Heston) and his two surviving fellow astronauts, who have made the voyage from our Earth in our time to what they believe to be some far-flung planet in another solar system some two thousand years hence, are greeted with a crushing answer to Taylor's hypothesis, adopted as the movie's brilliant tag line: "Somewhere in the universe there must be something better than man." These apes seem to embody humankind's worst tendencies, at least in terms of animal (human!) cruelty. By the end of the hunt, dead human bodies hang upside down, strung up like prize deer for the grinning gorillas to take souvenir photographs beside.

This disturbing vein of imagery, with its inescapable connotations of lynching and the Holocaust, resonated with me from an early age thanks to ambitious units in my public school on the civil rights movement and in my Hebrew school on World War II. And it is this imagery that the film continues to mine. Taylor, taken into captivity after the hunt as an experimental subject for chimpanzee "animal" psychologists and recovering from a wound to the neck that prevents him from speaking, is eventually subject to assault by a powerful water hose, just like I had seen civil rights protesters endure in photographs. Furthermore, he is gagged, shackled, and stripped naked, like a slave. One of his fellow crew members, a Black man named Dodge (Jeff Burton), is killed during the hunt and featured as a stuffed corpse in the apes' museum of natural history.

Once Taylor regains his voice, he is seen as a threat, a freak of nature who must be put on trial for the heretical fact of his existence; echoes of the 1925 Scopes "monkey trial" over teaching evolution ring loudly and ironically here. When asked to explain why all apes are created equal, Taylor fires back, "Some apes, it seems, are more equal than others." And it is true—the orangutans are a small elite who seem to hold all positions of political and religious power, the chimpanzees are the middle-class intellectuals, and the gorillas are the working-class soldiers and laborers. But like everything else in this funhouse mirror of a film, the fantastic, futuristic, otherworldly ape society bears more than a passing resemblance to our own. The film's now legendary punch line, delivered when Taylor comes across a half-buried Statue of Liberty at the movie's end and realizes this "planet of the apes" has been Earth all along, really does knock the wind out of us.

This is because our nagging sense that the inequalities and cruelties the apes express toward humans and one another is all too familiar—all too human—and gets validated by the film's quite stunning sense of history. According to the film's backstory, humankind annihilated itself in a nuclear war, effectively throwing humanity back to the Stone Age and allowing the apes to ascend. But the apes have erected their civilization on the ashes of man's, so they have inherited, in a sort of reverse-evolutionary psychosis, many of man's weaknesses. The apes are not our opposites; they are our doubles. Not only is there nothing better than man in the universe, but in addition, man himself is much worse than we thought. His self-destructive, self-hating poison crosses centuries and species. In the film's final moments, the quotations from ape scripture we have heard no longer sound paranoid or ludicrous but chillingly sensible: "Beware the beast Man for he is the Devil's pawn. Alone among God's primates he kills for sport, or lust, or greed. Yea, he will murder his brother to possess his brother's land. . . . Shun him. . . . For he is the harbinger of death."

The horror of *Planet of the Apes* stems from its insistence on curdling allegory to the point of bitter, frightening self-reflection. The distance between the apes and ourselves is constantly collapsing, until finally there is precious little sci-fi distraction left to take refuge in. It's not apes killing humans on the screen that's at issue; it's humans killing humans off-screen. It's not ape society mimicking human society's viciousness on the screen; it's human society's viciousness off-screen flooding the cinematic images. For me, a kid watching these films in a Reagan-era America where the Cold War often ran hot, man *did* seem like the harbinger of death. The real possibility, even the inevitability, of mutually assured nuclear destruction meant that death must hang over the future as much as it lives in the past and present. What was the use of learning all those hard-won lessons of the civil rights struggle and the Holocaust if humankind was set on an apocalyptic nuclear course?

The fascination the *Apes* films exerted on me was powerful enough to inspire my first real film research and/as collecting project around the age of twelve. While accompanying my father, a professor of social work at Rutgers University, to the college library, I began seeking out books and articles related to the *Apes* films. I would patiently photocopy each page and compile them in folders separated by each film's title. I wanted to know more about what these movies meant, how they were made, and how I could process their personal importance to me. I wanted to smudge the line between the on-screen world of the films and the off-screen world of social and personal history. I had reached an age when I could pursue this desire through a set of skills and resources of my own that were just beginning to feel within reach. I carefully saved my earnings and gifts to spend on things that I thought could bring the films closer to me. I combed used bookstores for weathered copies of novelizations of the films, attended comic book conventions where paraphernalia related to the series was for sale, and sent away for catalogs advertised in the classified ads of horror and science fiction movie magazines for movie posters, lobby cards, pressbooks, toys, even used props from the movie sets. My bedroom quickly came to resemble a sort of planet of the apes in its own right, the walls and even the ceiling plastered with so much of this memorabilia that it became difficult to discern the color of the paint underneath.

Yes, this was partly about the joys and satisfactions of research, but it was also about world-making or world-blending. There in my room, I could create a world of my own that was at once separate from the one outside—the one where my parents' arguments had grown louder, more frequent, and more frightening than ever before—and an intimate reflection of it. The *Apes* films were all about the need to recognize and respect those who differ from you, along with the tragic, often violent failure to fulfill this need. I felt this need and its failure over and over again, whether it was in the collapse of my parents' marriage, or in the history of the Holocaust that haunted our Jewish family, or in the story of the civil rights struggle still unfolding in my newly desegregated suburban public school. Immersing myself in a planet of the apes was not so much about fleeing the history of the world I lived in as learning to cope with it. I already knew that hoping for something in the universe better than humankind was futile. What I wanted, and needed, was a way to understand who I was and who we are so that the darkness would not be so impenetrable. For me, the films that scared me had become the light I could not live without. And my *Planet of the Apes* collection was my way of building bridges among cinema, history, and experience—bridges I still traverse today.

Walter Benjamin, reflecting on his own cherished book collection, speaks of how that collection stirs him not only on the level of "thoughts" but also of "images, memories." When Benjamin unpacks his library, he is transported to the times and places where he acquired each of the volumes. He recalls the cities, the bookshops, and finally his own "boyhood room" where just a handful of the books in his collection originated.[5] But one gets the sense that Benjamin's book collection, which included a special interest in children's books, allowed him to take that boyhood room with him wherever he went.

I would speak similarly about my own *Planet of the Apes* collection, with its occupation of every wall, shelf, and crevice of my childhood bedroom. The Benjaminian dimension of my collection, its power to transport me back to the realm of childhood experience no matter where or when I happened to be, now seems freighted with themes of alternate evolution suggested by the *Apes* films themselves: reimagining that evolutionary process commonly referred to as "growing up," where the ape within is not simply outgrown but constantly communed with through a bedroom-filling cinematic collection. Once I moved out of that room and left for college, the collection froze; it did not travel with me, nor was it added to. But the room stayed just as it was, as if I still lived there. When the house was sold, the collection went into a trunk, where it has remained ever since. But I feel as if that room and that collection is with me and within me wherever I go, and in whatever I write. For it's in that room that I first attempted to enact cinematic experience as a sensory surround immersion: a matter of sight, sound, smell, and touch stretching beyond the bounds of the film's running time and into the duration of lived time both personal and historical. And there is no doubt in my mind that if a *Planet of the Apes* breakfast cereal existed and I was able to track down a vintage box of it, I would have added taste to the sensory surround experience as well.

My collection was driven by my experience of the *Apes* films, my need to surround and immerse myself in that experience as deeply as possible. For me, the collection was fundamentally cinematic—without my relationship to the films, the collection would mean nothing. And in turn, the collection was protection against the potential evaporation of the cinematic experience, an enacted commitment to overcome the transient nature of watching a film. What the collection provided was a kind of immersive testimony, active at the level of my very senses, that what I felt while watching these films stayed with me and mattered to me long after the actual viewing ended. The fear, the horror, the trauma, the fascination, the thoughts, the images, the memories, the allegories, the history. These were the things I experienced when watching the films, so the collection performed a sort of endless renewal of the cinematic experience.

Benjamin senses the "childlike element" of the collector in a commitment to the "renewal of existence," a desire to "renew the old world." "Among children," he writes, "collecting is only one process of renewal; other processes are the painting of objects, the cutting out of figures, the application of decals—the whole range of childlike modes of acquisition, from touching things to giving them names."[6] My own collection was childlike not only in its creation during my life as a child and teenager but also in its dedication to renewing the cinematic experience—to touching that experience, to giving it a name. It was more important that my collection filled that boyhood room and surrounded me rather than imagining I was at work on completing a checklist that included every piece of *Planet of the Apes* memorabilia ever produced. I did not possess such a checklist, nor was I interested in devising it. The point was the sensory surround, the extension of the cinematic experience enabled by the collection's display.

That boyhood room was my living cinema, the space where the films were screened endlessly, not through a projector or a television but through my own senses. This was an era where my access to the films themselves was limited to TV airings, expanding eventually to VCR viewings (but even then, the videocassettes needed to be rented rather than purchased due to their expensiveness, and for years only the first two films in the series were available on videocassette at all as far as I could tell). What I relied on were painstakingly assembled recordings of the films that I made with my VCR during television broadcasts. I would stay up in front of the TV, often in the wee hours when the films would air, the wire from the VCR snaking to the remote control in my hand, hitting "pause" whenever a commercial break would begin and then resuming recording when the break ended. Dozing off even momentarily could and often did result in a "ruined" recording, because the whole purpose was to simulate a "cinematic" experience, without commercials, even though I had never watched these films in a movie theater. The theater was my room, my mind, my senses, my memories—the theater enabled by my collection.

If my room functioned as an experiential theater, then my collection functioned as an experiential film. Conceptualizing a collection in this way is rather different than many theoretical definitions of collecting. For example, Susan Stewart claims that a collection resembles a museum more than a library because the collection shares the museum's desire for "closure of all space and temporality within the context at hand."[7] But my collection, imagined as a bridge to cinematic experience, existed precisely to open space and time, not close it. My collection converted my room not into a museum or a library, but a movie theater. A movie theater that screened not just any film, and not just the *Apes* films, but a phantasmagoria composed of my experience with the *Apes* films in their personal and historical dimensions. The collection unmoored my cinematic experience from its originary coordinates in space and time, freeing it to roam in all of those spaces and times where the films lived through my thoughts, feelings, and senses.

There is a surrealist impulse embedded in this aim of my collection to unmoor the space and time of cinematic experience. This is not something I would have been aware of when I was assembling the collection, but as a scholar who studies the conjunction of surrealism and cinema, I can now reflect on the accidentally surrealist characteristics of my collection.[8] What I hear now in my collection are the echoes of André Breton's statement about the transformation of a movie theater into a dining room, where he and a friend would watch a film while "opening cans, slicing bread, uncorking bottles, and talking in ordinary tones, as if around a table, to the great amazement of the spectators, who dared not say a word." Like Breton's practice of slipping in and out of movie theaters at random, without any regard for making sense of the films that were screening, his goal was to forge a surrealist experience of cinema where the film became unhinged from its original context. The movie was no longer bound to its intended space and time, but reinvented as a battery for viewer fantasy exercising its power beyond the theater itself. "The important thing," Breton explains, "is that one came out 'charged' for a few days."[9] I now see my collection as an attempt, in its own way and on its own terms rather than simply duplicating Breton, to charge my cinematic battery. To extend the cinematic experience in space and time not just for a few days but ideally for an infinite array of spaces and times—wherever and whenever the collection could transport me in orbit around a planet of the apes.

This facet of my collection as a mode of cinematic transportation connects it not only to Breton but also to broader theories and practices of surrealist-influenced "enlargement" that include figures such as André Bazin and Roland Barthes. Bazin's "blind field" of cinema, where figures emerge from the screen as alive for the viewer, resembles Barthes's "third meaning," where he finds in the film still a horizon of reception where "film and still find themselves in a palimpsest relationship without it being possible to say that one is *on top of* the other or that one is *extracted* from the other."[10] For Barthes, then, the film still enlarges the cinematic experience when it "throws off the constraint of filmic time," permitting a sort of reverie for the spectator that takes shape between film and film still.[11] In *Camera Lucida*, Barthes will insist that this power of enlargement or expansion belongs to photography rather than to cinema, but the ghosts of "third meaning," or meaning located somewhere *between* and *beyond* the photography of the film still and the cinema of the film itself, remain.

In fact, there is something very Benjaminian about *Camera Lucida*, particularly in Barthes's emphasis on childhood as integral to the mode of transportation enabled by the collection. Barthes does not regard the photographs he meditates on as a collection per se, but he pores over his favorite photographs with the energy of a collector in Benjamin's sense: the mission is a childlike "renewal of existence" in general and to "renew the old world" in particular.[12] The photograph that pierces Barthes more deeply than any other, that transports him from his own life and into the life of his beloved, recently deceased mother, captures his mother herself as a child.

Barthes describes the transporting effect of this Winter Garden Photograph: "I arrived, traversing three-quarters of a century, at the image of a child: I stare intensely at the Sovereign Good of childhood, of the mother, of the mother-as-child."[13] But the transportation is not simply a window into his mother's life, but a bridge between Barthes's own life and the life of his mother. What he sees in the Winter Garden

Photograph is not just his mother as a child, but his mother in her final days, when she became so weak with illness that he had to nurse her. "She had become my little girl, uniting for me with that essential child she was in her first photograph."[14] In this treasured photograph for Barthes, as in those treasured books for Benjamin, space and time collapse while a form of transportation that bridges one's own life-time with the life-time of another is born. One's mother as a child, one's self as a child, one's mother in old age, one's self in old age—all of these temporalities mingle through the power of a collected object.

There is something stubbornly, intractably personal about Barthes's Winter Garden Photograph and Benjamin's book collection. Barthes refuses to reproduce the Winter Garden Photograph, just as Benjamin declines to furnish an inventory listing each of the books in his collection. Nor can I provide a photograph or an inventory of my *Planet of the Apes* collection that would convey its cinematic power for me, its capability to transport me across space and time, history and sensation. On a fundamental level, the collection cannot be communicated. But the attempt to *transmit* the collection's significance through writing matters, as Barthes and Benjamin demonstrate so beautifully. Much more clumsily, I also strive in my own work for something like that sort of transmission for my readers and students. I want each film I write about, and every film I teach, to transmit some suggestion for my audience of that childhood journey to the planet of the apes for me.

Among the many film stills in my collection, there is one that moves me especially deeply. It is a lobby card from *Planet of the Apes* depicting the film's hunt sequence, with gorillas trapping humans in nets. Against the backdrop of a lush green crop field, the apes and humans stand in stark contrast. The apes, dressed in blue-and-brown military uniforms, are walking upright while they manipulate the netting around their human prey with confident, organized precision. The humans, clad only in rags and cowering helplessly on the ground, revert to fetal positions while ensnared in the net. A gorilla on horseback trains a rifle on the captured humans, snuffing out any chance of escape.

Despite the sharp visual disparity between the apes and humans in this still, there is also a blurring between the two species. The hunt is

A lobby card captures the image of gorillas hunting humans in *Planet of the Apes* (Franklin J. Schaffner, 1968)

caught in motion, with the apes and humans all so intent on their kinetic actions as predators and prey that no individual face can be easily discerned. What moves me is this doubleness, with the apes and humans set apart as predators/prey and yet simultaneously conjoined as one faceless mass locked in endless motion. This is otherness revealed as a matter of constant, cinematic transformation—through a film still in my collection that returns me to my very first childhood encounter with *Planet of the Apes*.

While writing this essay, I opened that trunk in my basement for the first time in many years. I asked my nine-year-old daughter to accompany me. I wasn't having any luck persuading her to watch *Planet of the Apes* with me, so I thought that perhaps my collection could work for her in reverse: a bridge outward to the films through the objects rather than a bridge backward to the films that the objects had been for me. Her eyes widened when she saw how much stuff the trunk contained, and her hands reached immediately for the action figures. After surveying them quickly, she turned to me disappointedly and asked, "Are they all boys?" I was crestfallen for a moment but then directed her attention to the Zira action figure. Dr. Zira, the unforgettably fearless and brilliant "animal" psychologist of *Planet of the Apes*, played by Kim Hunter in chimpanzee makeup. She held her lovingly. I told her Zira was now hers. She looked at me solemnly and promised, "I will pass this down to my children."

We still haven't seen the movie together. But I think we are already on our way to the planet of the apes.

A publicity still featuring actress Kim Hunter, in makeup as Dr. Zira, between takes on the set of *Beneath the Planet of the Apes* (Ted Post, 1970)

NOTES

1. See Adam Lowenstein, *Shocking Representation: Historical Trauma, National Cinema, and the Modern Horror Film* (New York: Columbia University Press, 2005); and Adam Lowenstein, *Horror Film and Otherness* (New York: Columbia University Press, 2022).
2. See, for example, Vivian Sobchack, *Screening Space: The American Science Fiction Film* (New Brunswick, NJ: Rutgers University Press, 1997).
3. I have used this distinction in my teaching for many years. When I shared it with my longtime friend and colleague John Belton, he asked me if he could include it in his textbook *American Cinema/American Culture*, 3rd ed. (New York: McGraw-Hill, 2008), where I am happy it has found an adopted home.
4. See Eric Greene, Planet of the Apes *as American Myth: Race, Politics, and Popular Culture* (Middletown, CT: Wesleyan University Press, 1998).
5. Walter Benjamin, "Unpacking My Library: A Talk about Book Collecting," in *Illuminations*, ed. Hannah Arendt, trans. Harry Zohn (New York: Schocken, 1969), 67.
6. Benjamin, "Unpacking My Library," 61.
7. Susan Stewart, *On Longing, Narratives of the Miniature, the Gigantic, the Souvenir, the Collection* (Durham, NC: Duke University Press, 1993), 161.
8. See Adam Lowenstein, *Dreaming of Cinema: Spectatorship, Surrealism, and the Age of Digital Media* (New York: Columbia University Press, 2015).
9. André Breton, "As in a Wood," in *The Shadow and Its Shadow: Surrealist Writings on the Cinema*, 3rd ed., ed. and trans. Paul Hammond (San Francisco: City Lights, 2000), 75, 73.
10. André Bazin, quoted in Roland Barthes, *Camera Lucida: Reflections on Photography*, trans. Richard Howard (New York: Hill & Wang, 1996), 55–56; and Roland Barthes, "The Third Meaning: Research Notes on Some Eisenstein Stills," *Image-Music-Text*, trans. Stephen Heath (New York: Hill & Wang, 1978), 67. See also Lowenstein, *Dreaming of Cinema*, 11–42.
11. Barthes, "The Third Meaning," 67.
12. Benjamin, "Unpacking My Library," 61.
13. Barthes, *Camera Lucida*, 71.
14. Barthes, *Camera Lucida*, 72.

7

COLLECTING AND THINKING GENERICALLY

Barry Keith Grant

CHARLES FOSTER KANE, THE TITLE character of *Citizen Kane* (1941, Orson Welles), was, as different people tell us in the opening "News on the March" newsreel, a communist, a fascist, or, according to himself, an American. But he was also and emphatically a collector. At the end of the film, as the camera cranes over the vast collection of material belongings Kane had gathered during his lifetime, one of the journalists marvels, "He sure liked to collect things, didn't he?" and another replies, "Anything and everything." As a multimillionaire with money to burn, Kane collected statues and sculptures from around the world ("There's a Burmese temple and three Spanish ceilings down the hall"). Kane's collecting compulsion, though to my knowledge scarcely commented on by any of the film's numerous analysts, actually may explain much about his character. Earlier in the film, his assistant Bernstein receives a telegram from the towering tycoon informing him that he wants to buy the world's biggest diamond; Kane's friend Jed Leland responds that he didn't know Kane was collecting diamonds, and Bernstein explains, "He ain't. He's collecting somebody that's collecting diamonds. Anyway—he ain't only collecting statues."

In short, Kane treated people like things that helped shape his own narrative, his own identity. Like Kane, I have been a collector all my life, although I hope I have treated other people better than Kane did. And while I have had my own Rosebuds, without a Xanadu I have had to be more judicious than Kane in my collecting habits. As a young boy growing up in a New York City apartment, I collected the usual stuff of city kids—marbles, bottle caps, trading cards, comic books. Eventually, they all dropped away except for the comics. I'm not certain when the first large box of comics actually became a collection rather than a haphazard bunch, but at some point in preadolescence it did. The implications of this reconceptualization of material possessions as a collection are profound, for collections require, among other things, organization rather than random arrangement, a way of regarding cultural texts within webs of intertextual and paratextual contexts.

Eventually, I had complete or large runs of several titles, including Quality Comics' *Plastic Man* and a number of DC titles ranging from *Superman* offshoots such as *Superman's Pal Jimmy Olson* and *Superman's Girlfriend Lois Lane* to science fiction titles such as *Strange Adventures*. Of course, my collection included horror titles like *Weird Tales* (my interest in horror developed early); and there was *Mad* magazine, which was in a category of its own, imitators like *Cracked* paling by comparison. In retrospect, I realized that *Mad*, with its razor-sharp observation of movies, television shows, fads, and trends, was in fact my first exposure to the type of cultural criticism that I would later experience as a media scholar. With incisive observational wit, *Mad* demonstrated that cultural criticism could be entertaining as well as enlightening—indeed, it even parodied some of the other comics I collected—and it is a goal to which I've always aspired in my own work.

As I reached adolescence, it was my record collection that took precedence over others, the comics somehow disappearing into oblivion, and I have actively collected them ever since (although I concentrated more on albums than singles).[1] I didn't play an instrument—drum lessons had proven futile—but I was particularly fond of rhythm-and-blues and vocal harmony (what later was dubbed doo-wop), and I did of lot of singing (solo) in great acoustical spaces like subway stations and the shower. I collected 45s,[2] listening to them on my own little portable record player with speakers that swung out from either side of the turntable like earflaps. (I wince now to think of how I stacked records on the spindle for them to drop automatically after play, one upon another.) I actively searched out items for my collection, looking for records by particular groups or on specific labels (already I was developing a nascent sense of authorship and production contexts), scouring local candy shops and dime stores, trading them with friends, and reading newsstand magazines (the graphic pleasures of busy subway newsstands in the 1950s were immense) like *Hit Parader* and more specialized periodicals like Onyx's *Rhythm and Blues* to expand my knowledge. In Nick Hornsby's novel *High Fidelity*, a woman angry at her collector boyfriend says, "He just sponges off me and sits around all day on his fat arse staring at record labels."[3] I don't know about the fat ass, but I understand the contemplation of record labels. Ah, the original Ramas, with their bold block silver lettering and forced perspective set in a surreal landscape; the yellow Suns with the stylized rays and the circle of musical notes around the circumference; Chess labels, silver and blue with the three chess pieces; later Ends, in three colors with the bisected dachshund.

I could go on.

In her book on museum studies, Susan Pearce lists no fewer than seventeen motivations for collecting, as summarized by Mieke Bal: "leisure, aesthetics, competition, risk, fantasy, a sense of community, prestige, domination, sensual gratification, sexual foreplay, the desire to reframe objects, the pleasing rhythm of sameness and difference, ambition to achieve perfection, extending the self, reaffirming the body, producing gender-identity, achieving immortality."[4] Clearly, some of these drives have informed my own collecting habits. I had little interest in reading and none in collecting "girls'" comics, such as *Little Lulu*, *Archie*, or romance comics. The stories in these comics were more domestic in focus and dealt with relationships, the artwork less interesting to me (although later on I certainly appreciated Roy Lichtenstein's art). I had grander ideas about crime fighting and enforcing morality, unaware then, of course, of the extent to which that very morality had contributed to

Could Frankie Lymon's classic version of "Goody Goody" be on any other label than Gee, with its bold red color and dancing logo?

shaping my interests in the first place. Obviously, my comics collection, like me, was positioned according to the traditional binary construction of gender. But rather than reflecting on the formation of my masculine identity here, or whether I suffer from, as per Woody Allen, Ozymandias Melancholia,[5] in what follows I want to explore some of the ways being a collector, and what I collected, has helped shape my critical thinking and, consequently, my teaching and research in media studies.

I taught at Brock University, a midsize Canadian university located in Ontario's Niagara Peninsula, for four decades. I arrived there in 1975, one of four faculty members teaching in a film studies program, the first to offer a degree in film studies in Canada. Much of my research has focused on genre studies and authorship, which inevitably intersects with other areas of popular culture. And so, in the early 1980s I proposed and taught the first course on popular culture, to my knowledge the first such course in a Canadian university. Several years later I spearheaded the creation of a new undergraduate degree program in popular culture, based in part on the only other one then in existence, at Bowling Green State University in Ohio, and it was soon followed by a master's program. The new programs required working with library staff to develop their holdings in popular culture in a variety of formats, including records, and I also established a popular music archive, arranging for and receiving numerous donations of thousands of discs in all formats and musical styles from donors across Ontario. As a long-time collector, I was able to provide detailed appraisals of donations for the university to issue official receipts of charitable donations for income tax purposes. Students were employed to organize, catalog, and shelve materials. In these ways I was able to extend my collecting activity from the personal to the institutional, even to experience the joys of crate digging as part of my job, and to pass on my knowledge of collecting, cataloging, and preserving recorded materials to students whose interests were similarly inclined.

Among the comics I had collected as a boy was *Classics Illustrated* (you could be familiar with great literature without reading the books!), not only for the great stories but also for the gorgeous cover paintings that replaced the original pen and ink drawings of the earlier issues. I was fascinated with the work of color illustrators, especially those who were bold in their use of color, whether expressionist or realist, and used it in ways I found surprising. In *Mad* there were Kelly Freas and Norman Mingo (also pulp illustrators), Alberto Vargas and LeRoy Neiman in *Playboy* (I was a male adolescent in the 1950s, after all), and, of course, Norman Rockwell, whose illustrations for Coke ads during Christmastime festooned every local candy store in the neighborhood. Rockwell's imagery may have been all about a conservative, white America that existed only in fantasy, but his use of color was radical. Look, for instance, at the portraits he painted of the two musicians for the cover of their *Live*

Adventures of Al Kooper and Mike Bloomfield double LP (which I eagerly purchased when it was released in 1968): How do you paint faces with flecks of blue and still make it look real?

Film historian John Fell was one of the first to note the transmedial connections between film and comics, observing that the emergence of newspaper comics "accompanied the development of the motion picture. After the creation of the animated cartoon, the most successful comic artists worked both fields," and he goes on to show how both forms developed similar visual narrative techniques simultaneously.[6] The intimate connections between the two forms has only come to the fore with the recent cycle of superhero movies and the possibility that "the comic book movie" may have emerged as a distinct genre.[7] My father Sumner Grant was a graphic artist and an amateur cartoonist, with a cartoon feature in the US Army publication *The Forty-Niner* during World War II and a cartoon of army life featured on the envelopes of all the letters he sent almost daily to my mother, many of which have been preserved by the Library of Congress.[8] I had a similar interest in art and won several art scholarships in public school, and although my later academic interest in literature (my doctorate was about political ideology, democratic ideals, and style in nineteenth-century American literature) and film took me in a different direction, my appreciation of visual design significantly informed my understanding of and thinking about cinema, helping, I like to think, make me sensitive to mise-en-scène and frame.[9]

By the time I was twelve, I was making weekly pilgrimages alone by subway from the Bronx downtown to Forty-Second Street in Manhattan, weekly allowance clutched firmly in pocket, to enter the mecca for R&B collectors, Times Square Record Shop, owned by the legendary Irving "Slim" Rose. The shop was tucked away in a stairway alcove between the train level and the street, a liminal space between two worlds that was semiotically resonant, for it seemed like its own world with its own myths. One spoke, for instance, in hushed tones about the version of "Stormy Weather" by the Five Sharps, the holy grail for collectors.[10] Did this record even exist? That no one knew for sure gave it mythical status among collectors. But the actual records, from the fairly common to the very rare, were displayed in the shop's one plate-glass window, covering

The chess piece on the left may be confusing, but there is no mistaking the "deep feeling" of the label's rich blue-and-silver tones.

it almost completely and making for a patchwork quilt of beautiful shiny objects d'art. On the window, the records sat snug in their sleeves, taped to the glass, a mosaic of graphic delights that I could stare at for what seemed like hours.

In 1961, a great debate erupted among the patrons of Times Square Record Shop with the release of "Blue Moon," Richard Rogers and Lorenzo Hart's classic 1934 song, by the Marcels, a vocal group from Pittsburgh. According to the story, the group needed one more song for their debut album and "Blue Moon" was suggested to them by their producer, who also suggested adding the famous bass vocal introduction, borrowing it from the group's arrangement for another tune. The rest, as they say, is history: the record rocketed to the top of the charts as fast as any before it, reaching number one on both the pop and R&B charts and, in the United Kingdom, becoming a million seller. But was it true doo-wop? As Bernard Gendron defines the term, it is "a vocal group style, rooted in the black gospel quartet tradition. . . . Its most distinctive feature is the use of background vocals to take on the role of instrumental accompaniment for, and response to, the high tenor or falsetto calls of the lead singer."[11] But the bass line in "Blue Moon" is neither response nor instrumental imitation, but a vocal riff recognizable as such because of the extent of its nonsense syllables ("Bomp-ba-ba-bomp, Ba-bom-ba-bom-bomp, Ba-ba-bomp-ba-ba-bomp, A dang-a-dang-dang, A-ding-a-dong-ding"[12]), so many purists dismissed the song as a pop gimmick, albeit one with a great hook, rather than as authentic rhythm and blues.

Only later did I realize that this was essentially a debate about genre—about genre definition and boundaries, about what is acceptable within a tradition, and how one sees that tradition—but without the critical terminology. It would be less than two years until the Beatles broke in North America and the British Invasion followed, but already the Marcels' "Blue Moon" sounded like rococo embellishment of a waning style. As Gendron remarks (although without referencing "Blue Moon"), "A record that advertises its genre in a caricaturized way itself becomes a caricature of that genre."[13] For some genre theorists, generic change is conceptualized as a series of evolutionary phases. Tom Schatz, for example, following art historian Herni Focillon's *The Life of Forms in Art*, asserts that there are distinct "ages" to genres: "the experimental age, the classic age, the age of refinement, the baroque age."[14] While there is debate about the very concept of generic evolution,[15] if, as Schatz writes, that over time genres seem to "shift in emphasis from one cultural function (social, ritualistic) to another (formal, aesthetic),"[16] then the Marcels' "Blue Moon" would seem to be a clear example of the latter.

Ironically, the British Invasion helped make me, as it did for many white listeners, more aware of American roots music. Following the trail of credits on the labels for British Invasion covers of American blues and soul, soon I was exploring the history of American popular music and teaching courses on the subject (allowing me to justify, both to the university research and finance offices and to myself, acquiring yet more records as "research").[17] In addition to the music, I discovered new graphic delights to be found in jazz collecting, as with the covers sketched in ink by David Stone Martin or the ravishing designs of Reid Miles for Blue Note album covers. At its height, my collection consisted of eleven thousand LPs, with jazz, blues, and vocals forming the core, although, like its owner, it has been whittled away over time. As happens with many collectors, I've found myself drifting toward focusing on what I consider the core, the great recordings, and abandoning any drive for completism. The 45s and 78s, of which I also had several thousand, are now gone entirely, and I console myself with Spotify, even though for me there are glaring gaps in its generally impressive catalog. And the lack of physicality involved when listening to music delivered digitally still feels odd, for, as I knew even as a teenager, records and record collections are first and foremost tactile, material things, talismanic objects that require certain rituals for optimal performance and storage.[18] Digital clicking is hardly a satisfying substitute.

As I collector, being attuned to the material form of music as records inevitably and significantly informed my writing and teaching about popular music. For example, one of the lectures I developed for that first Introduction to Popular Culture course contrasted the Beatles and the Rolling Stones as cultural icons representing opposing cultural values. The lecture involved playing some of their music (prerecorded on cassette tape—other professors looked on bemusedly as I toted a boombox to class) and analyzing the covers of their North American LP releases. I avoided bringing actual records into class to save on wear and because I remembered with horror what happened to the unfortunate teacher who brought his rare Bix Beiderbecke 78s to school in *Blackboard Jungle* (Richard Brooks, 1955), but also because it was a large lecture class. (Because I taught the course in the 1980s and '90s, there was as yet no internet from which to draw visual images and, of course, no PowerPoint with which to show them. To give the lecture, weeks earlier I had to bring all the album covers to the university's photographic department, where slides were made, and then I arranged with what was then the Media Services department for a slide projector to be set up in the lecture hall at the specified date and time.)

On their records, the Beatles, like the Marcels and other rock groups that preceded them, followed convention in wearing similar outfits (and hair styles), while the Stones, iconoclastically, each dressed differently. The Beatles' emphasis is thus on togetherness and community, while the Stones express individualism. On the back-cover photo of their Capitol debut LP, *Meet the Beatles* (1964), George has one arm extended, resting on Ringo's shoulder. On the cover of *Beatles '65* (1965) the four of them are sitting together with open umbrellas, all "in the same boat"; on the *Beatles IV* (1965) cover, they are all laughing and holding the same object, like members of a sports team before a game; and on one of the inside gatefold photos of *Help!* (1965), the four Beatles are all wearing the same long scarf, literally tying them together. This same togetherness becomes a visual gag in the group's first film, *A Hard Day's Night* (Richard Lester, 1964), in which the four Beatles have different street entrances but live in the same house. The original infamous "butcher block" cover of the Beatles' 1966 LP *Yesterday and Today* (now a rare collector's item, which I once owned but sold in a moment of folly and penury as a graduate student), showing the group in butcher aprons arrayed with dismembered dolls and cuts of meat, was inconsistent with this image and so was withdrawn from the market.

While the Beatles albums tend toward bright designs, the Rolling Stones' covers, by contrast, emphasize a darkness, signifying somberness ("Paint It, Black"), mystery, and perhaps even danger. The first four albums all feature head shots of the group swathed in darkness and shadow. On the covers of *12×5* (1964) and *Out of Our Heads* (1965), their faces, pimples and all, are crowded into the frame—in *our* face, as it were. While the Beatles invite us on *A Magical Mystery Tour* (1967), the Rolling Stones enact *Their Satanic Majesties Request* (1967). Their infamous performance of "Sympathy for the Devil" at the 1969 Altamont concert, where the band seems to whip the audience into a frenzy before a fan is stabbed to death by a Hell's Angel bodyguard, captured in the Maysles Brothers' rockumentary *Gimme Shelter* (1970), is commonly understood as the culmination of their embrace of the dark

The dramatic sky, forced perspective, buoyant cumulus clouds, and bold lettering of the Rama label enhance the connotations in a song such as "Falling for You."

side.[19] If the Beatles played rock 'n' roll, the Stones played the blues, "the devil's music," the two genres carrying significantly different significations. The Beatles sang "I Want to Hold Your Hand," but there was little sexual sublimation with the Stones: "I'm just a King Bee, buzzing around your hive," they sang on their first album. By the time of *Sticky Fingers* (1971), their sexual appeal was incorporated directly into the record's packaging, as the front cover, designed by Andy Warhol, features a pair of jeans on a male torso with a functioning zipper that one could pull down.

Of course, many students had a sense that the two groups represented a tension between letting it be and letting it bleed, but it was less the meaning than the method that was important. Connecting visual evidence (close readings of album covers) and analysis, along with paratexts such as press coverage and film appearances with the music, had a greater impact than just listening to the music. Further, it allowed for speculation about other aspects of popular culture beyond the specifics of these two British rock bands, as influential as they have been, such as the importance of packaging, promotion and marketing, and reception. As well, concepts of authorship, ideology, mass culture, and the culture industry follow from such an analysis. The implications of the iconographical distinction between the two bands are readily contextualized within popular culture generally as cultural myth that addresses the human conflict between Apollonian and Dionysian modes of being, like *Star Wars'* two sides of the Force, and as an example of cultural dialectics. Such a lecture was generated by hours of handling and gazing at the record jackets that is part of collecting activity.

A similar awareness of records as objects informed my research on popular music as well, as evidenced by my pioneering essay on jazz "vocalese," a hitherto genre of jazz singing largely neglected by critics and scholars.[20] The essay depended on recordings—both for the creation of the genre and for my discussion of it. Vocalese involves the singing of lyrics (composed rather than improvised) that duplicates recorded jazz instrumentals, both melody and solo parts, arrangement and solos, note for note. Thus, vocalese is distinctly different from scat singing, the more familiar form of jazz singing, both because it is arranged and composed rather than improvised and because it relies on language rather than simply on rhythmic sounds that generate meaning by connotation rather than denotation. In order to learn the notes that were once improvised and then to substitute words for them, Eddie Jefferson had to listen to Coleman Hawkins's version of "Body and Soul" and King Pleasure to James Moody's rendition of "I'm in the Mood for Love" innumerable times on their phonographs. In turn, in order for a listener to fully appreciate any vocalese recording, they have to "know" the original recording—a record, originally and ironically, of a live improvisational performance. I had to listen to the recordings of both the vocalese sing-ers' records and the instrumental versions they were based on repeatedly in order to tease out the form's aesthetic and conventions with the tools of cultural theory and textual analysis.

My 1980 essay on popular music and authorship, focusing on the work of Frank Zappa, was one of the very first to consider the applica-tion of auteur theory (a theory of authorship pioneered in film studies) to popular music. There was, of course, scholarly and popular writing on the Beatles, Bob Dylan, and a few other pop musical artists at the time, but almost all of it was based on the thematic analysis of lyrics. As I wrote then, I was considering Zappa's music "not as music—that is, in terms of musical theory or structure—but rather, as an oeuvre of recorded material which exists as works of popular culture. In other words, his LP records will be considered as records," taking into account "essential properties of the LPs themselves—the order of songs on an album, the production, the jacket, and so on."[21] In addition, I considered live performances, interviews, and other paratexts to identify what later theorists might have called "the critical construct known as Frank Zappa." I took as the goal of the analysis Peter Wollen's observation that "the purpose of auteur criti-cism thus becomes to uncover behind the superficial contrasts of subject and treatment a hard core of basic and often recondite motifs."[22] In the essay I explain that I was focusing on Zappa's work because one of his major themes is precisely the relation of the individual musical artist to the constraints of commercialism. His pastiching of a wide range of musi-cal styles—incorporating, among others, blues, tin pan alley, heavy metal, free jazz, and yes, doo-wop—foregrounds his distinctive sound against a background of generic convention. The jacket illustration of Zappa's *200 Motels* soundtrack record (1971), the same image that appeared on the movie poster, depicts a giant Zappa face looming over a collage of events and characters from the film and its songs—a provocative image of the auteur's relationship to this material that perfectly captures what Andrew Sarris refers to as the essence of the auteur, "the tension between a director's personality and his material."[23] I approached the film from this perspective when, provocatively, I included *200 Motels* on the syl-labus for the Experimental Cinema course (it employed multiple video effects that were innovative at the time) along with the work of the more usual suspects such as Stan Brakhage and Maya Deren.

Listening to and collecting doo-wop recordings, because they were so much alike, so formulaic—the overwhelming majority followed the conventional 32-bar AABA structure of popular song—sharpened my ear for both generic similarities and subtle differences among them ("the pleasing rhythm of sameness and difference," to revisit Bal's words). Gendron notes that "for every doo-wop hit, there were hundreds of songs that failed. It is estimated that thousands of doo-wop groups were recruited from the streets to make records."[24] Yet like other aficionados of the form, I could distinguish a Philly sound from a New Orleans sound from a Los Angeles sound from a New York sound—even, I liked to think, a Bronx sound from a Brooklyn one. Such distinctions, like the generic "phase" the record represents (e.g., whether it was foundational or revisionist, as in the case of "Blue Moon"), were important for questions of inclusion/exclusion in my collection, and how it was organized. "If," as John Elsner and Roger Cardinal reason, "classification is the mirror of collective humanity's thoughts and perceptions, then collecting is its material embodiment. Collecting is classification lived, experienced in three dimensions."[25]

Collecting then, is often built on a sense of genre, however inchoate, sophisticated, or debatable the generic regimes in the mind of the collector may be. In order to organize one's collection, whether by artist, style, label, or another protocol,[26] the collector must necessarily be aware of what T. S. Eliot has called "tradition and the individual talent,"[27] viewing the individual text in relation to its antecedents. While a student of literature, I was influenced by the work of film critics who provided close, persuasive textual readings, including Victor Perkins, Robin Wood, and the champions of literary New Criticism, as well as by those who found broad patterns in multiple works, such as Roland Barthes, Leslie Fiedler, and Northrop Frye—these two tendencies characterizing my own defining interest in genre and authorship, whether I was writing on the work of Hollywood director John Ford, documentary filmmaker Frederick Wiseman, or iconoclastic musician Frank Zappa, on the one hand, or on broader topics such as gender in the horror film, the representation of rock 'n' roll in the film musical, or the negotiation of genre in New Zealand cinema, on the other.[28] But I have no doubt that even before my formal academic studies, my involvement in comic and record collecting helped develop the generic awareness that I have brought to textual analysis in film and popular culture.

NOTES

1   Long-play (LP) records, which superseded single-play 78s, allowed for multiple tunes on each side because of its microgroove technology. The LP, which played at 33⅓ rpm, was introduced first in 10-inch format in 1948 and was the industry standard until it was replaced by digital formats beginning in the 1980s (although it has never disappeared entirely and remains the preferred format of audiophiles).

2   The vinyl 45 rpm (7-inch) record (also called a single) was introduced commercially in 1949 and quickly became the universal format for the release of individual recordings (usually designated as A and B sides), replacing the earlier shellac 78 rpm records.

3   Nick Hornsby, *High Fidelity* (London: Indigo, 1996), 70.

4   Mieke Bal, "Telling Objects: A Narrative Perspective on Collecting," in *The Cultures of Collecting*, ed. John Elsner and Roger Cardinal (London: Reaktion Books, 1994), 97–115, 103.

5   Woody Allen invented the term in his film *Stardust Memories* (1980). Referencing Shelley's poem "Ozymandias" (1818), it refers to a feeling of depression arising from an overwhelming sense of the impermanence and futility of human endeavor in the context of time's relentless march.

6   John L. Fell, *Film and the Narrative Tradition* (Berkeley: University of California Press, 1974), 89.

7   See, for example, Liam Burke, *The Comic Book Film Adaptation: Exploring Modern Hollywood's Leading Genre* (Jackson: University of Mississippi Press, 2015).

8   Many of these envelopes have been preserved by the Veterans History Project at the Library of Congress and featured on its website, memory .loc.gov/diglib/vhp-stories/loc.natlib.afc2001001.20970/.

9   This influence is especially apparent in my essay "'Jungle Nights in Harlem': Jazz, Ideology, and Animated Cartoons," *Popular Music and Society* 13, no. 4 (Winter 1989): 45–57, and, more recently, in my anthology *Comics and Pop Culture: Adaptation from Panel to Frame*, coedited with Scott Henderson (Austin: University of Texas Press, 2019).

10   Even now it is not clear that this tune was ever pressed as a 45. Here is the note to be found under the listing for the Five Sharps in the *Goldmine Price Guide to 45rpm Records*, ed. Tim Neely (Iola, WI: Krause, 1996), 273, and reprinted in subsequent editions and other overlapping price guides: "Only released on 78 RPM (2 or 3 known copies, one of which is cracked); all known 45s are counterfeits. Even the cracked 78 would likely sell for $10,000; if a legitimate 45 would be confirmed, it could sell for more than any record ever made!"

11   Bernard Gendron, "Theodor Adorno Meets the Cadillacs," in *Studies in Entertainment: Critical Approaches to Mass Culture*, ed. Tania Modleski (Bloomington: Indiana University Press, 1986), 18–36, 24.

12   As transcribed by John Javna, *The Doo-Wop Sing-Along Songbook* (New York: St. Martin's Press, 1986), 15.

13   Gendron, "Theodor Adorno," 29.

14   Thomas Schatz, *Hollywood Genres: Formulas, Filmmaking, and the Studio System* (New York: Random House, 1981), 37.

15   See, for example, Tag Gallagher, "Shoot-Out at the Genre Corral: Problems in the 'Evolution' of the Western," in *Film Genre Reader IV*, ed. Barry Keith Grant (Austin: University of Texas Press, 2012), 298–312.

16   Schatz, *Hollywood Genres*, 41.

17   The appropriation of music by Black artists by white musicians and record company executives is an important aspect of the complex and significant dynamics of race and racism that inform the history of American popular music. I address this issue in the "Jungle Nights in Harlem" essay and in my book *The Hollywood Film Musical* (Malden, MA: Wiley-Blackwell, 2012), esp. 50–54.

18   I discuss my own adventures with the materiality of collections in "Music Halls with Walls: Record Collecting and Popular Culture," *Mid-Atlantic Popular Culture Almanack* 14 (2005): 17–28.

19   My knowledge of popular music and its iconography helped me provide a rich context for rockumentaries I regularly taught in the documentary film course and for the chapter on *Woodstock* (Michael Wadleigh, 1970) in Grant, *The Hollywood Film Musical*.

20   "Purple Passages or Fiestas in Blue? Notes toward an Aesthetic of Vocalese," in *Representing Jazz*, ed. Krin Gabbard (Durham, NC: Duke University Press, 1995), 285–304.

21   Barry K. Grant, "Frank Zappa and 'La Guitare-Stylo': Auteur Criticism and Popular Culture," *The Sphinx* 11 (1980): 27.

22   Peter Wollen, *Signs and Meaning in the Cinema*, rev. ed. (Bloomington: Indiana University Press, 1972), 80.

23   Andrew Sarris, "Notes on the Auteur Theory in 1962," *Film Culture* 27 (Winter 1962/63): 7.

24   Gendron, "Theodor Adorno," 33.

25   John Elsner and Roger Cardinal, "Introduction," in *The Cultures of Collecting*, ed. John Elsner and Roger Cardinal (Cambridge, MA: Harvard University Press, 1994), 1–6, 2.

26   See Hornby, *High Fidelity*, 52, for the narrator's discussion of the various possible ways of organizing his collection.

27   T. S. Eliot's "Tradition and the Individual Talent," published in 1919, was one of the first works to address the idea of an artist working with an awareness of generic tradition and is thus regarded as an important text of Twentieth-century modernism. The essay is included in Eliot's *Selected Essays*, new ed. (New York: Harcourt, Brace & World, 1950), 3–11.

28   See my works, respectively, on John Ford: *John Ford's Stagecoach* (New York: Cambridge University Press, 2002), and "Two Rode Together: John Ford, Fenimore Cooper, and Generic Cycling," in *John Ford Made Westerns: Filming the Legend in the Sound Era*, ed. Gaylyn Studlar and Matthew Bernstein (Bloomington: Indiana University Press, 2001), 193–219; on Frederick Wiseman: *Voyages of Discovery: The Cinema of Frederick Wiseman* (Urbana: Illinois University Press, 1992), *Voyages of Discovery: The Cinema of Frederick Wiseman*, 2nd ed. (New York: Columbia University Press, 2023), and *Five Films by Frederick Wiseman* (Berkeley: University of California Press, 2006); on Frank Zappa: "Frank Zappa"; on rock 'n' roll and the film musical: "The Classic Hollywood Musical and the 'Problem' of Rock 'n' Roll," *Journal of Popular Film and Television* 13, no. 4 (Winter 1986): 195–205, and *The Hollywood Film Musical*; and on New Zealand cinema and genre: "Kiwi Conventions: Genre and New Zealand Cinema," *Film International* 32 (2008): 14–22.

8

TO BE CONTINUED

Collecting Comics as Ouroboros /
Ouroboros as Comics Collecting

Blair Davis

THE MEDIUM OF COMICS HAS grown rapidly in recent decades, as have the possibilities for comics collectors. From the rise of original graphic novels that tell stories in a longer, nonserialized format (along with collections reprinting previously serialized issues of various comic book titles) to the birth of digital distribution, webcomics, and beyond, modern comics fans have more options than ever before for how their collections can take shape as the boundaries of what comics *are* continue to shift. In past generations, reading comics meant opening a newspaper to enjoy *Peanuts* or *Prince Valiant* as well as buying the latest issue of *Action Comics* or *Captain America* from a newsstand or drugstore. By the 1970s and '80s, fans could also turn to specialty retailers like Denver's Mile High Comics and Vancouver's Comic Shop but only if their town was lucky enough to have its own store. Collecting comics used to be a question of when and where you might find a coveted issue that you'd long sought after. Now it's usually just a question of what format you want to own a particular comic in and how soon you want to download it or place your online auction bid.

My own journey as a comics collector has paralleled the rise of these new platforms ever since I started collecting comic books in the early 1980s: I've bought, and often sold, my favorite comics in different versions and formats over the years, from single issues to fancy hardcovers to digital editions. At the same time, my experiences as a comics fan have been influenced by my role as media scholar over the past three decades, transitioning from first-generation university student to graduate student to adjunct instructor to the tenure track. I've gone from selling my collection on eBay to support myself in grad school to buying back much of it to use in my teaching and research as a now-tenured professor at DePaul University, be it in classes about comics themselves or adaptations thereof, or for the books and articles I've written about comics like *Movie Comics: Page to Screen/Screen to Page*.[1] In turn, my life as both a comics collector and a media scholar demonstrates how collecting is often a cyclical process resembling the figure of the ouroboros—the "Gnostic symbol of a snake eating its own tail."[2] Collecting, then, is not always a linear progression of simply acquiring more and more over time but instead an ouroboros-like ebb and flow of gain and loss, procurement and replacement.

ORIGIN STORY

I will admit that I have always been obsessed with comics. We didn't own a VCR that let me pause and rewind my favorite movies until the late 1980s when I was a teenager, so as a kid I loved the way that comics let me control how I experienced the temporal pace of visual narratives. Movies were fleeting experiences, but I could study and scrutinize my favorite comics panels again and again, for as long as I liked. Once I realized how comics held that advantage over movies, I was hooked. Comedian Jerry Seinfeld has a bit about Halloween revolving around kids' obsession with candy: "Your whole motivation in life when you're a kid is GET—CANDY. It was like a mantra running through every second of every day. . . . Friends, family, school. These were just obstacles in the way of getting more candy. You pretend that you're talking to people, doing things. But inside your head, candy is your only real goal," he says.[3] For me, the goal was comics, not candy. How could I get my hands on new issues of my favorite titles as well as those I'd always wanted to read but couldn't afford? If I held a garage sale at the end of our driveway to sell some of my old comics (which I remember doing at least twice), would I make enough money to buy new comics? If you'd told me when I was eight years old that someday I'd have a job that would not only pay me to teach about comics and write books about them but that they'd often give me money to buy the comics I needed to do that job, I would have looked at you dumbfounded.

I grew up in Burnaby, British Columbia, Canada, with the 1980s forming the basis for most of my childhood. Burnaby was the nearest suburb of Vancouver, and between the two cities there were a fair number of comic shops by the end of the decade. But it took a while. I didn't set foot in a retail establishment devoted primarily to the sale of comic books until the summer of 1983, when I was eight years old. My mum took me to the Comic Shop in Vancouver, which was the biggest in the city with its three levels of merchandise.[4] The nearly ten-mile trip took the better part of a day—three different buses to get there and three more back. It was the only experience I've ever had in my life that I would describe as a kind of pilgrimage. It truly was a life-changing experience, one that I point to as the secret origin of my scholarly career. In turn, I ended off the acknowledgments of *Movie Comics* by writing about how that trip "has proven to be an inspiring example of how to literally go to great lengths for your kids when they show an interest in something."[5]

Up until that trip, new comics were something that I could find only at a handful of the local drugstores or corner stores in my neighborhood. We had two drugstores within walking distance of my house in the early 1980s, and I remember them as usually carrying perhaps one or two dozen titles at one time at most. Not every corner store carried comics in those days, but there was one that was a short bus ride away that had a spinner rack full of issues that I always longed to spend more time perusing. It was on the same block as a used bookstore called Burnaby Books that kept a box full of older comics in the back of the building, well out of sight—on the floor, underneath some shelving. I was occasionally able to convince my mum to go there since it was near our local library, which we visited often. We had to walk past that corner store with the spinner rack beckoning in the window to reach the used bookstore, but since we didn't have a lot of money growing up, I have few memories of spinning that rack myself. I mostly just got to look through the window, like Tiny Tim outside the shops on Christmas Eve ("Did you have a nice time looking at all the wonderful things?" his mum asks in the 1951 film *Scrooge*).[6]

But I was mostly happy enough with the used comics at Burnaby Books, even if they weren't new or unread or unbent. It's probably why my comics collection still has a large number of books I buy each year from used-book sellers. For many people, collecting is often about the condition of the item. But for my teaching and research purposes, condition often amounts to an assessment of whether the cover is still intact and if any of the pages have been cut out. Mint condition is not a prerequisite for effective pedagogy or scholarship when it comes to comics. I want my students to handle the comics I bring into the class-room (usually enough to fill two huge tote bags at a time!). I need them to understand that the medium of comics encompasses a range of dif-ferent formats—some that are thin enough to roll up and put in your back pocket, others much bigger and heavier. Comics are distinct from visual media like movies and television in part because of their tactil-ity, and the material nature of my own comics collection has seen a wider and wider range of physical shapes and sizes in recent years. I bring in everything from thirty-two-page single issues (known as floppies among fans) to hardcover omnibuses reprinting more than a thousand pages of any given series, to oversize editions of early-twentieth-century comic strips that stand almost two feet tall like *Little Nemo in Slumberland* (in the original page size that they appeared in newspapers),[7] and I let them handle everything so they can better understand how the medium of comics involves a multitude of reading experiences. The process often means that my books return back to the shelf with more wear than they started off with before class, and I'm fine with that. Unlike some collec-tors who take pride in the condition of their collection, I treat my comics as the equivalent of lab materials; you expect that your equipment will take on some nicks and scrapes along the way.

Upon entering the hallowed grounds of the Comic Shop in 1983, what stood out to me among the thousands of new and old issues for sale were several publishing formats I had never seen before.[8] I was used to ongoing series from publishers like DC, Marvel, and Harvey. I had even come across the occasional annual featuring my favorite heroes, which were released once a year as a special issue with extra pages. But what I was most drawn to at the Comic Shop were the formats that I wasn't already familiar with: limited series and one-shots and reprinted collections. One-shots are stand-alone single issues, like the copy of *Marvel Tails Starring Peter Porker, The Spectacular Spider-Ham* I bought that day, which aren't followed by a second installment. Limited series are serialized titles featuring a predetermined number of issues (often four, sometimes six or twelve), like the first issues of *Hawkeye* and the *Falcon* that I brought home with me.

The anthropomorphic visage of a porcine webslinger in *Spider-Ham* was too good to pass up, because it was a new take on the traditional male superhero. I don't recall buying many titles with women in title roles (not that there were many to choose from); like most young lads, I likely overlooked series like *Wonder Woman* and *She-Hulk* in favor of the male heroes, which I had been socially conditioned to view as more relevant to my boyhood interests. But I do recall being interested in reading a series starring a Black hero when I saw the *Falcon* #1. I knew about characters like Black Lightning and Luke Cage in passing but often read the Falcon's adventures in issues of *Captain America* and *The Avengers*. The chance to own the first issue of a solo title—let alone one whose limited series status promised an ending rather than the need to buy additional serialized issues—featuring my favorite Black hero was an exciting moment. In turn, I have gone on to write numerous essays about Black comics characters and creators, proving how scholarly interests are often forged at a young age.[9]

What also stood out to me were the reprinted collections offering readers older issues and stories in a new package, such as the two *Marvel Illustrated Books* I bought that reprinted tales from *The Avengers* and *Uncanny X-Men*. As a kid, my local library had a few collections of reprinted comic strips like *Garfield*, *Broom Hilda*, and *Hagar the Horrible*, as well as

Reprinted Marvel collections through the ages, from Illustrated Books to Omnibuses

European titles like *Tintin*, *Asterix and Oblix*, and *Lucky Luke*. But reprints of American superhero comics were mind blowing to me because they meant easy access to a wealth of older (and narratively canonical) story lines that I had known about only in passing via how they were referred to in newer issues (by the editors in textual captions, by readers in the letter pages, or by the characters themselves within the story). My early fascination with past issues of ongoing series eventually led to my historical work in my books *Movie Comics* and *Comic Book Women*, which are focused on the origins of comic books in the 1930s through 1950s.[10]

Similarly, I presented a conference paper at the International Comics Art Forum about those same limited series I bought in 1983,[11] and the ideas in that presentation were then cited as part of the opening

Framed issues of important comics from my youth hang on the wall of my home office.

framework in one of my fellow comic scholars' essays in the anthology *The Other 1980s: Reframing Comics' Crucial Decade*.[12] Those same issues now hang framed on the wall of my home office. They are visible in the background whenever I record a lecture video or join a Zoom meeting, serving as a way of both branding my identity as a comics scholar and paying tribute to the role of my mum (who died in 2010) in my origins as a media studies scholar with that fateful daylong trip to the Comic Shop in 1983.

Perhaps collecting is a first step toward scholarship. Media Studies scholar John L. Sullivan notes that comic book collectors "perform the role of 'experts' in their field and distinguish themselves according to both their level of knowledge about comics and their personal collections of rare and unique comic books."[13] For some collectors, the process of gaining "knowledge" and expertise through building a collection can translate into the realm of applicable skills within academia. Building a collection also involves a process of curating, which can lead one toward an intellectual curiosity about the objects being collected. For comics collectors in particular, amassing a collection also involves a desire to put things into historical context, with one's comics often organized in a combination of alphabetical and chronological order. My volumes of Superman comics, for instance, begin in the 1930s and end in the modern era as they span three shelves. My scholarly instinct to draw historical patterns across various media texts was spawned in no small part by the regular, ritualistic process of considering the role of chronology as I add items to, catalog, and/or reorganize my collection.

GRAD SCHOOL ATE MY COMICS COLLECTION

My comics collection played a key role in my early academic days not only in terms of what I acquired but also what I gave up. By the late 1980s, a store called Tazmanian Comics opened up in Burnaby, mere steps away from both Burnaby Books and that wonderful corner store with the spinner rack. With a subscription service that let me request copies of my favorite titles rather than haunting local drugstores in the hopes of buying a random copy, Tazmanian Comics allowed comic book collecting to become both a practical venture as well as a source of subcultural identity in my teenage years.

As an undergraduate in the 1990s, I collected issues of the *Amazing Spider-Man*. I started with then-recent issues while also tracking down whatever back issues I could afford from local comic stores and at various conventions around the city. I also allowed my fascination with reprints to fill in the gaps of this collection, through issues of *Marvel Tales* featuring Spidey's initial adventures from the 1960s along with collected editions of *The Essential Amazing Spider-Man* in black and white. I used parts of this collection to write a paper for a media studies class comparing the formal conventions of comic book storytelling in the *Amazing Spider-Man* to those of Art Spiegelman's Pulitzer Prize–winning *Maus*—demonstrating the aesthetic and narrative differences in the latter. I included the essay as a writing sample when I applied to the master's program at my local university, a fact that I was brash enough to share with Spiegelman himself in person during a posttalk signing in 1998 while proudly presenting him with a copy of the essay. I don't know if he ever read it, but today he and I both serve as members of the editorial advisory board for *Inks: The Journal of the Comics Studies Society*.

My doctoral work at McGill University saw me living in Montreal while I did my course work and then returning to Vancouver, where I did my comprehensive exams and dissertation. But as I continued my doctoral studies, my collection soon served more urgent needs, like food and rent. As a first-generation university student, I supported myself throughout all my degree programs with a variety of jobs—machine operator at the various warehouses where my dad worked, ESL tutor, and then eventually adjunct instructor. I also turned steadily to eBay as a way of making enough money from my comics to live. I had given up buying new comics on a regular basis upon starting at McGill, instead buying the occasional single issue or graphic novel as I could afford them. I ended up selling nearly my entire collection on eBay between 2002 and 2008, keeping only those comics from the 1980s that I prized the most. I sold my entire *Amazing Spider-Man* collection, a vast array of *Batman*, *Superman*, *Star Wars*, and *X-Men* comics, along with sets of *Hate*, *Hellboy*, and *Madman*. Neil Gaiman's *The Sandman*, Paul Pope's *THB* and Dan Clowes's *Eightball* sold well especially well, as did early issues of *The Simpsons*.

Each transaction helped pay the bills for another week as I finished my dissertation. I also sold nearly all of my childhood toys (so long, 1985 *G.I. Joe* Snake Eyes figure complete with all accessories) and many of my collectible videos (fare-thee-well, bootleg *Star Wars Holiday Special*). In order to survive my doctorate financially, I had to sell off nearly every vestige of collectible media I had acquired up until that point. The very act of selling a collection that had inspired my scholarly career seemed akin to the ouroboros as the cost of my degree devoured the very types of pop culture objects that I was training myself how to study. Grad school certainly ate up most of my comic collection. But the end-career result of my PhD soon allowed me to buy parts of it back.

TENURE-TRACK LIFE

By the time I started as an assistant professor in the College of Communication at DePaul University in 2011, there were far fewer comics to move to Chicago than there had been when I began my doctoral work. Many comics collectors measure the size of their collections in terms of "long boxes"—cardboard storage containers that are over two feet long and hold more than two hundred issues. At its peak, my collection filled at least a dozen or more such boxes. By the time I was done with eBay, it filled little more than a single box. Nearly all that remained was from the 1980s—issues of *Blue Devil*, *West Coast Avengers*, *Hawkeye*, the *Falcon*, *Secret Wars*, and the *Legion of Substitute Heroes Special*. I also hung on to a full ten-issue set of Jack Kirby's *2001: A Space Odyssey*, as well as his oversize Treasury Edition adaptation of the film. Some comics were worth going a little hungry for in grad school.

When I started teaching, my collection began to grow once again— but often in new forms. I applied for grants to support the materials needed for new research projects and requested funding for teaching-related supplies. If I needed certain DVDs to teach a film studies class, I was often able to request them. When I taught classes on comic book movies, my department bought copies of the Marvel Cinematic Universe oeuvre, *Watchmen* (Zack Snyder, 2009), *Scott Pilgrim vs. the World* (Edgar Wright, 2010), and other such films so that I could teach our students how filmmakers make choices in adapting the content of one medium into another. If I needed certain books for a comics studies class, I could ask for those too in order to better teach our students about the materiality and medium specificity of comics in various formats. As I wrote books like *Movie Comics*, *Comic Book Women*, and my current project on how comics have represented Christianity, I was lucky enough to use grant money to buy the comics needed for my research. The fact that I now had a full-time job with a steady paycheck also helped to build back certain parts of my former collection (along with some of my favorite comics-related toys from my younger years to line my bookshelves), demonstrating how collecting is often a cyclical process tied to the ebb and flow of one's life circumstances and finances. Sometimes we all have to weigh the need for keeping or growing our collection against necessities like food and shelter; being a media scholar can require the additional layer of tying that collection to the needs of your research and pedagogy, and weighing your choices accordingly depending on where you are at in your scholarly career.

Most of the time, it was more economical for me to buy reprint collections than original issues for my research: black-and-white collections like Marvel's Essential Marvel and DC's Showcase Presents editions;

In my home office, collected editions of various formats are stored as their size allows, while single issues are stored in IKEA magazine holders.

hardcover omnibus editions; softcover trade paperbacks. Many of them were used copies (some bought at my local library's sale table, others at flea markets, used booksellers and, yes, eBay), in keeping with the role played by that cardboard box in the back of Burnaby Books in my humble collecting origins. The issues of *Hellboy* I had to sell during grad school became replaced by a set of *Hellboy* Library Edition hardcovers. My

My work office contains numerous bookshelves full of comics used for teaching. Not shown are the stacks and stacks of single issues piled on the floor, in filing cabinets, and elsewhere.

long-gone collection of *The Sandman* comics was replaced by two giant omnibus editions. Giant tomes now stood where single issues of *Bone* and *Eightball* once remained, as did Marvel Omnibus hardcovers collecting such 1980s story lines as "Atlantis Attacks" and "The Evolutionary War." Trade paperbacks now replaced single issues of *The Avengers, Black Panther, Dork, Fantastic Four, Green Arrow, Hate, Madman, Naughty Bits, Power Pack, Preacher*, the *Shadow, Sin City*, and *Usagi Yojimbo*.

As these new editions joined my now small but meaningful assortment of single issues, I've been able to use my collection not only as the basis of book-length manuscripts but also for various essays in anthologies edited by my peers. Often when I come across a call for papers, I'll turn to my shelves for inspiration to see what I already know about a given subject from my years as a collector. For Brannon Costello and

Brian Cremins's *The Other 1980s: Reframing Comics' Crucial Decade* (2021), I drew on single issues of *Blue Devil*, and *'Mazing Man* as well as reprinted Showcase Presents collections of *Ambush Bug* and *Captain Carrot and His Amazing Zoo Crew*.[14] For a semiotic analysis of Black superhero costuming in Frances Gateward and John Jennings's *The Blacker the Ink: Constructions of Black Identity in Comics and Sequential Art* (2015), I drew on single issues of *Black Lightning* and the *New Teen Titans* I'd managed to hang on to over the years, along with reprinted collections of *Justice League of America, Luke Cage*, and *Uncanny X-Men*.[15] For a comparison of class issues in urban and rural settings for Marc DiPaolo's *Working Class Comic Book Heroes: Class Conflict and Populist Politics in Comics*, I used my Essential Marvel collections of *Luke Cage, Power Man and Iron Fist*, and *Man-Thing*.[16] For Barry Keith Grant and Scott Henderson's *Comics and Pop Culture: Adaptation from Panel to Frame*, I used my long-treasured copies of Kirby's *2001: A Space Odyssey* to write about adaptations and extensions of movies to comics in the 1970s through the present, along with issues of Marvel's *Star Wars* and *Marvel Super Special*.[17]

In studying those latter two series, I turned to an entirely different material form than those in the physical collections in both my home and work offices: I used my digital subscription to Marvel Unlimited to read various issues online. Much as I learned at a young age that a comics collection can be comprised of both original and reprinted materials, so too have digital copies now supplanted many of the physical copies I once owned. As I turn toward new research projects, I find myself increasingly balancing the use of the physical texts on my shelves with the digital versions of comics in numerous online archives. I compile reading lists on Marvel Unlimited and download issues from the Digital Comic Museum, curating my own personal collection of files with the same care that I organize my bookshelves. I also assign comics for my students to read in both physical and digital forms, once again in aid of studying the materiality and formal qualities of the medium in classes offered within a media studies program.

As comics have been reprinted in new physical and digital formats, my collection has often taken on new forms that I could never have expected in my younger years. I can now read the beloved copy of *Marvel Tails Starring Peter Porker, The Spectacular Spider-Ham* that I bought in 1983 as a single issue (I own multiple copies), as part of a collected trade paperback (of which I own two different versions, in different sizes), and as a digital version online. I often do all three, as a way of reminding myself not only how much comics have changed since I was a kid but also about just how far I have come as a scholar. The figure of the ouroboros was "adopted by Gnostic sects as a symbol of knowledge and eternity," with some scholars seeing the ouroboros as "representing the unity of opposites in the formation of reality."[18] I certainly see "unity" in how I am able to balance the use of physical and digital copies of comics—sometimes turning to different versions of the exact same issue in class and in doing my research. In turn, I see this multiplicity of formats as enabling the medium of comics to endure regardless of the technological shifts which may arise in generations to follow. No matter what comics might look like in the future, and no matter what parts of their collections future generations of scholars might have to sell to fund their own studies, I have no doubt that collecting comics will prove to be an eternal process long after I have taught my final students and written my final words.

NOTES

1   Blair Davis, *Movie Comics: Page to Screen/Screen to Page* (New Brunswick, NJ: Rutgers University Press, 2017). See also Blair Davis, *Comic Book Movies* (New Brunswick, NJ: Rutgers University Press, 2018).

2   Micah Issat and Carlyn Main, *Hidden Religion: The Greatest Mysteries and Symbols of the World's Religious Beliefs* (Santa Barbara, CA: ABC-Clio, 2014), 80.

3   Jerry Seinfeld, *Is This Anything?* (New York: Simon & Schuster, 2020), 100.

4   The Comic Shop opened in 1974 and closed in 2019. See Craig Takeuchi, "After 44 Years, The Comic Shop Enters its Endgame," *Georgia Straight*, December 17, 2018, www.straight.com/life/1178351/after-44 -years-kitsilanos-comicshop-enters-its-endgame.

5   Davis, *Movie Comics*, x.

6   While my memories of collecting comics as a child are often bittersweet ones, the role of memory and nostalgia are often posited as foundational for collectors. Lincoln Geraghty writes, for instance, "Memories

are essential to the production of subjectivity therefore the memories embedded within the collection of toys, merchandise and collectibles are emblems of the self, markers of identity and symbolic of the cultural capital that fans accumulate in their life-long engagement with a media text." *Cult Collectors: Nostalgia, Fandom and Collecting Popular Culture* (New York: Routledge, 2014), 4.

7   See, for instance, Winsor Nemo, *Little Nemo in Slumberland: So Many Splendid Sundays, 1905–1910*, ed. Peter Maresca (Palo Alto, CA: Sunday Press, 2011); and Peter Maresca, ed., *Forgotten Fantasy: Sunday Comics, 1900–1915* (Palo Alto, CA: Sunday Press, 2011).

8   Arguably, I walked into the Comic Shop a dedicated reader of comics and left the store as a dedicated collector, more fully aware of the scope of what I might collect and the ways in which my collection might take shape. For more on the distinctions between reading and collecting comics, see Benjamin Woo, "Understanding Understandings of Comics: Reading and Collecting as Media-Oriented Practices," *Participations: Journal of Audience and Reception Studies* 9, no. 2 (2012): 180–99.

9   See Blair Davis, "Bare Chests, Silver Tiaras and Removable Afros: The Visual Design of Black Comic Book Superheroes," in *The Blacker the Ink: Constructions of Black Identity in Comics and Sequential Art*, ed. Frances Gateward and John Jennings (New Brunswick, NJ: Rutgers University Press, 2015), 193–212; Blair Davis, "All-Negro Comics and the Birth of Lion Man, the First African American Superhero," *Inks: The Journal of the Comics Studies Society* 3, no. 3 (2019): 273–97; and Blair Davis, "The Art of Alvin Hollingsworth," *Desegregating Comics*, ed. Qiana Whitted, forthcoming.

10   Peyton Brunet and Blair Davis, *Comic Book Women: Characters, Creators and Culture in the Golden Age* (Austin: University of Texas Press, 2021).

11   Blair Davis, "#1 In a Limited Series: Marvel Goes Mini" (paper presented at the International Comics Arts Forum, Seattle, November 2017).

12   See Aaron Kastan, "Amethyst, Meet Misty, and Angel Love: Historical Footnotes or Paths Not Taken?," in *The Other 1980s: Reframing Comics' Crucial Decade*, ed. Brannon Costello and Brian Cremins (Baton Rouge: Louisiana State University Press, 2021).

13   John L. Sullivan, *Media Audiences: Effects, Users, Institutions and Power* (Thousand Oaks, CA: Sage, 2013), 208.

14   Blair Davis, "The Lark/Light Returns: DC's Humorous Heroes of the 1980s," in *The Other 1980s: Reframing Comics' Crucial Decade*, ed. Brannon Costello and Brian Cremins (Baton Rouge: Louisiana State University Press, 2021).

15 Davis, "Bare Chests."

16 Blair Davis, "From the Streets to the Swamp: Luke Cage, Man-Thing and the 1970s Class Issues of Marvel Comics," in *Working Class Comic Book Heroes: Class Conflict and Populist Politics in Comics*, ed. Marc DiPaolo (Jackson: University of Mississippi Press, 2018), 149–68.

17 Blair Davis, "From Adaptation to Extension: A History of Comics Adapting Films, 1974–2015," in *Comics and Pop Culture: Adaptation from Panel to Frame*, ed. Barry Keith Grant and Scott Henderson (Austin: University of Texas Press, 2020), 36–48.

18 Issat and Main, *Hidden Religion*, 80–81.

9

THE *LEGO* MOVIES, A LEGO COLLECTOR, AND THE PROBLEM WITH REPRESENTATIONS OF COLLECTING IN FILM

Kara Lynn Andersen

ONE OF MY ACADEMIC AREAS of expertise is the representation of collecting in visual entertainment media (film, animation, television, and video games). It stemmed from my observation that many live-action and animated films rely on a trope of collecting that is at odds with reality of collecting practice. Museologist Susan M. Pearce found in her sociological work that approximately 30 percent of the population in the Western world engages in some form of collecting at any given time, making it a common activity. Furthermore, she found that collectors are more often female than male (of those surveyed and self-identifying as collectors, 42 percent are male and 58 percent female) and they are frequently well integrated into other aspects of society. The information about family and employment situations indicates that collectors are living personal lives which do not differ from those of non-collectors, and which are "normal" in terms of human sexual and familiar relationships. . . . The point is an extremely important one, because the stereotype of the collector is of a dispirited, anorak-clad loner who is unable to form personal relationships, especially with the opposite sex, and who uses collecting as a substitute for personal emotional satisfaction. This image recurs in the media and in cartoons, and forms part of the mind-set of most non-collectors.[1]

In films and other entertainment media, however, the stereotype Pearce references above is employed far more often than a more realistic portrayal of collectors or collecting. The stereotype appears to stem from the association of collecting with serial killers. This is demonstrated in a number of films about serial killers, including *Psycho* (Alfred Hitchcock, 1960), *The Collector* (William Wyler, 1965), *Silence of the Lambs* (Jonathan Demme, 1991), *The Bone Collector* (Philip Noyce, 1999), and Marcus Dunstan's *The Collector* (2009), *The Collection* (2012), and *The Collected* (forthcoming). They all capitalize on the fact that real-life serial killers are indeed known to collect souvenirs or trophies from their victims. But in the cinema, that association at times extends unrealistically beyond collections with a direct connection to the victim, to the idea that anyone who collects anything might have murderous impulses. Thus, entertainment media frequently employ the trope of collectors who kill to protect their collection or to acquire a new item for it. This is a repeated motivation for murder and other crimes in police procedurals and crime shows like *Law & Order* (1990–2010, 2022), *Law & Order: Criminal Intent* (2001–11), *Firefly* (2002), *CSI* (2000–2015), *Monk* (2002–9), *Justified* (2010–15), *Bones* (2005–17), and *Fargo* (2014–present). When collectors are not portrayed as criminals in the movies (or as victims of a crime related to their collection), they are still often characterized as social misfits of various kinds, which is not true to the profile of actual collectors. This occurs in Stephen Frears's *High Fidelity* (2000), where Rob Gordon's (John Cusack's) collecting is linked to stunted social growth; in Liev Schreiber's *Everything*

Is Illuminated (2005), where a socially awkward youth collects mementoes of family history; and in Judd Apatow's *The 40-Year-Old Virgin* (2005), where Andy Stitzer's (Steve Carell's) maturation into a sexually active adult is signaled by his willingness to sell his collection of action figures. In short, collectors have gotten a bad rap in the popular imagination, one that does not at all reflect the reality of the practice.

COLLECTING RESEARCH AND TEACHING ANIMATION STUDIES

Though the examples above were all drawn from live-action dramatic films, I have also found my research on collecting and its filmic representations useful in teaching History of Animation and Contemporary Animation, in several contexts. First, character merchandising (in the form of figurines, toys, clothing, objects, etc.) has been an important component of animation's financial success going as far back as Felix the Cat (first created in 1919), and understanding the way collectors are marketed to—and even created—by animated texts is important for any student who wants to work in or study the commercial animation industry. Second, collecting is an important component of fan culture, and any course that engages with audience studies must account for the role of both youth and adult collectors in the construction of fandoms (animated and otherwise). Additionally, an understanding of the way the representation of the collector was established and has endured is useful in screenwriting and other courses that examine how tropes are used in entertainment media narratives.

A particularly interesting case to consider is the image of the collector in the two recent LEGO movies—animated features built not around a particular character but around an established children's toy that has been internationally popular for decades.

THE LEGO MOVIE (2014)

When *The Lego Movie* (Christopher Miller and Phil Lord, 2014) was released, I went to see it in the theater because I am a fan and collector of LEGO merchandise, unaware that the film's plot was yet another example of the negative collector stereotype—this time one that hit very close to home. In *The Lego Movie*, the animated LEGO minifig[2] Emmet Brickowski (voiced by Chris Pratt) struggles to become a Master Builder and save the LEGO world from being destroyed by Lord Business/President Business (Will Ferrell), a corporate executive who wants to control the LEGO world by gluing the pieces together into his vision of a perfectly neat and organized world. This story line is mirrored in a live-action sequence of a young boy, Finn (Jadon Sand), and his father (known only as "the Man Upstairs" and played by Will Ferrell again) clashing over whether LEGO building sets should be mixed together and played with or glued in place and preserved. The Man Upstairs is an adult collector of LEGO sets who builds according to the instruction booklets and then glues the bricks in place. Finn would rather play with the sets, assembling and disassembling them in ever-changing permutations—and Emmet's narrative is meant to originate from Finn's imagination. Both Lord Business and the Man Upstairs are thus the villains of the movie in their respective realms, authoritarian figures whose impulse to collect and order their worlds is portrayed as oppressive and arbitrary. Finn ultimately persuades his father to his point of view: LEGO sets are meant for building a variety of things, real and imagined, and should never be fixed in place as a static collection. Emmet likewise defeats Lord Business by becoming a Master Builder, someone who can see the endless potential in any set of LEGO bricks and not need a set of instructions. As Madeleine Hunter observes, "At the heart of *The Lego Movie* dwell questions about the nature of play itself; what does it mean to 'play well'—a phrase which in Danish translates to 'Leg godt' and from which LEGO takes its name?"[3] The message of the film is clear: collecting is out (since it means a fixed object); creative play is in.

THE LEGO MOVIE 2: THE SECOND PART (2019)

Though Finn and his father come to an agreement at the end of *The Lego Movie*, the Man Upstairs notes that if Finn is allowed to play with the collection in the basement, he also has to let in someone else: Finn's little sister. In Emmet's LEGO world, the film ends with the appearance of DUPLO invaders (DUPLOs being bigger LEGO pieces for younger children), one of whom announces in a babyish voice: "We are from the planet DUPLO and we are here to destroy you."

The Lego Movie 2: The Second Part (Mike Mitchell, 2019) was released to continue the story. It is five years later, and Emmet and the other minifigs live in Apocalypseburg, named as such because the destructive play of Finn's younger sister made it impossible to maintain any structure intact. The Man Upstairs abandoned LEGO sets entirely because he did not want to deal with the children's squabbling. The promise of father and children playing together was only an empty hope, it seems.

Finn keeps the LEGO bricks in the basement. In the first movie, he wins the right to creative free play but still follows rules: LEGO bricks should be located together, and while different sets can be mixed and building instructions do not need to be followed, building is the ideal. In *The Second Part*, siblings Finn and younger sister, Bianca, fight over where the LEGOs can be kept and who can play with them, to the great annoyance of their mother, who wants to put all the LEGOs in the "Bin of Storajj," a location of stasis and death for toys. Over the course of the two films human characters learn to relinquish control and embrace untidy free play. The Man Upstairs, the collector from the first movie, doesn't even appear in *The Second Part*, only participating with a couple of voice-over comments. *The Second Part* focuses on Finn learning to share his love of LEGOs with Bianca just as his father learned to share with him, but evidently the Man Upstairs has had to give up playing with LEGOs altogether (a common theme in visual entertainment media narratives about adult collectors). He has taken up golf and leaves the children's mother to manage the siblings. She never gets to play.

Thus, the message in both films is that LEGO sets are for children's messy, chaotic, and inventive play. This is made clear in the LEGO Group's brand values: "Learning is about being curious, experimenting and collaborating—expanding our thinking and doing, helping us develop new insights and new skills. We learn through play by putting things together, taking them apart and putting them together in different ways. Building, un-building, rebuilding, thereby creating new things and developing new ways of thinking about ourselves, and the world."[4] These are aspirational claims meant to appeal to adults seeking quality toys for the children in their lives, and there is enough research on the value of creative play for children to back up their claims. There is far less research on whether playing with children's toys has a similar value for adults, but theorists like Pearce have likened collecting itself to play.[5] The *Lego* movies suggest instead that adults should neither collect nor play with LEGOs—they should grow up and do grown-up things, like golfing and refereeing sibling arguments. However, both LEGO playsets, specifically, and toys in general are highly collectible items, and there are many adults who continue to purchase and enjoy them.

ADULT LEGO COLLECTING

The LEGO Group is certainly a for-profit company motivated to produce the kinds of products that make money, and in the last two decades it has been targeting teens and adults as purchasers for themselves. In 1999, the LEGO Group released its first licensed theme sets: LEGO *Star Wars*. This franchise has great appeal to children, of course, but it is also known for its adult fans and collectors, and LEGO *Star Wars* sets have become some of the most collectible and expensive the company produces. The LEGO Group has continued to expand on its licensed theme offerings that straddle the line of catering to adults and children. The company encourages consumers to consider LEGO sets collector's items through production of franchised sets including not only *Star Wars* but DC Super Heroes, Disney, *Harry Potter*, Marvel, and Minecraft sets as well. All these franchises have proven mass appeal, and the complexity and price points of some of the LEGO-themed sets supports the idea that the LEGO Group is purposefully seeking older target consumers. For how many parents would be willing to spend $799.99 on LEGO set 75192, a replica of the *Millennium Falcon* from *Star Wars*, for a child?[6] That is the original price for the set, but rare out-of-production sets can sell for much higher prices. Indeed, in December 2018, Victoria Dobrynskaya and Julia Kishilova published a study that found LEGO sets might be a better investment than gold due to their high value to collectors, so much so that the LEGO Group has instituted quantity limits on purchases to help control price gouging; one can buy only five LEGO *Millennium Falcon* sets at a time.[7]

In 2008, the company introduced the LEGO Architecture range, given an age rating of 14 and up, and on August 1, 2020, it introduced LEGO Art sets. Designed for builders ages 18+, these sets include mosaic images of Marilyn Monroe, the Beatles, Iron Man, or *Star Wars'* The Sith.[8] Each set comes with a music podcast to listen to while building and has between twenty-nine hundred and thirty-three hundred pieces. With the release of the new adult sets, LEGO also began featuring adults interacting with LEGO models on its print catalog pages. This marked the first time the company openly advertised LEGO building sets as products for adults. The January 2021 LEGO catalog contains a page with the heading "Adults Welcome," and advertises two sets: a flower bouquet and a bonsai tree. In other words, while the *Lego* movies give lip service to the hackneyed idea that collecting is for children, the LEGO Group is clearly and actively designing building sets for adult LEGO collectors. Katriina Heljakka argues that "the ongoing gamification of many areas of culture seems to have contributed to an alleviation of the stigma previously associated with adult play."[9] And if, indeed, adults are more frequently or more openly playing with toys than in the past, why not design toys for adults? The LEGO Group also has a line of Serious Play kits that are geared toward improving creative thinking and innovation in business contexts. Serious Play is more than just a special set of bricks, however; it is a methodology for using LEGO bricks for strategy development, improving communication among employees, and sharing ideas. Heljakka further notes that adults have long been recognized as buyers of toys not only for the children in their lives but as *collectors*. Collecting, it seems, puts a veneer of maturity onto the idea of purchasing toys for the adult self. Now, however, "the most common way to identify, acknowledge and approve of adult toy play in reference to the toy industry . . . is still to name this type of play as *collecting*. Nevertheless, adult relationships and activities with toys often extend beyond the accumulation of toys that collecting is often recognized for."[10]

Page 28 from the January 2021 LEGO catalog features building sets geared toward adults.

MY LIFE AS A *LEGO* MOVIE

One of my earliest memories is of sitting at a low table, assembling and playing with LEGO bricks with my mother and father. It is one of a very few memories I have of my mother ever playing with me. I still have a handful of these original LEGO bricks. I never thought of myself as a collector of LEGO sets until I was much older and started keeping sets carefully separated in their individual boxes; but at some point, I picked these vintage bricks out and set them aside from the mass of mixed LEGO sets my brother and I shared growing up. As I recall, in my mid-teens I started keeping my LEGO sets in their original boxes—likely in part to keep them separate from those of my younger brother, although unlike Finn and Bianca in *The Second Part*, we rarely fought about LEGOs (just everything else). At some point in my teens, I made a display of my LEGO models on a low console table in my room. I had set 6085, Black Monarch's Castle, and set 6054, the Forestman's Hideout, reflecting a short-lived interest in medieval fantasy, and set 6386, Police Command Base, a LEGO Technic set I no longer have and can't identify anymore; the prize of my collection was set 1682, the Space Shuttle. The Space Shuttle represented a particular victory in my collecting as I had managed to wheedle my parents into gifting it to me long after they considered me too old to play with toys anymore.

I stopped collecting LEGOs for a while after high school but picked it up again in graduate school after preparing a class presentation on "interactivity" and Lev Manovich's *The Language of New Media*[11] tangentially led to my discovery of set 1349, LEGO Studios Steven Spielberg MovieMaker. The software it came with to make movies didn't work with my computer, and I think I bought it as much for the Steven Spielberg minifig as anything else—although I was interested in the idea of toys teaching children to make films. I next got set 4886, Designer Set, in 2004, one crafted so that you could build three different houses, and set 21005, the Architecture Fallingwater Set (since I lived near that famous Frank Lloyd Wright house). My last graduate school purchase was set 10184, Town Plan Set, from 2008, a multibuilding set I purchased primarily because it came with an Art Deco–styled cinema

Part of my earliest LEGO set, including three minifigs and two wheeled bricks, circa 1974

(including a marquee reading "Now Showing: *The 50 Year Brick*"). Again, I was attracted to it because it was movie themed.

Because LEGO sets can be expensive, I made only occasional purchases in graduate school. In the period between leaving graduate school and having kids, although I sometimes purchased new sets, I also gave away a few of my old ones to my nephew. But some of them still resided in my parents' house, and I would bring them back one at a time on my trips home. After having my own kids, LEGO collecting for myself dropped off for a while; however, I knew I was sitting on a gold mine in terms of toys my kids would want to play with when they got older. They went up on the high shelves, and until recently I had no time or space to build them.

However, since my son in particular has become interested in LEGOs, I have picked up a few more sets for myself while shopping for him, most notably set 75828, *Ghostbusters* Ecto 1 and 2, as both my children and I enjoyed Paul Feig's reboot, *Ghostbusters: Answer the Call* (2016). I keep that set in my office, because otherwise there is simply no

My LEGO cinema building and a curious pet lovebird

way to prevent my son from playing with it and thus losing some of the pieces. I also keep my Fallingwater set in my office, as well as set 21301, Birds, from 2015—although I have not yet found time to put it together. Most of the money I spend on LEGO products is for toys and other items for my kids, but I continue to have an interest in cinema-related LEGO sets myself, as well as those that have personal meaning for me, like my LEGO house, and Fallingwater.

MY SON'S LEGO HOARD—THE ANTITHESIS OF COLLECTING

I introduced both of my children to LEGO building sets at a young age, but they have only had enduring appeal to my son. His preferred way of playing with them is to build according to the directions, but at his current age he is unable to keep them organized by set. Once built, the pieces are gradually scattered all over the house, and LEGO building set designs have become more complicated over the years, with most containing unusual or unique bricks, and with many more tiny pieces than there were in past decades. We also inherited a huge bag of mixed LEGO bricks from a friend that overflows a 23 × 16 × 13-inch storage container. This makes finding specific pieces challenging. I refer to my son's accumulated LEGO sets and bricks as a "hoard." Since the term *collect* and its variations are applied to a wide variety of activities with meanings that range from "picking up items from a specific location" to "any gathering of items or people," there is often a slippage in understanding what qualifies as collecting. My preferred definition is "a gathering of items with some shared characteristic as defined by the person or institution doing the collecting," which is a wide umbrella that allows anyone who thinks they are a collector to be one. There is a distinction between collecting and hoarding, however, especially now that the fifth edition of the *Diagnostic and Statistical Manual of Mental Disorders* (DSM-V) has included hoarding as a discrete disorder. Hoarders value the objects in their hoard but do not value each item individually—they cannot, since they are overwhelmed with objects and are often not even aware of how many objects they have. Collectors, on the other hand, might have a collection that is poorly organized, messy, and even too large for the

My son's LEGO hoard, a jumble of LEGO bricks spilling out of a plastic container

space they have to store it in, but they are nevertheless selective about what they acquire and are aware of each of their objects individually. My son is not a pathological hoarder, but he certainly has a hoard of LEGO bricks. He cannot value each brick in the hoard because there are too many of them, and he cannot build and display the original sets because they are inextricably mixed together. His bricks also cause chaos in the house—they are on the kitchen counter when we want to cook, on the floor of every room, in the bathtub and the washing machine, and once even stuffed in the cheek pouches of his sister's hamster.

YELLING, STEALING, LOSING, BUYING, AND CRYING: YOURS, MINE, HERS, OURS

What does it really look like when an adult collector and child players cohabitate? And does it resemble the world of the *Lego* movies? The first thing I did when I had kids was to put all my LEGO sets away, and they stayed there until my kids were past the choking hazard age. I handed over some of my collection to them as they grew old enough to use them but only those that I was okay with having pieces getting mixed into the hoard. To value a set as a set, you have to keep it separate from all the rest. My son quickly learned that rebuilding a set that has been mixed in with other sets is an exercise in frustration. But he still lacks the organizational skills to keep sets separate from one another—even when he wants to. However, unlike the Man Upstairs in *The Lego Movie* I don't keep an elaborate display of assembled LEGO sets in my basement, and I don't glue them together. It is often said that collectors are always trying to foist their collections on unwilling adult child beneficiaries, but, so far, my son can't wait to get his hands on mine. But even now that he is eight, I have to keep my boxed sets hidden in the house—or else surrender them to the communal hoard, forever. For my son, the temptation to play with one of these sets is so great that when he finds my hiding places, he immediately begins playing with the set that he has found.

LEGO sets do appreciate in value with age, if you have the right ones, in the right condition, and I keep some of them with their resale price in mind. My son has inadvertently destroyed the monetary value of some of these sets as well. I had the 1985 Black Monarch's Castle with all the pieces, instructions, and box up until two years ago—when my son cut up the box and lost a number of its pieces. A listing for that set on eBay had a high bid of $142.50 with twenty-four bidders on November 28, 2020. The manufacturer's suggested retail price in 1985 was $68.00. I also had a new-in-box LEGO Indiana Jones Motorcycle Chase (set 7620) from 2018, purchased for $9.99. As of the time of writing, a new-in-box set is listed for $69.99 by an eBay seller who had previously sold three others for the same price.

What do I get from my LEGO collection that makes it important to keep it separate from my children's toys? For me, assembling a set using the directions is a stress-relieving hobby. The focus required is not unlike that for meditation; my mind is cleared of everything except the set in front of me. While I like to see the finished product, it is the process of building that I enjoy most. So it's not really the destruction of monetary value that bothers me when my son invades my collection but rather the pieces that go missing, which then prevents me from being able to complete the set when I build it myself. When I assemble a LEGO set, I am working on a task that I know I can complete—with a reassuring feeling of being *done* when that last brick is in place. It's like very little else in my life as an academic and single parent, and to achieve maximum satisfaction, every *original* piece needs to be there.

My son also enjoys building sets according to the directions, and I often have to manage his tears and anger when he cannot achieve this goal. But he furthermore likes to play with the finished set by driving LEGO vehicles, enacting chase scenes and crashes, or whatever else he might think of. He also builds inventively with pieces from his hoard and wants to make a photo book of his creations. Inevitably, his play process scatters pieces everywhere. There has been a lot of yelling, stealing, losing, buying, and crying as we cycle through new strategies to keep things organized. This involves new sets that arrive as gifts every holiday, new attempts on my part to encourage creative play rather than rote building, and continued efforts to navigate what is his, what is mine, what is his sister's, and what is all of ours together. It's more chaotic than Cloud Cuckoo Land itself here sometimes.

CONCLUSION

What conclusion can I draw from this rift between my experiences as a LEGO collector, my research on collecting, and the *Lego* movies' combined message that adults should leave toys to children and pursue banal adult activities? I'm tired of hiding my collection, tired of stepping on LEGO bricks in every room of the house, tired of siblings fighting, and indeed tired of collecting being portrayed in live-action and animated films as a childish pastime that adults must either renounce or else risk being associated with villains, murderers, and lonely eccentrics. As other chapters in this anthology demonstrate, adult colleting is not only common but also fulfilling and useful in a variety of ways. So let me take a page from the LEGO Group's corporate philosophy and use my creative thinking skills (which must surely be well developed after a lifetime of LEGO creative play) to formulate a different ending for my LEGO movie life. I will *not* take up golf and disappear from my children's lives like the Man Upstairs. Nor will I threaten to place their toys in the Bin of Storajj if they can't quietly resolve their own conflicts over them, like Finn and Bianca's mother. In fact, as part of my "research" for this chapter, my son, my daughter, and I built set 70820, *Lego Movie 2* Movie Maker, and made some silly animations together (and in full keeping with the imaginative chaos espoused by *The Lego Movie 2*, our hamster photobombed a few of them). I also justified the expense of purchasing set 10270, LEGO Creator Bookshop, by making it a family activity purchase, and I have made it a practice to set aside cooperative playtimes with each child, where they set the rules. Hopefully we will learn to value each family member's style of play. Except for the hamster's. One thing is certain, though: LEGO collecting and building may be chaotic and passionate in my home, but I am confident that it will not result in murder.

NOTES

1   Susan M. Pearce *Collecting in Contemporary Practice* (Walnut Creek, CA: Alta Mira Press, 1998), 27.

2   A LEGO minifigure, commonly referred to as a minifig, is a small plastic articulated figurine produced by Danish toy manufacturer the Lego Group. They were first produced in 1978 and have been a success, with over four billion produced worldwide as of 2020.

3   Madeleine Hunter, "Bric[k]olage: Adaptation as Play in *The Lego Movie*," *Adaptation* 11, no. 3 (2018): 273–81.

4   LEGO Group, "The LEGO® Brand: The LEGO® Brand Values," LEGO, accessed May 27, 2021, www.lego.com/en-us/aboutus/lego-group/the-lego-brand.

5   Susan M. Pearce, *Museums, Objects and Collections* (Washington, DC: Smithsonian Books, 1993), 50.

6   The LEGO group also sells a cheaper version of the *Millennium Falcon*, set 75257, for $159.99. Price as of May 2022 on LEGO's website, www.LEGO.com/en-us/categories/price-over-100-dollars?page=1&sort.key=PRICE&sort.direction=DESC.

7   Victoria Dobrynskaya and Julia Kishilova, "LEGO—The Toy of Smart Investors," Social Science Research Network, April 1, 2018, dx.doi.org/10.2139/ssrn.3291456.

8 "What are 18+ LEGO Sets and What Could They Lead To?" FirestarToys
   .com, August 16, 2020, blog.firestartoys.com/what-are-18-LEGO-sets-and
   -what-could-they-lead-to/#:~:text=This%20year%20LEGO%20released
   %20their,LEGO%20sets%20are%20being%20released.

9 Katriina Heljakka, "Rethinking Adult Toy Play in the Age of Ludic Lib-
   eration: Imaginative, Visual and Social Object-Interactions of Mature
   Players" (paper presented at the Eighth International Toy Research Association World Conference, International Toy Research Association, July
   2018), 2.

10 Heljakka, 6–7.

11 Lev Manovich, *The Language of New Media* (Cambridge, MA: MIT Press),
    2001.

II
COLLECTIONS OF OTHERS

10

ARCHIVAL SPOTLIGHT

Collectors' Contributions to Archiving Early Black Film

Leah M. Kerr

FILM HISTORIANS OFTEN MOURN THE large number of early silent and early Black films that have been lost, destroyed, or gone missing. Given the passage of time, the limited number of films printed, inadequate storage, deaths, bankruptcies, and the evolution of audiences' movie watching preferences, we should instead be celebrating the miracle of how much early film does exist. No magic was involved but rather the sweat, passion, research, and dogged hunting of a few dedicated film collectors who saved the treasures we have today. That they placed their gems in archives for preservation and future study speaks loudly to their primary mission, and their love of the medium.

Even though I was its first archivist, and left the Mayme A. Clayton Library & Museum as the Director of Collections, I never had the opportunity to meet the woman whose collection constantly astounded

This chapter originally published as Leah M. Kerr, "Archival Spotlight: Collectors' Contributions to Archiving Early Black Film," *Black Camera, An International Film Journal* 5, no. 1 (2013): 274–84. Published by Indiana University Press. Copyright © 2013. Reprinted with permission of Indiana University Press.

me. However, through my work there, I have been afforded historic opportunities to meet and speak with the keepers of the works and stories of early African American filmmakers. For this article, I was able to talk to Mayme A. Clayton's son, Lloyd Clayton; interview my friend and mentor Pearl Bowser and also my new acquaintance Henry T. Sampson Jr.,[1] who was clearly moved that others are continuing with the work of following scholarship of early black film. He is "depending on us to find new stories in the old films."

SHORT HISTORY OF EARLY BLACK FILMS: STORIES ABOUT US, BY US

Motion pictures have always been an intimate expression of how filmmakers see themselves and the world around them. In the early years of moving pictures, it was no small feat for African Americans to gain access to cameras, afford film stock, and orchestrate processing to capture their observations with a unique worldview. If not for the search and rescue by a few dedicated scholars and collectors, this history of early black films would have wasted away to ashy dust in forgotten vaults, closets, and basements. Thankfully, this is not the case, and we can celebrate the contributions of collectors such as Dr. Mayme A. Clayton (August 4, 1923–October 13, 2006), Pearl Bowser, and Dr. Henry T. Sampson Jr.

Moving images by and about African Americans became known as "race movies." The term may derive from "race man" or "race woman," which was a term of pride in describing successes of blacks. Photographers were among the first African Americans to take up the art of motion pictures. Addison N. Scurlock, Arthur Laidler Macbeth, and Jennie and Ernest Toussaint Welcome were well-known photographers who used motion pictures to document their communities. While only fragments of the films these individuals created still exist, descriptive accounts in newspapers tell us what they filmed. Around 1896, the public was treated to "actualities," many filmed and displayed by EDISON/ARMAT VITASCOPE, in New York, and later other venues around the country and world. Viewers were treated to titles including: *The Barber Shop, Boxing Match, Butterfly Dance, Serpentine Dance, Umbrella*

Dance, View of Venice with Gondolas, and *Walton and Slavin* (*Burlesque Boxers*). These short glimpses allowed Americans of all social strata to imagine adventures they may never have experienced.

The revelations when "race actualities" were released, beginning in 1910 by William Foster with *The Pullman Porter* (1910) and *The Railroad Porter* (1912) and Peter P. Jones with *The Dawn of the Truth* (1918) and *Rebirth of a Nation* (1915), were, as Bowser reflects, "attempts not just to address previous stereotypical images, but an attempt to present the black reality." Booker T. Washington hired George W. Broome to make a short film about the Tuskegee Institute, which was shown to potential New York investors in 1910 as an enticement for fundraising. Of the companies producing race films, Oscar Micheaux was the only one to successfully transcend from silent films to talkies. From 1919 (*The Homesteader*) to 1948 (*The Betrayal*), Micheaux produced approximately forty-one films. Today, fewer than a dozen can be seen. "Film," Bowser says, "was thought of as a good business for black people to be involved in. Black people spent a lot of money on the amusements in the movie houses." Box office numbers soared as many Americans streamed to motion pictures as a cheap escape, and amusing experience. Blacks were equally enamored but spent an inordinate amount of their earnings on the movies and still do today.

Experts suggest that 80 to 90 percent of all silent films have disappeared, leaving early black film little chance of survival. With the audience-pleasing innovations of sound and color, studios and distributors considered motion pictures made before 1950 to be without much commercial value. As these 35 mm prints were on highly flammable nitrate film stock and expensive to store, decisions were made to destroy them to retrieve silver from the negatives and prints. In California, many reels were taken to the pier and dumped into the Santa Monica Bay. With the lack of foresight for films that had been money makers, entertainment made by and for marginal populations was not even considered for preserving.

Among many lost race films, at least one was directed by a black woman. Unfortunately, the motion picture did not feature her name, and neither was it included in newspaper advertising. Bowser learned about her in *Half Century Magazine*, where she was unnamed, but there was a picture of her. Also lost were the works of Peter P. Jones, and now there are only descriptions of his films in the black press, where he was called a "fabulous photographer." His film *Rebirth of a Nation* told of the accomplishments of blacks since the end of slavery.

Perhaps the disappearance of many motion pictures could also be traced to a missing link that had traditionally held photographs and film prints—distributors. According to Bowser, aside from Sack Amusement and Toddy Pictures Company, there were few distributors working with African American filmmakers. In fact, "journalists sometimes shopped distributed films," with the likelihood they already had an engaged newspaper audience and could send viewers to theaters with a positive review. Micheaux used "runners" who would travel to towns ahead of him to book his films into theaters. They carried sample reels with them, a job that normally distributors would undertake. Those reels sustained frequent screenings and may have disappeared as well.

PEARL BOWSER: REDISCOVERING FORGOTTEN ARTISTS

Pearl Bowser (born in Harlem in 1931) spent much of her early years with her brothers in the theaters along 125th Street, watching the Hollywood Westerns, B-movies, and whatever black films were out at the time. Her mother would send Pearl and her five brothers to the movies as a type of six hour cheap childcare in the children's section of the movie theater. Fortuitously, she was influenced by the arts, culture and politics of the ongoing Harlem Renaissance, which were all parts of her education. She joined the Paul Robeson Club, and added the activist actor to her list of early teachers in her developing sense of identity and pride.

At the age of eighteen, Bowser moved to Brooklyn, attended Brooklyn College and worked at CBS tabulating the Nielsen Ratings for the soap operas, where she first learned of media manipulation of the public's perceptions of themselves and their reality. While at CBS, Richard Leacock, a proponent of the cinéma vérité style of documentary filmmaking, hired Bowser to work in his office at ABC. It was her first experience working with film, where she was running his office and was introduced to filmmaking from first concept to completion. Sitting in production meetings, editing sessions and meeting filmmakers such as Shirley Clarke and the Maysles brothers, Bowser learned from the pioneers of documentary filmmaking.

Bowser says her early black film research started in 1971, when she was working for ABC. One of her bosses, Charles Hobson, had found a little twenty-five-cent booklet on filmmakers which included a chapter on Oscar Micheaux. She began by searching around and uncovering forgotten films from vaults and motion picture cast and crew. ABC asked Pearl to do further research with some of the living performers from Micheaux's films. They gave her a tape recorder, a ticket to Hollywood, and a new adventure in her life.

Through her research Bowser met and interviewed actors, performers and extras who had been involved in working on race films in the 1920s and 1930s. They helped her to preserve film history through their conversations, but also by giving her scrapbooks and other ephemera they had collected. And they told her of their longing to get back into the business. Bowser states her interviewees were happy that she had come to speak to them, as no one else seemed interested in the work they had done.

Bowser's nearness to these links with nearly forgotten black film history is key. Many of her contacts had gone from watching the beginnings of American film history in the 1910s, to performing in the 1920s, to relating this information to an inquisitive researcher in the 1960s and 1970s. Given a few more years, this bridge would have been gated, blocked, or disintegrated due to the natural ravages of time.

Scar of Shame (1927) was the first race film Bowser saw as an adult. She understood how watching African Americans telling their own story was free from stereotype and related to her on a closer level, akin to the real stories she had seen from her neighbors and community. Here in 1970, a silent film from forty-three years earlier still felt relevant to her life. As Bowser followed her journey, she was able to see more race films and wondered how many of these she had seen already as a young child.

As a feminist, Bowser was also interested in the even more obscure information on the involvement of women in this poorly documented industry. She was surprised to find that women often worked as writers, editors and producers, although their names were generally missing from the sparse credits. More information could be learned from personal letters and diaries, and from reviews in the black newspapers from the time. Also, through interviews with women such as Harryette Miller Barton, who worked with William Alexander. Barton spoke of her work as a production manager, casting agent, screenwriter and even director of a few of the soundies, elucidating the overlooked roles of women's behind-the-camera work.

When the Lincoln Center Library was discarding materials, Bowser was there to scoop up stills and lobby cards. A lot of her collection also came from other companies dumping their pasts. Following the death of its founder, Astor Pictures employees tossed out boxes of stills and glass slides from early films, including images from their early race holdings, but Bowser was there to save them.

Bowser's research was only able to be completed with the aid of archives. She was "at the librarian's elbow every week" at the Library of Congress's reading room. She would request to see two films, and the librarian would bring out another five for her to watch. Bowser was watching films—mostly silents—including those by Orson Welles as well as Oscar Micheaux. As she says, "No question about it, I lived at the Library of Congress."

While she researched, her private collection grew. She collected titles in all formats—35 mm, 16 mm, Super8, and video. Then Bowser started to acquire projectors and other equipment to show the films in programs. Her collection of more than two hundred motion pictures included titles such as *Ten Minutes to Live* (1932), *Spying the Spy* (1918), *St. Louis Blues* (1929), *Broken Strings* (1941), *Go Down Death* (1941), and prints from filmmakers Julie Dash, Bill Gunn, and St. Claire Bourne, among a few of her contemporaries. All of her collecting and research led to scholarship; she taught courses, wrote journal articles, spoke on film panels, and served as curator for many festivals, including the landmark series, A Retrospective of Independent Black American Cinema, 1920–1980, at the Forum Les Halles in Paris. Her publications include *Writing Himself into History: Oscar Micheaux, His Silent Films and His Audience* (with Louise Spence) and *Oscar Micheaux and His Circle* (with Jane Gaines and Charles Musser). And in 1994 she directed the documentary film *Midnight Ramble: Oscar Micheaux and the Story of Race Movies.*

DR. MAYME A. CLAYTON: COLLECTING FILMS FOR THE FUTURE

As related by her son, Lloyd Clayton, Dr. Mayme Agnew Clayton recalled being very excited when she went to the cinema as a young girl and first saw black cowboys. At that time she considered it to be the greatest thing that had ever happened to her. Lloyd, Clayton's middle child, recalls that his grandparents wanted their daughters, Mayme and Sara Agnew, to be exposed to the world of culture. So the family traveled from their small town of Van Buren, Arkansas, to events miles away. In this way, the young woman was exposed to a concert by Marian Anderson and a talk by Mary McCloud Bethune, who became an early inspiration. Mayme told her son of her goal that "one of these days I hope that I'll grow up and make a contribution to my race."

Clayton thrived in academia. She attended Lincoln University of Missouri, transferred to the University of California, Berkeley, where she received a BA; worked at the University of Southern California in 1952; became a law librarian in 1957 for UCLA, where in 1969 she helped establish the African-American Studies Center Library, collecting hard-to-find, out-of-print works by authors of the Harlem Renaissance; and earned an MLS from Goddard College, in Vermont, and a PhD in Humanities from La Sierra University, in Riverside, California, in 1985. She felt education should be available to all youth. And she championed education based on filling the holes in history with the missing accomplishments of African Americans.

Already a book collector, Clayton often said she was sad to think of all of the wonderful films that we could never see because they were lost, destroyed, or misplaced. To remedy this loss, she collected any films by and about African Americans that she was able to locate. Living in Los Angeles undoubtedly aided in her access to movie ephemera. Her collecting started with movie posters she acquired as co-owner of the Universal Book Store in Hollywood. She picked up the gem of an original *Stormy Weather* (1943) poster featuring Lena Horne. When the store closed in 1974, Clayton was well on her way to collecting posters, photographs, lobby cards, scripts, and the odd movie reel.

As the black film collecting world was small, other film buffs would seek out Clayton to trade, barter, and sell movie ephemera featuring black-produced and white-produced all-black cast films. Lloyd mentioned that his mother used the now defunct *The Big Reel*, a bimonthly periodical (1974–2006), and would sit for hours scouring the ads to determine which film titles she would acquire next. She knew these films needed to be saved, and she began to stack the 16 mm reels in a cool closet in her garage, where the entire collection lived. Over forty years, her collection grew, and was noted by other institutions. At one point Lloyd recalls that representatives from the Schomburg Center for Research in Black Culture told Clayton that the number of titles in her film collection surpassed theirs. He also remembers an archive in Berlin offered $1 million for the Clayton film collection.

To continue with her educational mission, Clayton opened access to her collection under the banner of the Western States Black Research and Education Center (WSBREC). She encouraged students to come by for help to research and write their papers, and scholars and researchers to examine her primary source documents for their projects. One of the scholars who came in quite often turned out to be author Alex Haley, who was conducting research on Africa for his 1976 book *Roots: The Saga of an American Family*.

For a period, she operated the Third World Ethnic Bookstore from her garage, selling duplicates and books she felt the collection would survive without. Ultimately, as Lloyd relates, the Clayton family decided the collection was too valuable to be owned privately by one person. Instead, they arrived at the idea of the library and museum to hold the garage's contents. The collection was held under a 501(c)(3), relocated, and renamed the Mayme A. Clayton Library & Museum (MCLM).

FESTIVALS: BOWSER AND CLAYTON PRESENT AFRICAN AMERICAN LIFE AS RELATED BY AFRICAN AMERICANS

Once a few researchers excitedly wrote about the content and existence of early black films, it was time to take them on the road. That is exactly what Bowser did in New York in 1969 by organizing the First Black Independent Film Festival and, later, by programming films at the Museum of Modern Art. Bowser was determined to take her films on tour to any university or public meeting hall to spread knowledge of early black achievements as captured in film, much in the same way that the films had been seen in the past. As Bowser notes, race films were not just shown in movie palaces but in barns, tents, and churches across the country. Wherever people could gather and a projector and screen could be set up, that became a motion picture "theater." Bowser also collected posters and movie stills that she used for advertising and rented for publications. This grew into her company, African Diaspora Images.

On her film tours such as the Harlem Cultural Council, Third World Newsreel, and the Celebration of Black Cinema, Bowser's mission was to "wake up the public" about this very realistic film history that was fading away right under their noses. To provide context to the programming, Bowser included current works with the early black films, thereby highlighting the continuing traditions and the contrasts in historical outlook in both filmmaking and views of real life.

In 1976, on the West Coast, Dr. Mayme A. Clayton created the Black American Cinema Society (BACS), which served as the Film Archives of WSBREC. Black Talkies on Parade (BTOP) began as BACS's annual week-long film festival and celebration of past and present contributions by African Americans to the motion picture industry. To encourage future black filmmakers, the Claytons held a competition of independent and student films where the award-winning entries were screened at the festival. Sponsors including the Miller Brewing company, Kodak, and Roscoe's Chicken and Waffles funded the African American independent filmmakers' competition allowing scholarships ranging from one hundred to three thousand dollars for first, second, and third-place winners as well as three honorable mentions of the Black Filmmaker Foundation's Jury Prizes. As further encouragement to young filmmakers, they were also given Kodak film stock.

Showing the films during a festival once a year was Clayton's answer to providing the public an opportunity to see, discuss and discover early black films. The festival generally had morning cartoons for children—where kids flowed out of roughly a dozen buses—then afternoon and evening screenings, often at the Four Star Theater. Around the release of *Lady Sings the Blues* (1972), one student thanked Dr. Clayton for a screening of *The Emperor Jones* (1933). He was "blown away" to learn there was a real Billie Holiday.

As they had with Pearl Bowser, entertainers associated with early black film sought out Clayton wanting to share their experiences and to entertain once again. The Nicholas Brothers' daughters danced between screenings. Actor, composer, and singer Emmett "Babe" Wallace (who was left out of the credits for *Stormy Weather*) wrote and—for about five years—annually sang the "Ode to the Black American Cinema Society." In 1998, at the twenty-first-annual BTOP, the festival featured a Robeson "Sing-and-Look-Alike" contest.

Festival venues around Los Angeles included the Autry National Center of the American West, Director's Guild of America, the Cary Grant Theater on the Sony/Columbia lot, the Pacific Design Center, and the historic Ambassador Hotel. An auditorium at the Los Angeles Trade–Technical College could seat a thousand, but as Lloyd recalls, they still had people standing in aisles and sitting on the floor.

An impressive list of who's who of African American actors was recognized, and given either an Oscar Micheaux Award, Phoenix Award for Lifetime Achievement, or Paul Robeson Pioneer Award to recipients who made notable contributions to the film and entertainment industry. A few awardees were Julie Dash, Danny Glover, Beah Richards, Louis Gossett Jr., Virginia Capers, William Marshall, Pam Grier, Ivan Dixon, Brock Peters, Jada Pinkett, Bill Duke, Laurence Fishburne, Ester Rolle, Yaphet Kotto, and Cicely Tyson. As an added attraction, the Claytons displayed their vintage movie posters, lobby cards, and other related items from the collection. Avery Clayton (March 17, 1947–November 26,

2009), sold posters of his original renditions of Lena Horne and Dorothy Dandridge. It was a complete family operation, where Mayme Clayton did most of the planning for the annual events, and as Lloyd recalls, it was the "most exciting times of their lives." Although the galas and week-long festival have ended, the Black Talkies on Parade screenings continue at MCLM as a monthly event, allowing Mayme's collection to continue to introduce new audiences to the creativity and self-reflection of African Americans during the period 1909–47.

DR. HENRY T. SAMPSON JR.: RESEARCHING LEADS TO COLLECTING

There are differences between the goals of Pearl Bowser and Mayme Clayton's designs on saving early films, and Dr. Henry T. Sampson Jr.'s goal of researching them. However, the outcome is the same. Following years of research, teaching, screenings, and writing, Sampson has also created a large and important film collection. And this comes from a man who claims he was researching for himself, feeding his own curiosity, and "just collecting." Sampson's drive and curiosity fueled him throughout his career as an inventor and in his passion as a film historian. He was born in Jackson, Mississippi, in 1934, and attended Morehouse College before transferring to Purdue University and receiving his BS in 1956. Sampson then graduated with an MS degree in engineering from the University of California in 1961; continuing his education, he earned his MS in nuclear engineering from the University of Illinois Urbana–Champaign in 1965 and his PhD from the same university in 1967, making him the first African American to earn a PhD in nuclear engineering in the United States. Sampson's drive for education was set by the example of his father's accomplishments. Henry T. Sampson Sr. was a professor of mathematics at the historically black Jackson College, in Jackson, Mississippi, and later dean of the college.

As if his career in nuclear engineering was not time consuming enough, Sampson started researching black film while in graduate school at University of Illinois. His initial study was sparked by two things: his interest in how motion pictures were made and his early love of films with all-black casts. Dr. Sampson's research led to the publication of several books on early black filmmaking, including *Blacks in Black and White: A Source Book on Black Films* (1977), which examines often overlooked African American filmmakers and entertainers from the first half of the twentieth century; *The Ghost Walks: A Chronological History of Blacks in Show Business, 1865–1910* (1988); and *That's Enough Folks: Black Images in Animated Cartoons, 1900–1960* (1998). He also produced documentary films on African American filmmakers. His focus in collecting was on pre1950s films produced by black filmmakers. Sampson says he wanted to focus on performing arts, including minstrelsy; African Americans in radio and television; and black motion pictures.

The first film to enter Sampson's collection was a 16 mm compilation of spliced-together scenes from 1940s and 1950s films. Because he could not safely store nitrate films, Sampson only had one 35 mm film, which he later had transferred to 16 mm, the easiest format for a collector during the 1970s and 1980s. Like Dr. Clayton, Dr. Sampson also read *The Big Reel* for advertising sales and weekly collectors shows. At that time, the number of early black film collectors was small, so Bowser, Clayton, and Sampson all knew each other and were probably in competition for the same films, as they were significantly limited commodities. Many of the titles came from television stations and had been poorly stored and handled, often containing many extra splices cut in for commercial space. Sampson says he was also able to add to his collection by becoming an early eBay buyer. He did not have a vault for his film, but Sampson safely stored the reels in the cool recesses of his garage.

Sampson collected the films to show with lectures and seminars he gave at UCLA. He credits a black instructor in the UCLA film school who "paved the way" for him to begin lectures and seminars at the school. Later Sampson also showed his films and lectured at the University of Southern California. He also knew the Nicholas brothers and invited them to one of his lectures. Through his collecting, he was introduced to George P. Johnson, the founder of Lincoln Pictures in Los Angeles. Johnson was in a nursing home and was becoming senile, but at

106 years old he was able to relate stories to Sampson about starting the company, and knowing Oscar Micheaux. When he finished his draft of *Blacks in Black and White: A Source Book on Black Films* (1977), Sampson took it to Johnson to make sure he got the Lincoln Pictures portion correct.

He recently donated the collection to Jackson State University, to the library that bears his father's name. The Henry T. Sampson Sr. Library began processing the collection in 2008, with a grant to digitize much of it. Because of his curiosity, and desire to research, Sampson was able to donate 16 mm prints of Micheaux's *Homesteader* (1918); *Within Our Gates* (1920), *The Crimson Skull* (1921), starring Bill Pickett; black cast films *Hallelujah!* (1929), and *Hearts in Dixie* (1929); and later films such as Spike Lee's *Malcolm X* (1992). His donation also includes posters, lobby cards, still photographs, and videotapes to add to future scholarship.

ARCHIVES WITHOUT COLLECTORS

Imagine art magazines with no illustrations, history books with no primary documents, or reflections of culture without moving images. This is exactly the fate of an archive without the donation of a collector. Even if the term is broadened to include studios, or libraries, or vaults, someone must decide to hold on to reels of film rather than letting the deterioration of time take them away. Thanks to a small community of forward-thinking hunters and gatherers—including those profiled here among others such as New York's Edward C. Mapp and Detroit's James E. Wheeler—we can see early images of regular people doing regular things, actors portraying regular people, or even actors being regular people in their own home movies.

Surely, in early films such as *The Birth of a Nation*, we are given a distorted view of African Americans through the eyes of D. W. Griffith, but this is the vision he wanted to present. Just as Oscar Micheaux's stories would examine and reexamine the ideas of miscegenation, he too was communicating directly with the audience his concerns and projections of middle-class African Americans. Thankfully collectors have functioned as a concrete bridge between the artists of the past, and the scholars, historians, and film fans of the present, and even far future.

NOTE

1   Telephone conversations with Lloyd Clayton, April 25, 2013; Pearl Bowser, April 23, 2013; and Dr. Henry T. Sampson Jr., April 19, 2013.

11

ORIGINAL COPIES

How Film and Video Became Art Objects

Erika Balsom

IN THE EARLY 1930S, GALLERIST Julien Levy had a brilliant idea: to sell film prints as art objects. Levy is primarily known as the New York dealer who represented the surrealists; like them, he had a passion for cinema and for challenging what counted as an artistic medium. He was a powerful advocate for the filmic experiments of artists, hosting the first American screening of *Un chien andalou* (Luis Buñuel, 1929) on November 17, 1932. He exhibited works such as *Rose Hobart* (Joseph Cornell, 1936) and *Anemic Cinema* (Marcel Duchamp, 1926). In 1932 and 1933, he served as the president of the Film Society of New York, a not-for-profit organization that aimed to show films that might be too unconventional to attract a broad public. Taken by this enthusiasm for cinema, Levy wrote in his memoirs, "As part of my program to promote camera work as an art I hoped to be able to sell short films in limited editions to collectors."[1] He saw this model of sale as essential to the valorization of cinema as an

---

This chapter originally published as "Original Copies: How Film and Video Became Art Objects" by Erika Balsom in *Cinema Journal* 53, no. 1 (2013): 97–118. Copyright © 2013 by the University of Texas Press. All rights reserved.

artistic medium: "I had formed a collection of films reprinted on 16 mm stock, with two purposes in mind: films conceived by such important painters as Duchamp, Leger, or Dali should command much the same value as a canvas from their hand, and if a collector's market could be organized, I thought to persuade other painters to experiment in this medium."[2] Levy tried to promote the venture, but there is no record that he ever succeeded in selling a single print.[3]

Levy's initiative may be understood as participating in two seemingly contradictory impulses that marked the era: first, the desire to claim for cinema the status of art, something associated with French impressionist film theorists and filmmakers, as well as burgeoning film society movements in France and the United States; second, the desire to use cinema, with its basis in mechanical reproducibility and mass culture, to challenge the institution of art, something one might align with the filmmaking activities of the historical avant-garde. Steven Watson describes Levy as a "Harvard modernist," an individual who, like Alfred Barr Jr., "saw the traditional art hierarchy—which granted museum status only to painting and sculpture—as insufficient and inaccurate."[4] Although Levy's interest in cinema perhaps best embodies his desire to confound high and low and to rethink the status of the art object, his questioning of the hegemony of painting and sculpture extended beyond his involvement in avant-garde film. He sold books and periodicals, as well as found tchotchkes he called "kinack kinacks."[5] Levy was keenly interested in the sale of photographic prints, but it never generated enough income to keep his gallery afloat—this duty fell to the tried-and-true medium of painting.[6] Given the lukewarm reception collectors gave Levy's photographic offerings, the notion that there might be a market for limited-edition film prints seems unthinkable. After all, like a photograph, film problematizes the notion that the work of art is founded in uniqueness, but unlike a photograph, a film print cannot simply be hung on a wall.

How different the situation appears today. Over the past two decades, as the popularity of film and video in contemporary art has soared, the limited edition has finally proved itself as not only a viable model of distribution but also as perhaps *the* model of distribution for moving-image art. Today, films and videos are regularly sold as art objects, most often in an edition of three or four plus artist's proofs.[7] Though still nowhere near the salability of more traditional art objects, film and video are attaining a new market viability that has drastically changed the ways in which moving-image art is bought, sold, valued, and seen. Though most editions are sold to institutions, a growing private collectors' market for moving-image art nevertheless exists. In 2005, the *New York Times* profiled San Francisco video-art collectors Pam and Dick Kramlich, who have numerous works of video art installed in their home: "As eccentric as the Kramlichs' domestic situation may seem today, 10 years ago it would have been a downright oddity. . . . But now, video art is widely bought and exhibited by collectors and museums alike, and there are those who say flat screens may soon be as common on household walls as picture frames."[8] Film and video art is now collected like painting, and central to this enterprise is the artificial imposition of scarcity effected by editioning.[9] The widespread espousal of the limited-edition model represents a reining in of the inherent reproducibility of moving-image media and its wholesale recuperation into the symbolic economy it once compromised, that of the unique work of art. Authenticity—a concept that had never mattered much to film and video—becomes paramount. For some, this represents a betrayal of the specific qualities of film and video and the utopian hopes invested in them; for others, it represents the only way that film and video will be taken seriously as artistic media, and the most viable economic model to support the livelihood of moving-image artists.

When purchasing a video edition, the collector usually receives an archival master (often Digital Beta); exhibition copies in a current format; digital files; a signed and numbered certificate of authenticity; and a contract specifying the rights to exhibition, duplication, and format shifting. In the case of film, the collector usually acquires a master in the form of an internegative; a number of prints; a digital preview copy of the work; a signed and numbered certificate of authenticity; and a contract specifying the rights to exhibition, duplication, and format shifting. In some cases, the technological support required to display the work might be included as a part of the edition, though such a practice is relatively rare. Editions sometimes also include ancillary materials such as still photographs or sculptural packaging, included so as to endow the work with objecthood, but more commonly such objects (when they do exist) are sold separately from the edition. When one buys an edition, one purchases a rather curious combination of rights, content, and technical support—the specifics of which are all closely regulated by the contracts accompanying the acquisition. This makes the accession of film or video into a museum collection distinctly more complicated than would be the case with most traditional artworks. Though moving-image media do possess a kind of objecthood, it is crucial to recognize that what is for sale is less this object per se than a set of permissions, privileges, and responsibilities concerning the exhibition and guardianship of a given work over time.

Between Levy's inaugural attempt to sell film prints and the recent embrace of the limited edition, there have been a host of efforts to sell film and video as art objects. This article examines the roots of the limited edition in late-nineteenth-century printmaking and bronze sculpture before tracing its persistent rearticulation in relation to film and video throughout the twentieth century, by Bruce Conner in California, Gerry Schum in Düsseldorf, Castelli-Sonnabend Tapes and Films Inc. in New York, and others. Although these attempts to edition film and video differ in their geographical and historical locations, they share something in common: they were failures. The limited-edition model fails and fails again until the 1990s, when it finally begins to meet with success. How can one explain this particular trajectory? Concentrating primarily on the American context but offering a broader international perspective when possible, the following pages advance several hypotheses in an effort to account for this important shift in the distribution and valorization of the moving image in art. To conclude, the article examines both the benefits of this model and the criticisms it has provoked.

Questions concerning the sale and pricing of art are frequently left out of scholarly discourse; they are presumably thought to be vulgar and tasteless, a disavowed part of a business that never wants to recognize itself as such. However, as the following will show, such practices in fact have an intimate relationship to the symbolic value attached to a given art object, as well as a direct impact on how that object may be collected and archived. As Isabelle Graw has noted, the notion that there is a strict separation between the lofty ideals of art and the more earthly concerns of the market is patently false, though often assumed.[10] Although not isomorphic, the financial valorization of art and the cultural and symbolic valorization of art are inextricably tied together. The discipline of cinema studies, whether dealing with experimental film or a blockbuster megaproduction, has consistently embraced questions concerning the economics of circulation in a manner that has largely eluded contemporary art history.[11] When dealing with an interdisciplinary object like artists' film and video, it is imperative that one follow the enthusiasm of the former rather than the reticence of the latter. Understanding editioning is key to making sense of the past, present, and future of moving-image art and to parsing the distinctions between the two strands of artistic practice that are encompassed by that heading, experimental cinema and artists' cinema. It sheds light on art's ongoing fetishization of the unique object and on how conceptions of the authenticity, reproducibility, and value of film and video have changed over time and continue to change in our present moment.

ORIGINS

The practice of escalating the price of the art object and inciting consumer desire through the artificial cultivation of rarity existed before the moving image was used in an art context, but it is curiously contemporaneous with the invention of cinema. The turn of the century saw the development of this model in the arena of bronze sculpture and prints. These first instantiations of the limited edition display several key characteristics that would reappear as film and video artists adopted that model of sale in the late twentieth century. Throughout the nineteenth century, reproducible artworks were largely issued in unlimited editions. As Élisabeth Lebon notes in her study of French bronze foundries, at that time "the impulse was not to limit production—on the contrary. Fairly early in the century, some founders simply tried to number their casts without limiting how many could be made, something that can only be understood as an attempt to better manage production."[12] When clients became reluctant to purchase a bronze with a high number stamped on it, the initial move was not to restrict the size of the edition but to eliminate numeration altogether.[13] Artistic production at this time inhabited what Rosalind Krauss has termed an "ethos of reproduction."[14] At the beginning of the twentieth century, however, this was to change. As images attained a new reproducibility, the attributes of scarcity, authenticity, and originality began to be prized as never before.

According to Walter Benjamin, the advent of mechanical reproducibility threatened an economy of art founded in aura and uniqueness.[15] With the invention of photography and cinema, cult value gave way to exhibition value, and the work of art was made possessable through the proxy of its reproduction. The history of bronze editions and fine-art prints suggests a different narrative: a shift from an unrestricted number of castings to a largely artificial imposition of scarcity, precisely as the reproduction of images and goods attained a new facility. Rather than a preexisting value that was compromised by reproducibility, originality emerges as something *produced* by reproducibility. It was amid the new threat of the copy, of endlessly reproducible images, that originality took on the status that it retains today, even after decades of vanguardist assaults on its hegemony. In a world of surfeit, rarity triumphs. Or in Krauss's words, the copy is nothing other than "the *underlying condition of the original*."[16]

The limited edition was, then, a turn-of-the-century invention that rescued compound arts such as bronze sculpture from succumbing to the degraded status of mere copies in a new economy of desire. Henceforth, the number of objects produced would be restricted so as to generate an aura of quasi uniqueness. In the case of the compound arts, value was ensured by what Jean Chatelain has called "systematic rarefaction";[17] though artificial, this rarity possesses a true market agency, particularly as it becomes convention through consensus of the actors involved. The practice of numbering editions as, for example, "1/3" dates only from the first decade of the twentieth century, at which time Ambroise Vollard began to sell limited-edition bronzes. In a striking prefiguration of later attempts to sell film and video as art objects by drawing on the artist's established reputation in more traditional artistic media, Vollard also began to sell limited-edition engravings made by painters such as Cézanne and Munch. These prints participated in the new culture of reproducibility by extending high art into the domain of bourgeois accessibility. But they did so while reconfirming the values of rarity and artistic originality produced as a reaction to this culture of consumption, by insisting on the limited availability of prints. In a second parallel between Vollard's moment and our own, just as the tectonic realignment of image circulation proper to the late nineteenth century spawned rearguard efforts to reconstruct uniqueness, so the new mobility of images following the digitization of media in the 1990s would result in the countermovement of restricting the circulation of moving-image artworks by instituting the limited edition as market standard.

In the early twentieth century, however, the limited edition was not simply a question of rarity for rarity's sake. Until the passage of a French law in 1968 that would restrict bronze casting to an edition of eight plus four artist's proofs, the most frequent edition size was six, something that Lebon speculates is in all likelihood linked to the life span of the gelatin mold.[18] In the case of lithographs, limiting the edition size could also be justified as guarding against the possibility of degraded prints. In its initial employment, then, the "systematic rarefaction" of the limited edition was both a question of fabricating the status of a quasi original and of ensuring quality control—which, in something of a catch-22, would have been increasingly important when dealing with the augmented prices that resulted from limiting the size of the edition. Here one encounters a crucial difference from moving-image media, which can produce many more copies before image degradation becomes a concern. In the case of bronze sculpture and certain printing processes, editioning finds partial motivation in the material limitations of the media involved; in the case of film and video, it goes against what is the most potentially revolutionary attribute of their material base. Nevertheless, in another echo from the turn of one century to another, the rhetoric of ensuring the quality of the work will quite interestingly reappear, mutatis mutandis, in the 1990s as a justification for the necessity of restricting moving-image art to a limited-edition model of sale: major galleries will insist that editioning is necessary to ensure that a given work will not be viewed in unfavorable circumstances, such as on a laptop screen or in a highly compressed digital file format. In a span of roughly one hundred years, the very media that exemplified the supreme threat and radical promise of the copy would be, through a series of expectations and agreements, transformed into de facto originals.

AN ECONOMY OF THE MULTIPLE

In 1957, a year before making his first film, *A Movie* (1958), Bruce Conner wrote a letter to his gallerist, Charles Alan:

> New horizons, Unexplored territory. There is a potential patron of The Experimental Film. He hasn't been touched. I don't mean [a] patron who finances a film. Someone who buys a "print" of a film. People can be found who will purchase experimental films as they would a print or a painting. They have to know that these films can be considered as valid works of art as well as paintings and sculptures and musics [*sic*] and dances etc. This means apart from the mass public phenomena called movies.[19]

Resurrecting Levy's dream of a model of film distribution that would be more aligned with the realm of fine art than "the movies," Conner put into writing his plans for the sale of such films before even having one ready to offer to collectors. Kevin Hatch notes that the Alan Gallery "stopped short of investing money in selling artist-made release prints. In short, it is fair to say that Conner's letter did not prompt the sea change he had envisioned."[20] Once more, a proposition to sell prints as art objects—though not specifically as limited editions—remained unrealized. While this failure might be in part because of the lack of an established market for the sale of prints, it is also linked to the absence of a provision to limit the number of prints that would be available, as well as to the proposition that the collector would purchase a single print for exhibition rather than a master format (such as an internegative or interpositive) from which prints could be made. Celluloid film is an eminently fragile material, inescapably subject to wear and the possibility of damage at each projection. What motivation would a collector have to purchase an artwork that would degrade each time it was exhibited, particularly one that countless others might own? The model of the film limited edition that emerged in the 1990s would provide solutions to both of these problems by limiting the number of certified copies and providing collectors with a master from which to strike exhibition prints.

Nonetheless, the notion that a viable distribution model for experimental film could be found in selling prints to private collectors was not something that Conner immediately abandoned. In his 1963 application for a Ford Foundation grant, Conner reiterated his conviction: "I do not rent my films. I sell prints. I conceive of them as an engraver might conceive of an etching and then sell copies of it in a gallery. . . . I consider film distribution, as it is now, to be antagonistic to artistic process."[21] Conner believed that his films were best suited to repeat viewings in a domestic setting, so that the viewer might discover something new each time. There is, however, an element of disingenuousness in the statement that Conner did not rent but rather sell prints. Rather than a private collectors' market, rentals from distributors such as Cinema 16, the Museum of Modern Art, the Film-Makers' Cooperative, and later Canyon Cinema constituted the primary method of circulation for Conner's films from the time they were produced until close to his death. His statements on the possibility of selling prints as art objects nevertheless serve as a reminder of an untaken path of experimental film history; for one of the primary characteristics that distinguishes experimental film from artists' cinema is the former's commitment to a rental model of distribution rather than a limited-edition model of sale.[22]

The origins of experimental film's rental model of distribution are found in the late 1940s. As an increasing number of individuals began to make what would come to be known as avant-garde or experimental films, it became necessary to build distribution networks to support this fledgling field of practice. Amos Vogel's Cinema 16—which took on *A Movie* immediately after its release—was founded in 1947 and became the first major distributor for contemporary experimental films in the United States. At a time when film was by no means an accepted medium of institutionalized artistic practice, the channels of distribution and exhibition developed to nurture the emerging art were by necessity outside of the gallery context. Rather than imitating the art world and selling prints as collectible objects, Cinema 16's adoption of a rental model based on a per-screening fee mimicked an organization with which it had much more in common: the circulating film library established at the Museum of Modern Art in 1935.

Cinema 16 served as a crucial precursor for the establishment of artist-run organizations such as the New York Film-Makers' Cooperative (1962), the London Film-Makers' Co-op (1966), and Canyon Cinema (1967, of which Conner was a cofounder), which would support experimental film as a distinct mode of production that continues to this day. Such organizations charge a per-screening rental fee, determined largely by the format and length of the work. That fee is split according to a preexisting agreement between the distributing organization and the filmmaker.[23] Institutional sales sometimes occur, but they constitute a small fraction of overall income.[24] Central to the founding ethos of the cooperative model was an emphasis on access and the conviction that film possessed a democratizing potential. Rather than being sequestered away as the private property of a wealthy collector, a film could be shown to the public for a modest admission fee. However, the result of this belief in the democratizing status of the film medium was severe financial difficulty. Experimental cinema has historically been marked by financial hardship, with most filmmakers turning to other forms of employment, such as teaching, to supplement the meager income gleaned from rental receipts.

Though many experimental filmmakers defined their practice in opposition to feature-length narrative filmmaking, they also staked out an often-antagonistic position with regard to the established art world— a sphere in which film was beginning to make significant inroads. The entry of film into fine-art practice occurred under the sign of democratization and a leveling of hierarchies. The Fluxus artists, for example, turned to film precisely for its capacity for circulation and reproduction: issuing unlimited film editions as a part of the Fluxboxes was a way of intervening in the symbolic economy of the work of art, of refusing the notion of the original in favor of the industrially produced multiple. Fluxfilms were available for sale both on their own and as a part of the Fluxboxes; in 1965, for example, *Zen for Film* (Nam June Paik, 1964–66) was sold on its own as a loop in a small plastic box for $3 (roughly $20 in 2010) or as part of a Fluxkit for $100 ($683 in 2010).[25] In addition to these initiatives, the films were shown at festivals and deposited with the Film-Makers' Cooperative in New York City for rental distribution. At this time, the moving image provided a way of pursuing the same dematerialization of the art object that was occurring in performance, happenings, and conceptual practice alike. Even Warhol's prolific film production remained outside of any real sales initiative: despite the mention of plans to sell 8 mm loops of selected screen tests as "living portrait boxes," no such thing took place.[26] However, despite this emphasis on accessibility and the desire to reconsider what counted as "art," the Fluxus artists nevertheless prefigured later efforts to edition moving-image art by conceiving of film as an object that could be sold and possessed rather than simply experienced. With their 8 mm loops and handheld viewers, the Fluxfilms suggested that, despite conventional thinking on the matter, film was something that could be owned. Within a decade, the unlimited, quasi-industrial mode of production the Fluxus artists had embraced would begin to be rejected in favor of the limited-edition model of sale that dominates today.

PIONEERS: SCHUM AND CASTELLI

The advent of video drew an increasing number of artists to the moving image. Though the new medium was by no means wholly accepted by the artistic establishment at the time, it did enjoy a closer relationship to the gallery world than did experimental film, largely because many of its practitioners simultaneously produced work in other, more salable media. Like experimental film, early video did not derive funding from the sale of individual works. But whereas experimental filmmakers often held teaching positions to secure an income, video art was largely funded by grants, residencies, and the sale of the artist's nonvideo works. Despite these differences, video shared with experimental film the sense that it was a noncommodifiable, reproducible medium invested with a democratizing potential that would revolutionize artistic production. Both these utopian hopes and the medium's subsequent recuperation by the regime it sought to challenge are clearly visible in Gerry Schum's twin ventures in Düsseldorf, the Fernsehgalerie (1968–70) and the videogalerie schum (1970–73). With the Fernsehgalerie, Schum escaped the objecthood of the work of art and the elitism of the gallery; rather than a physical location, the Fernsehgalerie consisted of films and videos broadcast on television. Schum's first commission, *Land Art*, was broadcast on the West Berlin television station SFB on April 15, 1969, and included artists such as Walter de Maria and Robert Smithson. To introduce the program, Schum explained, "The Fernsehgalerie was born of a wish to directly confront the broadest possible audience with the current trends of international art production."[27] Some one hundred thousand viewers watched the broadcast.[28] After a second commission, *Identifications*, in 1970, Schum was unable to secure the necessary continued support of broadcasting agencies and reconceived his enterprise with a striking about-face. The videogalerie turned away from dematerialized mass dissemination and issued videotapes in both limited and unlimited editions, complete with signed and numbered certificates of authenticity, as well as a precisely formulated pricing model. Schum believed that the relative simplicity of video technology made moving-image art into a saleable object in a manner that was impossible with film: "Crucially, one doesn't have the same problem with video that one has with 16 mm film. . . . The problem with films is that one has to have a darkroom and someone who knows how to project the film. Television is, by contrast, a part of our everyday milieu: there are no difficulties with its presentation since one is familiar with the medium."[29] A 1971 price list for the videogalerie schum shows unlimited editions priced between DM500 and DM800, while an edition of six of *Filz-TV* (Joseph Beuys, *Felt TV*, 1970, shown in *Identifications*) is listed at DM9,800 and an edition of four of *The Nature of Our Looking* (Gilbert and George, 1970) is priced at DM4,800 and declared sold out.[30]

Ian White has proposed that Schum's videogalerie embraced "an effectively untested financial model" in its foray into the video limited edition.[31] It is a model, however, that would have to undergo its true test not in Düsseldorf with Schum but in New York with Leo Castelli: Schum decided to close the gallery as a result of financial difficulties in late 1972, and he committed suicide in March 1973. Castelli, meanwhile, had begun to deal in film and video in 1968 for the simple fact that several of the most prominent artists he represented—such as Bruce Nauman and Robert Morris—had begun to produce work in those media. In 1974, a joint venture with Ileana Sonnabend would legitimate the sale of videotapes as art objects while still keeping a foot in the rental model of distribution. Run by Nina Sundell and Joyce Nereaux and initially based in a loft on Greene Street, Castelli-Sonnabend Tapes and Films Inc. became the first organization devoted to selling moving-image art in the United States, offering both film and video for sale to private collectors and institutions. *Art-Rite* magazine publicized its inauguration:

> Most of their tapes sell according to length and whether they are b & w or color (rather than by the status of the artist). Prices tend to be under $250. A distribution system is just beginning to be set up. Castelli-Sonnabend will control the showing and rental of the tapes (and film) while other galleries will be able to buy for resale at a gallery discount. The market at this time is almost exclusively universities and museums, but the number of collectors who are interested is slowly growing.[32]

Like many bronze editions in the late nineteenth century, prints and tapes were numbered solely for administrative purposes and produced as the demand presented itself. If a purchase became damaged or worn, the collecting institution could have it replaced for the cost of copying and shipping. In most cases, only a handful of copies were produced, and even the most popular offerings—such as *Vertical Roll* (Joan Jonas,

1972) and *Television Delivers People* (Richard Serra, 1973)—made it to just over fifty.[33] The organization also issued a very small number of videotapes (but no films) as limited editions of twenty, priced at $1,000.[34] Interestingly, although these are marked as such in volume one, number one, of the Castelli-Sonnabend catalog, by 1982 none of the works marked as editions of twenty retains that designation—though all retain their elevated price. The financial records of the organization show that rentals far outweighed sales and that the artificial scarcity imposed by limiting the number of tapes available did not incite increased demand; on the contrary, the editioned tapes did not sell as well as many of the uneditioned tapes, presumably because of their inflated prices. As early as 1977, the venture was experiencing serious financial difficulty. A memo dated September 30, 1977, states that the organization had $14,415.23 in outstanding bills and owed $29,539.33 to artists. By February 1979, there was serious discussion about alternative ways of running Castelli-Sonnabend, which consistently posted an annual deficit of some $10,000. The ideas floated included obtaining not-for-profit status or reabsorbing the organization back into the Leo Castelli Gallery. Despite these ongoing difficulties, Castelli-Sonnabend continued its activities until ceasing operation on July 1, 1985.

After the shuttering of Castelli-Sonnabend, video found continued support in public and private granting agencies and in not-for-profit distributors. Uneditioned works could be rented through organizations such as Electronic Arts Intermix (EAI), founded in 1971 by Howard Wise after the closure of his eponymous gallery, and Video Data Bank (VDB), founded in 1976. In fact, after the dissolution of Castelli-Sonnabend, many of the tapes distributed by that organization found their way to EAI and VDB, where they were made available for rent.[35] In the British context, video also stayed outside the commercial gallery circuit. David Curtis notes that although galleries such as Lisson Gallery, Nigel Greenwood, Jack Wendler, Robert Self, Angela Flowers, and others began to dabble in video in the early 1970s, they soon became aware that no market for it existed.[36] Furthermore, Curtis writes that the arrival of selections from Castelli-Sonnabend at the Video Show: First Festival of Independent Video in 1975—evidence that a commercial gallery might stand behind video—was at odds with the UK experience: "Interest by British galleries had been limited; many British artists disapproved of limited-edition works in principle; certainly any hope that a market might develop in Britain proved premature."[37]

In experimental film, though the rental model stayed strong, some individuals began to display frustration about the limited possibilities for remuneration stemming from that form of distribution. Seeing the increased acceptance of film and video in the art world, certain experimental filmmakers began to look to that realm for financial support. In the late 1970s, Kenneth Anger made a series of limited-edition films for private collectors that were never publicly exhibited.[38] After a visit to Amsterdam, where he had come into contact with successful efforts to sell film prints, Larry Jordan published a polemic titled "Survival in the Independent—Non-Commercial—Avant-Garde—Experimental—Personal—Expressionistic Film Market of 1979." Jordan advocated not joining the art world per se but adopting some of its practices, such as the sale of films to private collectors. "Film artists," he wrote, "have been too long intimidated by their own countercultural identifications on the one hand and fear of the art 'establishment' on the other."[39] Jordan ruefully acknowledged that the elevation of a work's monetary value can lead to an augmented respect and to increased possibilities of archival preservation, as well as the fact that the sale of films as art objects was perhaps the only way that filmmakers would be able to secure a livelihood from their practice without resorting to other forms of employment, such as teaching.

Unlike Conner before him, he recognized that the sale of a film for the life of that print only would not succeed: "Purchase of film *prints* has never greatly interested art collectors for the very real reason that a *print* is of no real value as an investment. Only one-of-a-kind originals (from which the collector can make prints or not) have saleable value—saleable, that is, at prices which will be of any sort of real help to the film artist. Progressive collectors *will* collect films (as they do Video) under the right conditions."[40] Jordan recognized that collectors wanted to be able to display their acquisitions while also maintaining the work in pristine condition—something that would be impossible through the sale of prints alone. He also acknowledged the pull of the unique object. Though Jordan does not elaborate on what would count as a "one-of-a-kind original"—the negative, perhaps?—he identifies solutions to two key problems that had obstructed the sale of films as art objects in the past. If film were to become collectible, it would have to bend to the demand for scarcity proper to a collector's market, much as video had done before it. Jordan's proposal received no substantial attention within the experimental film community. And yet he looked forward to the day when the "first sale of a five minute film original for $10,000 or more" would change "the face of the art world. . . . Film would be a valuable commodity, which at present it is not. And no one could ever shrug it off again."[41]

TOWARD MARKET VIABILITY

The 1990s witnessed a tremendous explosion of moving-image art. With improvements in projection technology, video was no longer restricted to the small image of the television monitor. The digitization of media spurred a new mobility of images and offered artists a new ease with production and postproduction techniques. Analog film found itself under threat of obsolescence and reappeared as a major component of artistic practice for the first time since its displacement by video. Moving-image art had finally accumulated an aesthetic history, with pioneers such as Bruce Nauman, Richard Serra, and Andy Warhol firmly canonized. Many of the decade's most prominent emerging artists, such as Matthew Barney and Douglas Gordon, worked extensively in video, and major museums endorsed the moving image as never before.

Amid this flurry of activity, the old idea of the limited edition, which had never entirely disappeared, gained new life—and this time, both private and institutional collectors were ready to invest. Major New York galleries such as Barbara Gladstone, Marian Goodman, and David Zwirner began to represent an increasing number of film and video artists and to edition their work. As moving-image art began to increasingly mimic the structures of independent film and production costs soared, this investment was more necessary than ever.[42] After roughly sixty years of existence at the margins of the art market, what accounts for the ascendance of the film and video limited edition in the 1990s? Three factors of varying importance worked together to create market viability.

The first factor is economic. Noah Horowitz emphasizes the crash of 1990 as instrumental in the creation a new market for video. He writes, "Galleries increasingly began exhibiting video largely because, according to Barbara London, associate director in MoMA's Department of Film and Video, 'they had nothing to lose'; sales had dried up and the opportunity cost of showing video and other alternative practices diminished."[43] While the new viability of cheaper, less object-oriented work may be ascribed in part to the severe price deflation at this time, other key factors were at play. These factors demonstrate the extent to which market valorization is never a matter of economics alone but rather is deeply shaped by elements of the art world—elements which, at first glance, operate far from the transactions taking place at auction houses and commercial galleries.

The second factor is linked to technological innovation and changes in the speed and facility of image reproduction and circulation. While the mainstream adoption of the Internet in the early to mid-1990s spurred a significant artistic trend of remaking and recycling existing cultural forms, it also resulted in a qualitative leap in the transportability of images and sounds that induced a crisis of authenticity comparable to that of the late nineteenth century. Just as was the case for printmaking and bronze sculpture in the late nineteenth century, the film and video limited editions that emerged at the turn of the millennium were attempts to reconstruct authenticity and (near) uniqueness amidst a new proliferation of copies. During this period, edition sizes shrink dramatically: while Castelli-Sonnabend Tapes and Films offered editions of twenty, by the 1990s this number had dropped to fewer than ten and often as few as three. At a time when images were more mobile than ever before, the limited edition provided a way of guaranteeing that the work would circulate only within authorized channels and would be seen only in the proper setting. While it was, of course, always possible to duplicate videocassettes, the 1990s and 2000s heralded a qualitative shift in the ease of moving-image reproduction. Jack Valenti of the Motion Picture Association of America had cause to assert that his organization was fighting its "own terrorist war" against copyright infringement—a war it continues to lose.[44] Unlike the film industry, the art world had access to radical measures that would successfully ensure the integrity of its product. Rose Lord, director of Marian Goodman Gallery, has stated, "All our artists want their works to be shown under very specific circumstances, where every aspect is carefully calibrated. That's why we have collectors sign purchase agreements that insure that the works will be shown as per the artist's wishes."[45] The open circulation of a Steve McQueen work on DVD would result in a flood of copies of varying quality that could be consumed on laptops or as ambient background at a loft party. It is in this manner that quality control is asserted as a motivating factor behind the limited edition, albeit in an entirely different way from the bronze sculpture or lithograph before it: the rarity of the work is constructed not simply to entice collectors but also to guard against the possibility of a degraded image.

The third and perhaps most important factor in the rise of the limited edition is again a matter of technological change, but also one of institutional politics: it concerns the advent of high-quality, low-cost video projection and its tremendous institutional endorsement from the early 1990s onward. The moving image might have once challenged the traditional museum, but in the 1990s, endowed with a new, large-scale mode of display, it was recruited by museums to secure relevance in an increasingly competitive marketplace demanding breathtaking, immersive experiences. And where institutions go, the market follows. Institutional endorsement can have a profound effect on the price of an art object, a fact clearly demonstrated by the controversy surrounding the New Museum for Contemporary Art's *Skin Fruit* exhibition of trustee Dakis Joannou's private collection in 2009.[46] In the case of photography, the J. Paul Getty Museum's June 8, 1984, purchase of five major private collections of vintage prints for a reported twenty million dollars forever changed the market possibilities of the medium.[47] While no single event comparable to the Getty purchase may be cited in the case of moving-image art, the 1990s and 2000s saw an institutional investment in film and video without parallel in the history of art. The cavernous spaces of newly opened or newly renovated museums, many of which are devoted exclusively to contemporary art, called for colossal installations and big box-office receipts.[48] The turn away from monitor-based presentation and toward projection resulted in a greater sense of monumentality and an increased assertion of presence in the space of the gallery. It pulled video art away from associations with television and its domestic banality, and instead aligned it with a medium by then possessing increasing cultural cachet, the cinema.[49]

While projection had been possible since even before the invention of video recording technology, it was seldom used in art practice until cheap, bright, crisp projectors came to market in the late 1980s and early 1990s. In 1992, video installation featured heavily at Documenta IX, the biggest, costliest, and best-attended Documenta since 1959.[50] As a major international exhibition occurring once every five years and tasked with taking stock of contemporary artistic practice, Documenta provides a useful barometer for evaluating the changing status of the moving image. Responding to Documenta IX, one critic wrote that the curator Jan de Hoet "knows that there is an almost desperate need now to bridge the worlds of high art and popular culture in a new way, and that using massive exhibitions like this one to attract hundreds of thousands of people is certainly a part of that process."[51] In 1996, both *Hall of Mirrors: Art and Film since 1945* (Museum of Contemporary Art, Los Angeles) and *Spellbound: Art and Film* (Hayward Gallery, London) were huge shows bringing together contemporary video artists with Hollywood directors in a drive for accessibility. Museums such as the Museum of Modern Art, the Tate Modern, and the Whitney Museum of American Art greatly expanded their moving-image holdings during this time, purchasing historical and contemporary work and also commissioning temporary projects from moving-image artists.[52] Christopher Eamon, former curator of the Kramlich collection, has stressed the extent to which the institutional endorsement of the installation format—rather than the 1990 market crash—is key to understanding the ascendance of video art within the 1990s and 2000s art market.[53] An installation, after all, cannot be easily rented, and it more clearly asserts its difference from mass circulating films and tapes through its claiming of gallery space. It was a reciprocally beneficial situation: major museums looked to the moving image for scalar intensity and relevance and began making commissions and purchases, and in turn, this institutional legitimation accorded the moving image a new status on the primary market.

OPPOSITION AND ADVOCACY

The increased visibility of the limited-edition model has brought with it increased criticism. For some artists, such as Martha Rosler, the solution is to opt out, to continue to issue unlimited editions that will be distributed through organizations such as EAI and VDB.[54] For others, the popularity of the limited edition is something to be attacked outright. Produced anonymously and distributed online by the activist and artist collective ®™ark (pronounced "art mark"), *Untitled #29.95: A Video about Video* (1999) is a fifteen-minute work that constructs a schematic history of video art based on the changing relationship between the medium and the market. It embraces a low-tech collage aesthetic that appropriates various clips of the video art of the past forty-five years and rephotographs them from television monitors. On the soundtrack, a computerized female voice-over offers a narrative of the medium as subject to a tragic fall into market exploitation. As *Untitled #29.95* would have it, upon its introduction to artistic production, video was used to "challenge the authority of the mass medium and the materialism of the art world." The narrator continues, "Video was born under radicalism and from the beginning it was used as an instrument of resistance." A brief interval of black gives way to Martha Rosler stabbing a fork into the air, with her *Semiotics of the Kitchen* (1975) playing on a television screen. Castelli is singled out as the great villain who tried to commodify video by making it into a limited edition, but the narrator tells us, "It didn't work. Thank God. Perhaps they thought video was too much like TV, the ultimate in low-brow culture."

Untitled #29.95 follows the development of video through the late 1970s and 1980s, asserting it as a rich, and decidedly anticommercial, field of practice closely linked to activism. The video posits the decimation of National Endowment for the Arts funding for media art as the event that put an end to politicized video practices circulating outside of the institutional art world. In its place, a gallery-bankrolled video art emerged that eschewed political commitment in favor of productions deemed decadent (Matthew Barney) or trivial (Lucy Gunning).[55] The video cites a 1998 *New York Times* article by Roberta Smith, "Art of the Moment, Here to Stay," as signaling the new acceptance of this brand of video in the gallery establishment. Smith proclaims the importance of 1990s video art by comparing it to pioneers like William Wegman and Bruce Nauman. The narrator intones, "She does not even mention the eighties, as if an entire decade of incredible video production around race, class, gender, sexuality, media, politics and power relations never even existed. Now videos are being sold in limited editions in New York galleries and not for $29.95." White text scrolls on black screens, listing works that have been editioned and their prices: "Stan Douglas, *Overture*, $150,000, limited edition of 2. Diana Thater's *China* $60,000. *Cremaster* by Matthew Barney, limited edition of 2, $25,000. Gillian Wearing's *10–16* I heard went for $60,000. It's just a videotape, for God's sake."

Untitled #29.95 is not alone in arguing that the existence of the limited edition fundamentally contradicts the medium-specific qualities of video. Pierre Huyghe has said, "For videos, editions are fake. . . . When Rodin could only cast three sculptures of a nude before the mold lost its sharpness, it made sense. But all my works are on my hard drive, in ones and zeros."[56] And yet Huyghe issues his films and videos in limited editions through Marian Goodman Gallery, which suggests that despite being "fake," editioning is still worthwhile. In a similar vein, Dieter Daniels has remarked that "the principle of the signed, limited-edition video cassette or DVD is absurd. A signature does not impart an image carrier with the character of an original, but only stands for a commercial agreement to limit the edition to a certain number of copies, whose extent depends not on the reproducibility of the medium as for woodcuts or etchings, but merely on market-strategy factors."[57] Certainly, the aura of rarity that surrounds the limited-edition film or video is an artificial construction—but it is one with real effects, both positive and negative. Editioning is no more "fake" than the convention of delaying the DVD release of a film until after its theatrical run has been completed; it is, like the delayed DVD release, a mechanism to generate value. These are conventions that are agreed on by market actors, conventions that possess a certain truth despite their status as historical constructs.

The critique of editioning advanced in *Untitled #29.95* greatly oversimplifies the relationship between moving-image art and the market that exists today. Nowhere does the video confront the difficult question of how artists might make a living from their art if not by editioning. The recent movement of many individuals associated with the experimental film tradition into the gallery context testifies to the possibility of the financial support that private and institutional collectors can provide. Isaac Julien, Jonas Mekas, Ben Rivers, Leslie Thornton, and Emily Wardill are but a few examples of individual artists who have decided to edition their work. Matthias Müller, another such filmmaker, has stated that, because of financial realities, "there is no alternative *but* a gallery, which demands that works be sold as limited editions."[58] Similarly, although Anthony McCall has expressed that he has "some problems with the idea of editioning" because "[t]he scarcity value is created quite artificially since there is no technical limit to the number of copies that could be made," he simultaneously recognizes it as a sustainable model that allows the sale of one work to finance the next.[59] It resolves the problem that had perennially faced avant-garde film: the lack of a viable economic framework.

At stake in the sale of film and video as limited editions is not only the artist's present but also the artwork's future. When a collector buys a limited edition—sold not as film print or as DVD but as a set of archival materials and rights governing the usage of those materials—he or she also takes on responsibility as to the care and preservation of that work. Many museums, such as the Tate Modern, will collect only editioned artworks—which means that the limited edition is not simply a way of cashing in but also a way of ensuring that the artwork will be amenable to institutional structures that participate in the writing of art's histories and that enable the preservation and exhibition of the work for posterity. It is without question that much work remains to be done to grapple with the particular challenges that film and video pose to the practices of acquisition, collection, and exhibition at major institutions, and there may be cases in which such institutions will have to adjust their policies to cater to the needs of these media. However, the limited edition constitutes a site at which film and video art is meeting art institutions halfway—and vice versa. While certainly some rental-based distribution organizations, such as Electronic Arts Intermix, are engaged in serious preservation activities, the involvement of collecting institutions is necessary to ensure the stewardship of vulnerable media artifacts. Freely circulating VHS tapes, DVDs, or high-compression computer files are unable, for reasons of quality and longevity, to function as archival masters. It is expensive and time consuming to engage in processes of digital migration from format to format. Preservation is a costly business, and an institution is more likely to invest in a given work if it has the secure knowledge that it is one of a limited number of stakeholders in that work. For the films and videos that currently circulate as moving-image art, editioning is perhaps the best way of ensuring long-term safekeeping.

Like any good manifesto, *Untitled #29.95* ends with a call to action. Over rephotographed footage of *Cremaster 5* (Matthew Barney, 1997), the viewer is told that by going to the ®™ark website, he or she can purchase "liberated" copies of limited-edition videos for only $29.95. Viewers are also asked to send whatever "liberated videos" they may have in their own collections to the ®™ark website so that they can be made available for free downloading.[60] The Robin Hood(s) of Chelsea, the maker(s) of *Untitled #29.95* plan to "steal video art from the rich and give it away for free, or at least for the reasonable cost of $29.95." The viewer is advised, "Remember: video was meant to be a democratic medium." Since the release of *Untitled #29.95* in 1999, many works of moving-image art have indeed been "liberated," though not precisely as urged in the video's closing call to action. Alternative economies of circulation have emerged precisely as the limited-edition model has gained in popularity. Though *Untitled #29.95* proposes its initiative as an intervention that would contest the way that videos are "held captive" by editioning, these unauthorized channels of circulation exist parallel to the sale of official editions rather than in any antagonistic relationship with it. The circulation of editioned artworks on the Internet is exceedingly common, whether through illegal YouTube postings, DVD trading networks, or members-only BitTorrent sites. Artists frequently supply screeners of editioned works—neither a part of the edition nor a designated artist's proof—to curators and scholars. Through these unofficial channels, interested individuals can access the works for their personal and/or professional use—with no harm done to the official editions in the possession of galleries and museums. Without the signature or certificate—inscriptions imparting authenticity and uniqueness—a DVD copy is simply a DVD copy.

Rather than an overturning of the limited-edition model, Sven Lütticken has advocated for the growth of this parallel economy of distribution grounded in the notion of "viewing copies" that would be distinct from collectible, certified copies.[61] Lütticken notes that the viewing copy tends to circulate "confidentially and in semi-secrecy" rather than through official channels of distribution. And yet these unsanctioned copies tend to be more common than official DVD releases. *Zidane: A 21st Century Portrait* (Douglas Gordon and Philippe Parreno, *Zidane: Un portrait du 21e siècle*, 2006) was issued as a mass-market DVD and as a limited edition of seventeen that paired a DVD of the film with rush footage from one of the seventeen cameras trained on Zidane throughout the football match, but this case is something of an exception. In an effort to come to terms with why this may be the case, Lütticken has speculated, "The emergence of over-the-counter viewing copy editions was halted not so much by fears that the 'real' work would be tainted artistically and/or financially, but by the fact that there was big money to be made from exclusive limited editions. Even if unlimited viewing copy editions do not threaten the aura of such gallery pieces, why bother with them when the returns are bound to be marginal at best, or, more likely, non-existent?"[62] Indeed, while in 1997 the David Zwirner Gallery had a waiting list for Stan Douglas editions costing up to $150,000, a group show of uneditioned videotapes priced between

$20 and $100 sold only five copies.[63] These uneditioned tapes do not promise the same return on investment as a Douglas edition might; issuing mass-market DVDs promises no lucrative financial returns, simply the exposure of moving-image art to potentially less-than-favorable viewing conditions. However, in the case of artworks that do not rely on substantial installation components, such viewing copies can serve as important resources for scholars and educators. At present, it remains difficult to teach contemporary moving-image art given the very limited availability of many of the most significant works produced during the period. If prominent commercial galleries wish to truly support artists' film and video, ensuring that such works are available to students and scholars is of utmost importance.

In the meantime, LUX, the London-based not-for-profit distributor of artists' film and video, has proposed another way of mediating between the exclusivity of the limited edition and the conviction that film and video are democratic media. LUX was founded in 2002 as an amalgamation of three predecessor organizations: the London Filmmakers' Co-operative, London Video Arts, and the LUX Centre. As such, it has a strong historical connection to the rental model of distribution and its focus on access, often taken to be antithetical to the practice of editioning. And yet LUX has not eschewed editioned works altogether. Director Benjamin Cook has said, "We realized a few years ago that [the cooperative] model was becoming increasingly anachronistic in terms of the market and the institutional art world, which is informed by the market. We really felt like we needed to rethink our position in relation to those things."[64] The result involved devising a novel compromise that acknowledges the financial and archival benefits of editioning while also insisting on the need to ensure availability and circulation. Though LUX does not sell editioned works, it partners with artists and galleries to serve as a renter of such works, thereby forging a hybrid space between two otherwise-separate modes of distribution. If, for example, a work is issued in an edition of three plus artist's proofs, one of those artist's proofs will be deposited with LUX and be available for rent. While this model is suited only to single-channel works, it represents a true step forward in the attempt to find innovative solutions in the collection and display of moving-image art. It preserves the cooperative spirit while making use of the benefits of the limited-edition model, without succumbing fully to its fetishization of rarity. As Cook puts it, "We really believe that one thing about film and video, in its very nature, is that it needs to circulate and be seen. What we are trying to do here is to create a system that equally values the need for works to be sold in limited editions—in a way so that the institutional art world can understand the value of those works—and that has built in a respect for the fact that these are theatrical works that need to continue to circulate in the world."[65]

The example of LUX and its hybrid model is instructive: it speaks to the need to move beyond existing models to develop better and more sophisticated ways of collecting, preserving, and exhibiting moving-image art. Commenting in 2010 on his 1979 proposal to sell experimental films as originals, Larry Jordan remarked, "I never thought that the exact idea I proposed in that article would be *the* idea, but I wrote the article to provoke those ideas. The mechanics were up for grabs."[66] Without a doubt, the mechanics remain up for grabs today. Though initiatives such as Matters in Media Art have done crucial work in setting out guidelines for the acquisition and loans of media art, a clearer set of best practices is necessary.[67] There is still a considerable amount of trepidation and uncertainty concerning the sale and acquisition of media artworks, particularly to private collectors. The narrative of the ascendance of the limited edition presented here is not one of unqualified triumph; when compared to painting, sculpture, and photography, film and video remain relatively unsaleable. Ensuring the market viability of film and video as artistic media among others involves building a knowledge base and advocating for greater transparency at all stages in the process. Writing the history of attempts to edition film and video is a first step in this direction.

Since its invention, the moving image has espoused a plurality of modes of distribution and exhibition that variously operate parallel to, in tandem with, and in opposition to one another. This remains the case today more than ever, when the most unregulated forms of circulation, such as BitTorrent, coexist with the most restricted, such as the limited edition. As new technologies revolutionize the dissemination of the moving image, understanding the institutional, economic, and medium-specific dynamics of distribution networks is more necessary than ever before. Cinema studies scholars have done well to chronicle and investigate numerous forms of moving-image circulation, whether they are traditional or untraditional, legal or illegal, mainstream or underground. The brief history of editioning presented here is intended as an addition to this rich body of work and a contribution to ongoing efforts to understand the historical and contemporary relationships between artists' cinema and the sphere of practice known as avant-garde or experimental film and video. It is, however, only a beginning. Substantial research remains to be done concerning the history of the limited-edition model in other geographic contexts beyond those considered here. Theoretical questions of value, authenticity, reproducibility, and medium specificity should be explored at length. Continued attention must be paid to the ongoing adoption and evolution of this model and whether it will meet with success on the secondary auction market, where it, as of yet, has no substantial presence. Specific case studies deserve close scrutiny: the Barbara Gladstone Gallery's 2008 acquisition of the Jack Smith estate and its 2010 offering of a set of eleven of Smith's films in a retroactive edition of ten to institutional collectors is an ideal starting point. In short, the end of the narrative of failed attempts to sell film and video as art objects is merely the beginning of new set of questions and research problems confronting scholars in both film studies and art history.

NOTES

Special thanks to Erica Levin, Federico Windhausen, and the anonymous reviewers at *Cinema Journal*.

1   Julien Levy, *Memoir of an Art Gallery* (Boston: MFA, 2003), 68.
2   Levy, 168.
3   A letter from Joella Levy, Julien's wife, to Paul Vanderbilt dated April 18, 1932, reads, "We do give performances of short Avant-garde and Amateur movies in the Gallery, they are all on 16 mm film, and we do rent them and sell copies." Joella Levy lists *Ballet mécanique* (Fernand Léger, 1924),

L'étoile de mer (1928), *Le Château d'If* by Man Ray (1929; which one presumes is *Les mystères du Château de Dé*), *Spirale* by Marcel Duchamp (presumably *Anemic Cinema*, 1926), and *Sportfilm* by V. Albrecht Blum (presumably *Quer durch den Sport*, 1929). She quotes a rental fee of $10 for *Ballet mécanique* but writes that "for the others we have to arrange a price as we've never rented before." According to Marie Difilippantonio of the Jean and Julien Levy Foundation, this is the sole extant reference to the sale of films as art objects. Joella Levy to Paul Vanderbilt, April 18, 1932, letter, Levy Gallery Archives, courtesy of Marie Difilippantonio.

4   Steven Watson, "Julien Levy: Exhibitionist and Harvard Modernist," in *Julien Levy: Portrait of an Art Gallery*, ed. Ingrid Schaffner and Lisa Jacobs (Cambridge, MA: MIT Press, 1998), 86.

5   See Ingrid Schaffner, "Alchemy of the Gallery," in *Julien Levy: Portrait of an Art Gallery*, ed. Ingrid Schaffner and Lisa Jacobs (Cambridge, MA: MIT Press, 1998), 22–23.

6   On Levy's difficulties in selling photographs, see Levy, *Memoir*, 59, 68–69.

7   The artist's proof—often abbreviated as "AP"—is a term that comes from printmaking. It originally designated a print made to test quality but has since come to refer to copies retained by the artist that exist outside of the numbered edition and are generally not for sale. They do, however, sometimes appear on the secondary market, where they can attract higher prices than the numbered edition.

8   Edward Lewine, "Art That Has to Sleep in the Garage," *New York Times*, June 26, 2005, www.nytimes.com/2005/06/26/arts/design/26lewi.html.

9   It is worth noting that true, rather than artificial, rarity also exists in moving-image art, whether because of the financial cost of striking prints, the availability of film stock, or aesthetic choices (such as the decision to work in performance or with camera originals). I plan to explore such rarity in my future research.

10   Isabelle Graw, *High Price: Art between the Market and Celebrity Culture*, trans. Nicholas Grindell (Berlin: Sternberg Press, 2009), 9.

11   Exceptions include Graw's *High Price* and Noah Horowitz's *The Art of the Deal: Contemporary Art in a Global Financial Market* (Princeton, NJ: Princeton University Press, 2011). In the domain of cinema studies, the body of scholarship that would fall under such a heading is far too large and diverse to cite here. However, of particular relevance are Lucas Hilderbrand's *Inherent Vice: Bootleg Histories of Videotape and Copyright* (Durham, NC: Duke University Press, 2009), and Haidee Wasson's *Museum Movies: The Museum of Modern Art and the Birth of Art Cinema*

(Berkeley: University of California Press, 2005). Many discussions of the economics of circulation in experimental film take place in informal channels—such as the Frameworks e-mail Listserv, which has been the site of lively debate on the issue of the limited edition in recent years—but even here, the issue remains underexplored.

12   Élisabeth Lebon, *Dictionnaire des fondeurs de bronze d'art: France, 1890–1950* (Perth, Western Australia: Marjon Editions, 2003), 56 (translation mine).

13   Lebon, 57.

14   Rosalind Krauss, "The Originality of the Avant-Garde," in *The Originality of the Avant-Garde and Other Modernist Myths* (Cambridge, MA: MIT Press, 1985), 153.

15   Walter Benjamin, "The Work of Art in the Age of Its Technological Reproducibility: Second Version," trans. Edmund Jephcott and Harry Zohn, in *Selected Writings, Volume 3: 1935–1938*, ed. Howard Eiland and Michael W. Jennings (Cambridge, MA: Belknap Press of Harvard University Press, 2002), 101–33.

16   Krauss, "Originality," 162 (italics in original).

17   Jean Chatelain, "An Original in Sculpture," in *Rodin Rediscovered*, ed. Albert E. Elsen (Washington, DC: National Gallery of Art, 1981), 278.

18   Lebon, *Dictionnaire*, 67.

19   Bruce Conner, letter to Charles Alan, April 1957, in Alan Gallery Records at the Archives of American Art, reprinted in Kevin Hatch, "Looking for Bruce Conner, 1957–1967" (PhD diss., Princeton University, 2008), 115.

20   Conner, 155–27.

21   Bruce Conner, application for a Ford Foundation Grant in Film Making, 1963, BANC MSS 2000/50 c, Bruce Conner Papers, Bancroft Library, University of California, Berkeley, 2.

22   My distinction between artists' cinema and experimental film follows Jonathan Walley's in "Modes of Film Practice in the Avant-Garde." The term *artists' cinema* by no means suggests that experimental filmmakers are not artists; rather, it designates a mode of production tied to the economic structures of the art world that makes use of the museum and gallery as primary sites of exhibition. For a further elaboration of this distinction, see Jonathan Walley, "Modes of Film Practice in the Avant-Garde," in *Art and the Moving Image: A Critical Reader*, ed. Tanya Leighton (London: Tate Publishing & Afterall Books, 2008), 182–99.

23   Currently, the New York Film-Makers' Cooperative returns 60 percent of rental income to the artist; Canyon Cinema returns 50 percent.

24 In 2006–7, the last year for which data are available in Scott MacDonald's *Canyon Cinema: The Life and Times of an Independent Film Distributor*, Canyon made $11,225 from film sales, $6,860 from video sales, and $112,395 from rentals. See Scott MacDonald, "Appendix 2: Canyon Cinema's Gross Rentals and Sales, from 1966 until 2006–2007," in *Canyon Cinema: The Life and Times of an Independent Film Distributor*, ed. Scott MacDonald (Berkeley: University of California Press, 2008), 433.

25 Jon Hendricks, *Fluxus Codex* (New York: Harry N. Abrams, 1998), 72–73.

26 In 1965, a reporter for the *Nation* wrote that John Palmer and Gerard Malanga informed him (while Warhol was on the telephone) of some films in progress, including 8 mm loops of *Living Portrait Boxes* (i.e., the screen tests), "which might sell for $1,000 or $1,500 each." See Howard Junker, "Andy Warhol, Movie Maker," *Nation*, February 22, 1965, 206–7.

27 Gerry Schum, "Einführung in die Sendung," in *Ready to Shoot: Fernsehgalerie Gerry Schum, videogalerie Schum*, ed. Ulrike Groos, Barbara Hess, and Ursula Wevers (Düsseldorf: Kunsthalle Düsseldorf and Snoeck, 2003), 69 (translation mine).

28 Ursula Weavers, "Leibe Arbeit Fernsehgalerie," in *Ready to Shoot: Fernsehgalerie Gerry Schum, videogalerie Schum*, ed. Ulrike Groos, Barbara Hess, and Ursula Wevers (Düsseldorf: Kunsthalle Düsseldorf & Snoeck, 2003), 31.

29 "Video Tappa Gerry Schum: Interview mit Gerry Schum in der Zeitschrift *Data* (Mailand), Marz 1972," in *Ready to Shoot: Fernsehgalerie Gerry Schum, videogalerie Schum*, ed. Ulrike Groos, Barbara Hess, and Ursula Wevers (Düsseldorf: Kunsthalle Düsseldorf & Snoeck, 2003), 313 (translation mine).

30 Converted to 1971 US dollars, the unlimited editions would be priced between $144 and $230.40, the Beuys at $2,822.40, and the Gilbert and George at $1,382.40. Conversion calculated at a rate of DM0.288 to the dollar, per the 1971 average interbank exchange rate given at www.oanda.com/currency/historical-rates. This price list is reprinted in Groos, Hess, and Wevers, *Ready to Shoot*, 300.

31 Ian White, "Who Is Not the Author? Gerry Schum and the Established Order," in *Afterthought: New Writing on Conceptual Art*, ed. Mike Sperlinger (London: Rachmaninoff's, 2005), 69.

32 "Castelli-Sonnabend Tapes and Films, Inc.," *Art-Rite*, no. 7 (Autumn 1974): 21.

33 Castelli-Sonnabend numbered its copies by assigning each a letter of the alphabet. While most tapes didn't make it past D, Serra's *Television Delivers People* goes up to copy UU, his *Hand Catching Lead* (1968) to EE,

Robert Smithson's *Spiral Jetty* (1970) to FF, Jonas's *Vertical Roll* to AAA, and William Wegman's *Selected Works: Reel #4* (1972–73) to PP. These listings include all copies sold, available for rental, lost, or destroyed from wear. All information on Castelli-Sonnabend is courtesy of Leo Castelli Gallery Records, Archives of American Art, Washington, DC.

34 Vol. 1, no. 1, of the Castelli-Sonnabend catalog shows nine videos offered as limited editions of twenty: Vito Acconci's *Full Circle* (1973), *Stages* (1973), *Theme Song* (1973), and *Walk-Over* (1973); Christian Boltanski's *Life Is Gay, Life Is Sad* (1974) and *(Some) Memories of Youth* (1974); Joan Jonas's *Merlo* (1974); Richard Landry's *Terri Split* (1974); and Charlemagne Palestine's *Body Music* (1973–1974). Simone Forti's *Untitled* (1973) was offered as an edition of 100, priced at $470. *Castelli-Sonnabend Videotapes and Films* vol. 1, no. 1 (1974).

35 Some film prints went to Anthology Film Archives and the Film-Makers Cooperative, some films and videos were returned to the artists, and works by artists represented by the Leo Castelli Gallery continued to be available for sale and rental from Castelli.

36 David Curtis, *A History of Artists' Film and Video in Britain* (London: BFI, 2007), 20.

37 Curtis, 20.

38 These include *Senators in Bondage* (edition of thirteen, 1976) and *Matelots et menottes* (edition of twelve, 1977).

39 Larry Jordan, "Survival in the Independent—Non-Commercial—Avant-Garde—Experimental—Personal—Expressionistic Film Market of 1979," originally published in *Cinemanews* 79, nos. 2–4 (1979), reprinted in *Canyon Cinema: The Life and Times of an Independent Film Distributor*, ed. Scott MacDonald (Berkeley: University of California Press, 2008), 337.

40 Jordan, 334.

41 Jordan, 338.

42 Walley has noted that rather than the artisanal mode of production that characterizes experimental film, "a more proximate point of reference for artists' films might be independent art cinema, as it is there that the division of labour in production is subsumed under the rubric of the *auteur*." See Walley, "Modes of Film Practice," 186.

43 Horowitz, *Art of the Deal*, 44.

44 Jack Valenti, quoted in Amy Harmon, "Black Hawk Download: Moving beyond Music, Pirates Use New Tools to Turn the Net into an Illicit Video Club," *New York Times*, January 17, 2002, www.nytimes.com/2002/01/17/technology/black-hawk-download-moving-beyond-music-pirates-use-new-tools-turn-net-into.html.

45 Rose Lord, quoted in Paul Young, "Black Box White Cube," *Art+Auction*, February 2008, www.artinfo.com/news/story/26655/black-box-white-cube.

46 See Deborah Sontag and Robin Pogrebin, "Some Object as Museum Shows Its Trustee's Art," *New York Times*, November 10, 2009, www.nytimes.com/2009/11/11/arts/design/11museum.html.

47 See Peter C. Jones, "High Times and Misdemeanors," *Aperture*, no. 124 (Summer 1991): 68–70.

48 The *Treasures of Tutankhamun* exhibition organized by the Metropolitan Museum of Art in 1976 is frequently cited as the beginning of a trend in museum exhibition to favor the guaranteed box-office revenues provided by accessible material and a well-stocked gift shop.

49 Dominique Païni has selected 1990 as the year that signals a change in the conception of cinema from one tied to mass culture to something that possesses a patrimonial value. The transformation is, he writes, "one from industry to art." It is also a time that sees a generalized waning of direct political investment on the part of many video artists. See Dominique Païni, *Le temps exposé: Le cinéma de la salle au musée* (Paris: Cahiers du cinéma, 2002), 26.

50 David Galloway, "Documenta 9: The Bottom Line," *Art in America*, September 1993, 55.

51 Dan Cameron, "The Hassle in Kassel," *Artforum*, September 1992, 86.

52 For a full list of collections of the Tate and the Whitney and the dates of acquisition, see Horowitz, *Art of the Deal*, 218–56.

53 Eamon sees the market-crash account as too New York–centric, especially given that the key figures in early 1990s video are not "New York painters turned video artists" but come from other parts of the world, such as Canada (Stan Douglas), Scotland (Douglas Gordon), and Switzerland (Pipilotti Rist). Interview with the author, March 8, 2011.

54 On Rosler's opposition to the limited edition on the grounds that it reduces access, see Ilana Stangler, "Interviews with Visual Artists: Martha Rosler," New York Foundation for the Arts Business of Art Articles, www.nyfa.org/level4.asp?id=120&fid=1&sid=51&tid=167.

55 As Cynthia Chris has noted, the advancement of this art historical narrative both conflates media art and media activism—overlapping but distinct areas of practice—and neglects to consider the real persistence of activist video into the present. See Cynthia Chris, "Video Art: Stayin' Alive," *Afterimage* 25, no. 7 (2000), www.highbeam.com/doc/1G1-61535391.html.

56 Pierre Huyghe, quoted in Greg Allen, "When Fans of Pricey Video Art Can Get It for Free," *New York Times*, August 17, 2003, www.nytimes.com/

2003/08/17/arts/art-architecture-when-fans-of-pricey-video-art-can-get
-it-free.html.

57 Dieter Daniels, "Video/Art/Market," in *40yearsvideoart.de, Part 1. Digital Heritage: Video Art in Germany from 1963 until the Present*, ed. Rudolf Frieling and Wulf Herzogenrath (Ostfildern, Germany: Hatje Cantz Verlag, 2006), 46.

58 Matthias Müller, quoted in Scott MacDonald and Matthias Müller, "A Conversation," in *The Memo Book: The Films and Videos of Matthias Müller*, ed. Stefanie Schulte Strathaus (Berlin: Verlag Vorwerk 8, 2005), 255.

59 Anthony McCall, "Round Table: The Projected Image in Contemporary Art," *October*, no. 103 (2006): 95.

60 As of May 14, 2012, the ®™ark website had not been updated since 2004. The no-longer accessible site for "liberated videos" states, "This page is continuously updated with new 'liberated' art videos made available for download or streaming," but the only two listed are Barney's *Cremaster 5*, with a price listed of US$25,000, and Lucy Gunning's *Climbing Around in My Room* (1993), with a price listed of US$4,000. The links to the videos are broken.

61 Sven Lütticken, "Viewing Copies: On the Mobility of Moving Images," *e-flux journal*, no. 8 (September 2009), www.e-flux.com/journal/view/75 (URL inactive).

62 Lütticken.

63 Marina Isola, "An Uncertain Market for Video Art," *New York Times*, February 15, 1998, www.nytimes.com/1998/02/15/arts/an-uncertain-market -for-video-art.html.

64 Benjamin Cook, interview with the author, November 29, 2010.

65 Cook.

66 Benjamin Cook, interview with the author, December 10, 2010.

67 This project was initiated in 2003 as a collaboration among the Museum of Modern Art, New York; the San Francisco Museum of Modern Art; the New Art Trust; and the Tate Modern. For more information, see www.tate.org.uk/research/tateresearch/majorprojects/mediamatters/ (URL inactive).

12

THE CLOTHES MAKE THE FAN

Fashion and Online Fandom when *Buffy the Vampire Slayer* Goes to eBay

Josh Stenger

People will pay anything to get into Sarah Michelle
Gellar's jeans!

—Fan post on alt.horror

SYNDICATION SECURES FOR SELECT TV series a media afterlife, as it extends a program well beyond its initial network run. But syndication constitutes only the most longstanding, most official form by which to prolong a series. Today, fan communities accomplish nearly the same task.

As Henry Jenkins has usefully explained, fandom is a "participatory culture," one in which people are bound together by a wide range of desires and expressed through an equally wide range of practices. Thus, even though the official text of a show constitutes an ineluctable

---

precondition of fan devotion, fans nevertheless frequently relate to programs, characters, and actors in ways that expand on and move well beyond official narratives, imagery, and relationships. Borrowing from Michel de Certeau, Jenkins describes such unauthorized acts as forms of "textual poaching." To the extent that they are undertaken by fans outside the space of official consumption, poaching can constitute a somewhat paradoxical subversion, recognition, and legitimization of the commodity status of a show and its stars.[1]

The World Wide Web has multiplied both the commercial and noncommercial forms in which television programs can survive beyond the period of their original broadcast; so too has it exponentially increased opportunities for fans to find one another and to express and cultivate their devotion to a series, character, or actor. That the maturation of internet fan culture has coincided with the increasing popularity and profitability of DVD box sets, online auctions, and entertainment memorabilia has given rise to a highly negotiated détente between corporate media interests that produce, own, and distribute programming content, on the one hand, and fans who frequently engage in unsanctioned appropriations of that content, on the other. Because online fandom and e-commerce alike are rapidly evolving cultural phenomena, their intersections become especially useful in refining our understanding of fans and their relationship to both the internet and consumerism. Such intersections are especially instructive when, for example, a program that at once embraced and satirized conspicuous consumption as well as its own cult fan following auctions off props on a website famous for combining the anything-goes ethos of the wild frontier with the name-your-price spirit of the bazaar and the ersatz optimism of the world's largest mall. Thus, when Twentieth Century Fox auctioned props from *Buffy the Vampire Slayer* on eBay when the series wrapped in 2003, the auction and the concomitant online reception occasioned a unique and enlightening collision of fandom, consumption, and internet culture.

Buffy's long-standing emphasis on style and the program's robust online fan presence had converged in many ways and on many sites, to be sure. But the Fox eBay auction of props served to consolidate this nexus. Far from mere attire, the clothes auctioned on eBay served, alternately, as collectibles, fetish objects, and opportunities for role-playing, dress-up, and fantasy production. The auction's emphasis on wardrobe items, combined with the routine yet diverse forms of overvaluation of these items, provided a key register along which to gain an understanding of television and internet fandom generally, and of online fan practices relating to *Buffy the Vampire Slayer* more specifically. Given the multifaceted reception of the auction among online fans, the *Buffy* auction crystallized tensions that had existed throughout the show's run. In what follows, I address several of these tensions, paying special attention to how each either revolved around or was catalyzed by fan fetishization of wardrobe items cast members wore. Specifically, these tensions include disputed notions of authorship and ownership between fans and producers; the struggle to reconcile a viable feminist politics with the recurring sexualization of the cast and characters, both on the show and in fan discourse; and the conflict between the egalitarian model of community idealized by the Scooby Gang[2] and aspired to in countless online fan spaces versus the explicitly competitive and hierarchical structure of the auction.

ONLINE FANDOM, TV FASHION, AND THE ROAD TO EBAY

To appreciate either the conjunction of fashion and internet culture in the eBay auction or the impact of that conjunction on online *Buffy* fan communities, it is important to consider how the series itself understood the imbrications of these aspects. From the first season forward, *Buffy the Vampire Slayer* positioned style and the internet as constitutive elements of adolescent identity, social belonging, and community.

Early into the series premiere, "Welcome to the Hellmouth," prom-queen-in-waiting Cordelia (Charisma Carpenter) guides the newly arrived Buffy through the school's social landscape; along the way, she derisively greets the nerdy bookworm, Willow (Allyson Hannigan), at a water fountain: "Willow! Nice dress. Good to know you've seen the softer side of Sears."[3] The series' eighth episode, "I Robot, You Jane," spoofs the dangers of internet dating when Willow's new online "boyfriend" turns out to be an appropriately named demon, "Moloch the Corrupter," who corrupts students' hard drives and sex drives alike.

The centrality of these aspects of teen life and lifestyle resonated with audiences and figured prominently in the series' quickly earned reputation as a "cult" phenomenon. Although it averaged only about six million weekly viewers in its five years on the WB (1997–2001) and its last two on the UPN (2001–3), *Buffy's* fiercely loyal and highly participatory fan base endowed the program with a popular cultural significance that far surpassed the size of audience. As Boyd Tonkin noted on the occasion of the series finale, "[*Buffy's*] impact and influence have always outpaced the viewing figures. . . . [A]bout 1,200 dedicated websites testify to the show's hold on near-obsessive fans, who range from the cult-hungry teens of the first target audience to hopelessly ensnared writers and academics. . . . More than any previous TV cult, *Buffy* sparked a state of creative synergy with the internet generation."[4]

As with other shows that developed their own intricate internal mythologies—for example, *Xena: Warrior Princess*, *Twin Peaks*, *The X-Files*, and, of course, *Star Trek*—*Buffy* was able to cultivate its multidimensional fan base in part through the savvy use of ancillary media, conventions, and internet forums. These in turn provided both products and spaces by which to multiply and strengthen fans' consumption of, and engagement with, the show. Tonkin's nod to the "1,200 dedicated websites of near-obsessive fans" is a reminder that even though the number of *Buffy*-related sites may change, the internet has, from the outset, played the most important role in securing and, to a large part, determining the coordinates of the series' cultural purchase. In their essay "www.buffy.com: Cliques, Boundaries and Hierarchies in an Internet Community," Amanda Zweernik and Sarah Gatson maintain that in an important way, the internet actually centralizes fan activity, for it "accelerate[s] a process that took the original highly public fan-based community—the fans of the original *Star Trek*—decades to achieve [because it] made it easier to find like-minded people on at least one issue: *Buffy*."[5] In short, *Buffy the Vampire Slayer*, like its core cast of high school do-gooders, came of age with the internet.

As the laptop-toting Willow reminded viewers in episode after episode, fighting demons was made immeasurably easier by a good web connection—a lesson lost neither on the show's wired teenage audience nor its many academic fans who could easily identify with Willow's penchant for "online research." With over a million threads on Usenet newsgroups and thousands of sites dedicated to star gossip, spoilers, fan fiction and role-playing games, it would be difficult to overstate either the scope or the importance of *Buffy*'s web-based fan activity.

There is more than a little irony that fans of the show are so active in (for fan culture) traditionally noncommercial ways, given that the show repeatedly affirms consumerism, especially in the realm of fashion. To be sure, just as the internet has been a staple component of *Buffy*'s reception, so too have conspicuous consumption and an emphasis on style been recurring elements of the program's narrative and mise-en-scène. As one editorial to the *New York Times* blithely remarked, the upwardly mobile adolescent Scooby Gang "always battled evil wearing great clothes."[6]

Though a self-evident and inconsequential observation, it is important to understand that, initially at least, "battling evil" and "wearing great clothes" denoted two incongruous lives for Buffy (Sarah Michelle Gellar) and friends. For example, early in season two, Angel (David Boreanaz) tells a very stressed-out Buffy he thought they had a date, to which she can only reply in exasperation: "Dates are things normal girls have. Girls who have time to think about nail polish and facials. You know what I think about? Ambush tactics. Beheading. Not exactly the stuff dreams are made of."[7] When Buffy temporarily joins a paramilitary demon-hunting group called The Initiative in season four, the group's leader sends her on a reconnaissance mission with the warning that she "might want to be suited up for this." Now seeming able to juggle more effectively the fashion and make-up rituals of "normal girls" and the "ambush tactics" required of a Slayer, Buffy dismisses the advice: "Oh, you mean the camo and stuff? I thought about it but, I mean, it's gonna look all Private Benjamin. Don't worry, I've patrolled in this halter many times."[8]

By late in the series, the one-time tension has become something the characters themselves not only resolve but begin to satirize. In "Once More with Feeling," the much-touted musical episode in season 6, Buffy offers Giles (Anthony Stewart Head) some perspective on the recent tendency of Sunnydale residents to burst into song and dance: "I'm not exactly quaking in my stylish yet affordable boots, but there's definitely something unnatural going on here, and that doesn't usually lead to hugs and puppies."[9] As the comment suggests, during the course of the series, Buffy and friends not only evolved into formidable fighters who can implement "ambush tactics" while wearing "stylish yet affordable boots," they also became exemplary, often self-consciously ironic catalog models for the teens and young adults who composed the official target audience of WB and UPN prime-time programming. This evolution gave rise to an interesting inversion late in the series. Early on, *Buffy* eschewed typical high school hierarchies, organizing the adolescent landscape not around the cool kids, jocks, and cheerleaders but around the misfits, nerds, and outcasts. By the end of the series, however, the Scooby Gang had become fashionable and cool in their own right, so much so that the villains of season 6 are not blood-thirsty monsters, demons, or hell-gods with visions of world destruction, but a trio of nerdy, maladjusted boys who use their intelligence, penchant for role-playing games, technological savvy, and knowledge of the occult to live out popular fantasies about masculinity, sex, and social and financial power.

The program's investment in fashion was central from the very outset. The series' premiere introduces Buffy as someone who, while hardly obsessed with fashion, trends, and popularity, clearly understands they constitute valuable cultural capital in the American high school. Newly arrived in Sunnydale, Buffy scores an invitation to join Cordelia at the local teen hangout, The Bronze. Preparing for her first extracurricular social experience in Sunnydale, Buffy stands in front of the mirror trying on different outfits. As she holds up several dresses, she provides her own commentary as to how each might define her, struggling to decide whether to go with the "Hi, I'm an enormous slut" allure of a skimpy black dress or the "Would you like a copy of *The*

Watchtower?" librarian look. She settles on a pair of pants and a blouse, arguably a more functional choice for a Slayer.

Though she struggles with her own style and look, Buffy understands the significance of "wearing great clothes"—or failing to—when it comes to identifying evil. At the Bronze, she encounters her Watcher, Giles, who insists that Buffy practice her powers of observation and perception so that she can intuit a vampire's presence. Buffy rejects Giles's call for mental focus and instead spots a vampire using her ability to decode the semiotics of teen fashion:

> **Giles:** You should know. Even through this mass and this . . . din, you should be able to sense them. . . . Well, try! Reach out with your mind. You have to hone your senses, focus until the energy washes over you, until you, you feel every particle of . . .
>
> **Buffy:** There's one.
>
> **Giles:** Where?
>
> **Buffy:** Right there, talking to that girl.
>
> **Giles:** You don't know . . .
>
> **Buffy:** Oh, please! Look at his jacket. He's got the sleeves rolled up, and the shirt! Deal with that outfit for a moment.
>
> **Giles:** It's dated?
>
> **Buffy:** It's carbon dated. Trust me, only someone living underground for ten years would think that was still the look.[10]

Moments such as these inaugurate one of the series' most enduring and least progressive tropes, solidifying a link between style and a specific class position. As Anne Millard Daugherty elaborates in her essay "Just a Girl: Buffy as Icon," "obviously affluent . . . [Buffy] never [wears] the same outfit twice. She dresses in tight, sexy clothes. . . . She rarely wears 'old' clothes. Often dashing home to change before going on patrol, she frequently slips into leather pants . . . which look comfortable and hard-wearing but also convey a message of prosperity."[11] Daugherty's exposition is useful here in that it strikes close to the show's early acknowledgment, then gradual effacement, of any tension between Buffy-the-feminist-monster-destroyer and

Buffy-the-sexy-clothes-horse—a tension the show and its fans actively negotiated in both highly affective and intellectual ways.[12]

The show itself seemed cognizant of the fact that narrative arcs frequently explored the (in)compatibility of an empowering, teen-friendly feminism and an entrenchment in a consumerism that historically has worked to objectify girls and women. Indeed, the series ended by paying homage to both of these totemic concerns. The final episode, "Chosen," sees the Scooby Gang struggling to vanquish the First Evil. Facing insuperable odds, Buffy asks Willow to perform a spell that will transfer her hitherto singular powers to girls and women around the world. As Buffy explains to her small "army" of "potentials": "To every generation a Slayer is born, because a bunch of guys who died thousands of years ago made up that rule. They were powerful men. This woman is more powerful than all of them. So I say we change the rule. I say my power should be our power. From now on, every girl who might be a Slayer will be a Slayer. Every girl who might have the power will have the power." The spell ultimately succeeds and the First Evil is defeated; yet while Buffy waxes grrrl-power communitarian, the series ends not with a feminist bang but with a consumerist whimper. Gathered around the crater where Sunnydale used to be, the group contemplates what to do next:

> Xander: We saved the world.
> Willow: We changed the world. I can feel them, Buffy, Slayers are awakening all over.
> Buffy: We have to find them.
> Willow: We will.
> Giles: Yes, because the mall was actually in Sunnydale, so there's no hope of going there tomorrow.
> Dawn: We destroyed the mall? I fought on the wrong side.
> Xander: All those shops gone. The Gap, Starbucks, Toys "R" Us. Who will remember all those landmarks unless we tell the world about them?[13]

While the rumination on the recently obliterated mall is played for laughs in the show, Twentieth Century Fox, which owns the rights to the program, lit upon a more earnest plan to exploit the long-standing confluence of fans' internet savvy and the program's prêt-à-porter fashion sensibility: BuffyAuction.com—a high-stakes, high-priced "For the Fans" fire eBay auction of *Buffy* props. During the summer of 2003, the auction sold off hundreds of items used over the seven years of production. These ranged from instantly recognizable, narratively significant props—like "Olaf's hammer," which Buffy uses to defeat the fashion-forward hell-god, Glory, in season five[14]—to more obscure fare, such as "assorted candleholders" and a "slightly broken" flower pot.

Of all the props, the cast's wardrobe dominated the list both in terms of sheer number and money spent. These items also regularly ignited the fiercest bidding wars and the most spirited online discussions. As fans' sense of ownership of, and devotion to, the show collided with the cash- and competition-based economy of eBay, it quickly became clear that in the space of BuffyAuction.com at least, the clothes made the fan. Far more than a prescient marketing ploy, Fox's deal with eBay effectively transmuted the finale's universalizing feminist impulse into an occasion for free-market enterprise, fantasy production, role-playing, and (commodity) fetishism. If you couldn't be a Slayer in real life, thanks to the *Buffy* eBay auction, you could at least dress like one.

CONSUMING FAN(DOM)S AND OWNING THE SHOW

Fox aggressively advertised BuffyAuction.com throughout May and June during commercial breaks on multiple networks, including the WB, UPN, and Fox, the three networks on which the show had aired either in original broadcasts or syndication. Ads offered home viewers the *Buffy* auction as a perfect solution for how to shop—and what to shop for—in a land without brick-and-mortar retail and a media landscape without new installments of *Buffy*. The commercial spots framed the auction as being "For the Fans," explicitly addressing the fans *as consumers*. In doing so, the auction at once embraced and elided the many unofficial, often unsanctioned forms of production, revision, and "poaching" in which fans routinely engage. Thus, it worked to bridge a divide that Matt Hills identifies in his book *Fan Cultures* as underpinning fandom generally: the fan's tendency to favor "anti-commercial ideologies," on the one hand, and the expression of fandom through "commodity-completist practices," on the other.[15]

The auction collapsed this opposition in part because fans, not a marketing department, determined the value of each item, giving rise to an anticommercial veneer under which the auction's commodification *of fandom* was effectively, if ironically, cloaked. For Hills, eBay is at once a singular and a representative online space in which fandom can express itself. This owes centrally to the fact that as with so many fan practices, eBay radically destabilizes any facile sense of "value," making muddle of traditional notions of the commodity in the process:

> Many commodities offered for sale on eBay should, according to the conventional logic of use and exchange-value, be almost worthless. However, due to many of them having been intensely subjectively valued by fans, such commodities take on a rede-fined "exchange-value" . . . created through the durability of fans' attachments, and through the fans' desire to own merchandise which is often no longer being industrially produced.[16]

Hills focuses on the phenomenon of fans' overvaluation of "mass produced" items (e.g., action figures, board games) surrounding a show or film. But the *Buffy* auction items were "one-of-a-kind," having been used in the production of the official text. This not only amplified the overdetermined status of the prop, but it also authenticated the object, lending each prop a kind of Benjaminian originality or aura it could not otherwise possess.[17] Consequently, when props are made available for private purchase in a public auction, the items' value becomes at once increasingly unstable and highly expansive. Even a heretofore mass produced "item" becomes an irreproducible "prop" from its birth as a set piece.

The worth of a mass-produced prop-object proved to be an oft-contested issue, however. For instance, when a phone that retails for under $20 appears on the auction and sells for over $1,000, a disagreement about "value" ensues among some fans. One person writes in disbelief, "The phone from the Summers house is going for just over $1,000. Who the hell's going to believe someone that it's the Buffy phone anyway? 'Hey Todd, yeah, do I sound any different? Really. Damn I just bought a thousand-dollar phone.'"[18] Another fan reveals a wholly different relationship to the phone's value: "[The phone is] the one thing I would actually want . . . I'd probably like to own any piece of crap they offer (ok so the phone isn't the only thing I'd want) if I could point to it in an episode and say 'look, this is it!'"[19]

If fans' abilities to set the material worth of each item destabilized the fan-producer binary, this binary broke down further around the issue of ownership. To be sure, a key allure of the props was the promise of "owning a piece of the show," no small thing, for as Henry Jenkins reminds us, ownership over content, characters, and imagery is a hotly contested issue.[20] The status of legal and intellectual ownership of any program's content usually amounts to an intractable division between fan and producer, yet the *Buffy* auction worked in part to bridge this gap. With each sale, the producers transferred legal ownership of a piece of the show to a fan.[21] As fan posts made clear, each prop served as a metonymy for the entire franchise, allowing the buyer to cross the line from viewer to part owner. If, as the feminist film scholar Mary Ann Doane once wrote of product placement in cinema, "metonymy is the trope of the tie-in," in the space of BuffyAuction.com, it was the trope of the *buy-in*, allowing bidders, literally, to invest in the "official" show from which their status as fans had previously served to keep them.[22]

While each prop afforded buyers a sense of ownership of the show, and many sold for considerable sums—the set of three rubber stakes sold for roughly $5,600 and the battle-axe from the series finale garnered over $15,000—it became clear that the most dearly prized and highly valued among fans and buyers alike were wardrobe items worn by cast members.

"B.Y.O. SUBTEXT": (AD)DRESSING DESIRES

The appeal of wardrobe items proved to be sui generis. In part, this owed to the fact that the clothes afforded fans such rich opportunities for fantasy production and role-playing, as well as for the focused fetishization of favorite characters and actors. Closely linked to gender identity and sexual desire, to the authentic and the performative, the body and the gaze, these items promised the chance to close—or at least to clothe—the distance between fan, character and actor. To begin, the relationship of fans to the clothing for auction crossed quickly from the structured distance of voyeurism to the more "polymorphously perverse" proximity of fetishism. No longer a mere spectator, the fan who owns a piece of clothing from the show has few if any restrictions on the types of desire in which she or he can indulge. Props of all sorts entered into the overvaluation of the commodity fetish within the space of the auction, to be sure. However, as Stella Bruzzi maintains in *Undressing Cinema: Clothing and Identity in the Movies*, clothes offer unique occasions for fantasy production and fulfillment. In her work on cinema fashion, Bruzzi contends that clothes can have a "substitutive effect" commensurate with Freudian understandings of the fetish object, working to signify and in some cases even replace the impossible-to-consummate sexual attraction to an actor or character. Moreover, she argues that fashion allows spectators to connect to an object outside the stable gendered hierarchy of the Mulveyan gaze, thereby producing a greater level of gender and sexual mobility.[23]

Bruzzi's model for understanding the function of fashion in cinema extends to the clothes on BuffyAuction.com in interesting ways. For instance, in both spaces, the attachment to the clothes can be eroticized in ways that lend themselves to a high degree of play, both in terms of gender and sexual desire on the one hand, and in terms of the conflation of the actor and the character, on the other. One very short post on the alt.tv.buffy-v-slayer newsgroup encapsulated the appeal of corporeal proximity invited by wardrobe items, while also revealing the multiple forms of desire enunciated in fantasy scenarios where ownership becomes tantamount to sexual contact: "I want EVERYTHING that Faith [Eliza Dushku] has EVER worn. Including Xander [Nicholas Brendon]."[24]

As was clear quite early in the auction, fantasies like this were available for bidding, but they often came at dizzying prices. Authenticity and proximity cost far more than mere dress-up; that is, dressing like Faith and having the clothes Eliza Dushku actually wore involved two vastly different sums of money. This was especially true for the actors/characters with the largest fan following, with outfits worn by Gellar/Buffy, Hannigan/Willow, and James Marsters/Spike fetching the highest prices. When one of the first Buffy/Gellar outfits appeared on the auction and sold for over $5,000, a disbelieving fan on alt.horror exclaimed, "People will pay anything to get into Sarah Michelle Gellar's jeans!"[25] And the poster was not far wrong. Of course, that the jeans were, in fact, Sarah Michelle Gellar's, was the key to their worth, for again, the distinction between mass-produced clothing and one-of-a-kind artifact derived entirely from the fact that merchandise otherwise easily acquired was actually worn or used by a cast member on screen.

Further, the more closely an article of clothing was associated with a star or character the higher the item's price. For instance, James Marsters had among the largest fan followings of all the cast members. Marsters first appeared as Spike in season two but was not a regular until season four. During four years as a leading character, Spike is rarely seen without his signature full-length black leather coat which, as the final episode of season four jokes, is instrumental to his star persona. The episode, "Restless," is one of the series' most self-conscious installments; at one point, it takes time to send up Marsters's newfound status as the show's reigning male sex symbol by literally having him "vamp" in front adoring fans who want to photograph him in his leather coat.[26] When fans eagerly speculated on how much his coat would go for once it came up for auction, several wrote in to share that the coat was actually Marsters's own and hence would not be for sale. No matter. Fans moved on to the next best thing: if they couldn't have *Marsters*'s coat, at least they could have what *Spike* was wearing when he acquired it in the show's diegesis.[27] In the end, that outfit sold for $13,000.08.

If the value fans place on an item's relationship to a character or star cannot be overstated, neither can the value of an item's relationship to existing fan discourse about said character or star. For instance, of all the wardrobe items put up for auction, few generated more buzz or a higher winning bid than an outfit worn by Hannigan in two episodes in season three, in which her character, Willow, appears as a vampire. Consisting of leather pants, a bustier, and long-sleeve top, the "Willow Vamp" outfit sold for over $8,000. When it became clear that the outfit was too expensive for most fans, one person posted to alt.tv.buffy-v-slayer with plans to reproduce the item, asking: "Do you think the outfit was a custom job . . . or was it purchased off the rack somewhere? . . . I'm just wondering how hard it would be to put together a facsimile outfit."[28] Yet, as others would point out, to think in such terms would be to miss the whole point. One fan parodied the discourse of a popular consumer credit card campaign in order to remark on the irreproducibility of the costume: "Similar Willow-Vamp shirt: $200. Similar Willow-Vamp pants $350. . . . 'THE' outfit that was on the show . . . 'PRICELESS.'"[29]

The Willow Vamp outfit not only occasioned some of the most pointed discussions about authenticity, it also revealed a correlation between an item's appeal to fans and its significance to both official and unofficial narratives. Hannigan wears the outfit in "The Wish" and "Doppelgangland,"[30] episodes that marked *Buffy* producers' direct responses to online fan fiction and comments widely circulating in the "Buffyverse" during season three. Series creator Joss Whedon and other members of the Mutant Enemy production company often participated in online discussion boards, especially the "official" board known as The Bronze. On several notable occasions the series' writers, directors, and producers responded to fan suggestions and queries from The Bronze posting board by incorporating them into stand-alone episodes.[31] As Justine Larbalestier has noted, such episodes "provided responses to fan speculative scenarios," responses that demonstrated the degree to which "[s]ome ways of reading the show are dependent not only on familiarity with previous episodes but also on participation in *Buffy* fandom."[32] "The Wish," for instance, answered fans' desire to see "what would happen if Buffy Summers never came to Sunnydale" and the "what if Willow and Xander were vampires" scenario.[33]

"The Wish" is a relatively dark episode, while "Doppelgangland" proved far more light-hearted, reveling in the playfulness of Vamp Willow to which fans responded so positively. In this episode, Good

Willow accidentally causes Vampire Willow's return to Sunnydale. At one point, a sultry and sexually liberated Evil Willow confronts—and sexually propositions—her bookish, sexually naïve doppelganger in a heavily eroticized staging of a slash fiction[34] scenario, to which the real Willow can only remark, "This just can't get any more disturbing." When Vamp Willow is finally subdued, Willow explains to Buffy her disbelief at her alter-ego: "I'm so skanky and evil. Plus I think I'm kinda gay." Buffy tries to assuage Willow's concern, assuring her that "a vampire's personality has nothing to do with the person it was." When Angel moves to disagree, "Well, actually," the disapproving glance from Buffy signals his need to change course mid-sentence, "That's a good point."[35] In the fourth and following season, however, Willow begins the series' only significant, long-term same-sex relationship when she falls in love with Tara (Amber Benson).

In its own way, "Doppelgangland" can be read as a piece of fan fiction, a producer-as-fan response to a fan-as-producer reading. The episode allowed a popular unofficial subtext to quickly become the official text, thereby making good on one of Whedon's most frequently cited credos about the show. Just two months prior to the airing of "Doppelgangland," Whedon responded to a fan's post about the homoerotic tension between Buffy and Faith on the Bronze VIP discussion board. Channeling the language of Freud to sanction fan rewritings of *Buffy*, Whedon wrote:

> Okay, so I guess I must apologize . . . I just read the piece on Buffy and Faith . . . and by God, I think she's right! I can't believe I never saw it! . . . But then, I think that's part of the attraction of the Buffyverse. It lends itself to polymorphously perverse subtext. It encourages it. I personally find romance in every relationship . . . so I say B.Y.O. subtext![36]

It is no coincidence, then, that the Willow Vamp outfit became the most expensive item of Alyson Hannigan's on the auction. Not only did it crystallize an over-determined narrative history within the program, it also functioned as a site where the fan-producer distinction was abrogated (by Whedon himself no less) and where sexual mobility and gender masquerade were foregrounded rather than suppressed.

A number of fans actively anticipated the outfit's arrival on eBay. Shortly after it appeared, one fan posted to alt.tv.buffy-v-slayer, shouting: "IT'S UP FOR AUCTION!!! *FAINTS* . . . whoever gets that is the luckiest fan in the world."[37] When another fan writes, "I'll probably be sorry I asked but what in the hell would you do with it?," the gauntlet is thrown.[38] "Let's see, my wife's about Alyson's size . . . ," writes a presumably male poster, to which the original questioner replies, "Well, that I can understand, but couldn't you play dress up a lot cheaper . . . ?"[39] Across several discussion threads, a consensus is reached that the outfit is not worth $8,000 even to "play dress up" with one's own sexual partner, at which point talk turns more directly to sexualizing Hannigan herself. "For what they've got the vamp Willow outfit selling for, I'd want to have it delivered with Alyson inside it. (And be allowed to take it off her)."[40] "If Aly came with it for a night, I certainly would [pay that kind of money]," insists a self-identified male poster with a thinly veiled desire for a sexual experience with Hannigan.[41] Others delve into more particular forms of arousal. One fan wonders, "Has it been washed yet? Oh wait . . . don't answer that. Does it still have Aly scent?"[42] It is worth noting that not all self-identified male fans regard the clothes as occasions for fantasy and fetishism; indeed, as one demurred, "I shudder to think what some people may do with SMG or Eliza Dushku outfits that are up for sale."[43]

In the seemingly all-male discussion that evolved from suggestions of fantasy fulfillment with one's own partner to fantasy projection involving Hannigan herself, one self-identified female poster offered a subtle challenge to the men in the thread in the form of a sarcastic prescription for how everyone can enjoy "his" own particular "need": "My suggestion: Get a co-op together and go in on it together. Once a week, the person that has it boxes it up and sends it to the next name on the list. Included is a diary to keep track of the adventures of the Vamp Willow outfit."[44]

As a cultural phenomenon, *Buffy the Vampire Slayer* garnered both popular and academic praise for its efforts to promote an image of strong girls and women. The show's feminist gender politics, however, are fraught with contradictions; importantly, these contradictions surpass the simple fact that the show's cast of strong female characters are also conventionally beautiful, thin, white, and upper-middle-class. In her essay "'Action, Chicks, Everything': On-Line Interviews with Male Fans of *Buffy the Vampire Slayer*," Lee Parpart explored online male fan reception of the program and notes that she was "struck by the number of men who seem able to enjoy the series while feeling no need to concern themselves directly with issues of female empowerment."[45] According to Parpart, for many online male fans gender was either ignored or an occasion for eroticization. However, online posts about the *Buffy* auction reveal a more complex picture of how self-identified male fans relate to gender identity and objects of desire, the earlier discussion of Alyson Hannigan notwithstanding.

For instance, although many fans engaged in the production of sexual fantasies involving the female cast members and their clothes, others displayed an equal if less overtly sexual fascination with the men. One writes, "I really hate Anthony Head . . . the man still wears size 34 . . . pants."[46] In the posts that follow in this thread, male posters routinely pay close attention to the changes the cast members' bodies undergo over the course of the show as signified by the sizes listed on auction items. In these conversations, male cast members are subjected to playful ribbing, as posters ruminate on masculinity and its relationship to a body that changes over time. One fan points out: "It's pretty funny to see that Xander went from a size 30 to a size 38. (I thought he looked like he had put on a few pounds). And Spike went from 32 to 34 (that isn't bad at all though. The guy is 41 years old.)" He goes on to note that "oddly enough, the females in the show all LOST weight. Weird."[47] Such discussions allow a glimpse into a more complex relationship between fans and gender, one that is not easily reducible to the uniform sexualization of cast members. Indeed, some fans engage in explicit gender play, as when another begins with a remark that is vaguely objectifying— "Emma Caulfield [who plays Anya] is a size five. Any size she is is fine by me"—only to sign the post, "Philip, who wonders whether or not he could squeeze into the vamp Willow outfit."[48]

And squeezing into these clothes, especially the women's, is what most people would have to do. Observing that Sarah Michelle Gellar wears an XS top and has a 25-inch waist, one woman noted the virtual impossibility of buying anything to actually wear: "I suppose there are other women out there who are virtually non-existent enough to wear SMG's wardrobe, but I'm sure not one of them."[49] If most fans couldn't fit into the actors' clothes, however, this was not their fault, one man comforted. Rather, the blame lays on all actors who are, apparently, remarkably undersized: "You'd be surprised, most male actors are short but the females . . . good god it's like standing by a 12 year old."[50] The obviousness of the dilemma was not lost on other fans: twelve-year-olds were an important part of the WB and UPN audience, after all, yet how many of them could afford $5,000 for a pair of jeans and a blouse?

FANS VS. FOX: VALUE, COMPETITION AND COMMUNITY ONLINE

In the fine print accompanying each auction item, Fox made it clear that these clothes were not, in fact, for wearing and certainly not for smelling "Aly scent" or engaging in any other kind of sexual pleasure. In a legal disclaimer, Fox warned: "[Items] are not to be used for their seemingly functional purposes and are only intended to be sold as collector's items. DO NOT use the items purchased through this Auction for any functional use." While the disclaimer may have been Fox's effort to avoid any erstwhile "wardrobe malfunctions," many fans nevertheless interpreted the subtext of the disclaimer—along with the undemocratic nature of the auction and the astronomic prices of the items—as signs that the "For the Fans" auction was actually aimed at, and ultimately priced for, merchants and collectors.

This soured the reception of the auction for many who berated its competitive nature and in so doing idealized the perceived egalitarianism of other online fan spaces. Some complained that the show's artifacts were being poached by feckless opportunists, and it quickly became clear that eBay had created a material basis for hierarchy among people who use the internet, in part, to form non-hierarchical communities.[51] Thus, the *Buffy* auction compelled fans to reassess the limits and potential of the web as a truly classless space. Given the prohibitive cost of many items, the auction dramatically altered the currency by which one demonstrated one's fan devotion. Fans used a range of strategies to reconcile the fact that, in the space of the auction, one's bank account trumped one's love for or knowledge of the show, its characters, or even its fans. Early into the auction, posts oscillating between dismissive and resentful began to appear. One fan wrote, "Some people have got more money than sense. 'Ooohhhh look at me I have $8,000 sitting around doing nothing . . . I think I'll use it to buy a Spike outfit.' I'm not bitter I just think it's too much money."[52] A few hours later, another pushed further: "I AM bitter! It's not fair! All of us Buffy fans want something but the rich bitches'll get it all!"[53]

One post to alt.tv.buffy-v-slayer proclaims that had Fox really intended the sale "for the fans," they would have leveled the playing field by hosting a lottery rather than slating the props for sale on an inherently in-egalitarian auction: "The rich fans get what they want (or are willing to spend) and the rest of us (who can't afford even the cheapest of the items) get nada . . . If they were doing it for 'The Fans' they should have sold raffle tickets over E-Bay for $10 bucks each. . . . And they should limit the # of tickets any one E-Bayer can buy to a max of 10 for any one item."[54] To be sure, fan concern over the unequal distribution of goods was well founded. During the auction, users posted feedback on Fox for 482 items; these came from 231 discrete users (or at least discrete user names), many of whom won multiple auctions. The top two individual bidders, for instance, accounted for 48 purchases, or roughly 10 percent of the total number of items for which feedback was posted. The top 10 percent of bidders posting feedback (23) accounted for over 37 percent of the items.

Of course, it is difficult to know what users will do with their merchandise. At least one multiple-item winner turned out to be an amateur collector in Florida who curates a collection of entertainment memorabilia and items used in television and film production and who maintains a website (MoviePropKing.com). Though this person's (relatively) deep pockets may have rankled some less fortunate bidders, one could hardly impugn his fan credentials. Still, fans' worst nightmares were realized when it became clear that other buyers were essentially destroying the props for a profit. Several eBay merchants began to offer one-inch swatches of wardrobe items framed alongside an image of the cast member wearing the outfit, transforming what was once, according to one fan, "a giant uncut diamond," into so many pieces of worthless glitter.[55]

At this moment in popular entertainment culture, however, the collector class has got to be expected by most fans. Ever since the Hard Rock Cafe and Planet Hollywood codified a consumer habitus and a spatial logic around the exhibition value of entertainment memorabilia, collecting props has become an increasingly popular and expensive undertaking.[56] Combine rising interest in props with what *Variety* identifies as the "confluence of more careful accounting of property by studios, an explosion of do-it-yourself auctioneering, and a growing awareness . . . that production detritus is worth something," and the potential to profit from the sale, resale and display of entertainment memorabilia seems nearly limitless.[57]

In the end, BuffyAuction.com clearly represented a shrewd business decision on Fox's part more than an altruistic gesture "for the fans," many of whom make little secret about their distaste for the network. Indeed, throughout the many discussions about the auction, Fox emerged as the unifying target of fans' discontent. As Sue Tjardes notes in her essay "'If You're Not Enjoying It, You're Doing Something Wrong': Textual and Viewer Constructions of Faith, the Vampire Slayer," fans' relationship to a show's creators can take the form of "worship or antagonism, as fans attempt to balance their conceptions of characters and plots with the creators' legal and cultural authority."[58] With respect to *Buffy*, such reactions were extremely bifurcated. Fans' adoration of the cultural authority of Whedon and Mutant Enemy was nearly as uniform as their distaste for the legal authority of Fox.

Relations between Fox and fans were tense throughout the show's run, seeming to hit their nadir in the spring of 2000 when Fox issued cease and desist orders to fan-operated websites using copyrighted images, sound, or characterization from *Buffy*.[59] Fans of the show banded together to organize a one-day blackout on May 13, 2000, asking hosts and webmasters to shut down for the day in protest. One group,

"The Buffy Bringers," led an internet campaign against Fox, posting banners across the Buffyverse reading: "The Buffy Bringers. Buffy saves the world . . . We save the World Wide Web. Fox doesn't get it."[60] Whether Fox didn't "get" to control web content or didn't "get" that fans "spend many unpaid hours building Web sites [that] enhance the value of the franchise" was unclear, but fan resentment of Fox was not.[61]

While fans pouted that items were bid up too high for them ever to buy a meaningful item from the show, what clearly angered them just as much was that the considerable proceeds were not, as the initial online consensus mistakenly held, going to charity but rather right back to Fox. Many fans howled, pointing out that cast members like Gellar and Nicholas Brendon had sponsored their own charity auctions in the past. One of the members in a *Buffy* forum on the Television without Pity website calculated that the first 400 items auctioned off yielded Fox roughly $563,000, news that made many fans even more resentful of the high prices for which items were selling.[62] One wrote in to alt.tv.buffy -v-slayer, "$13,000.08 for an outfit and $11,000 for a script all going back to Fox. Now, I'm . . . glad I'm too poor to bid."[63] Another adopted a more resigned perspective: "Now, for most fans, we'd given up on Fox a long time ago . . . any online fan of Buffy will hear the name 'Fox' and most likely issue a derisive snort in that direction. (And that's if we're being kind.) So when this broke amongst us, we mostly just threw up our hands and thanked Fox for one final slap in the face."[64] Thus, even as the auction seemed to be a golden opportunity to work toward a rapprochement between the two, the auction instead exacerbated an already tense relationship with *Buffy* fans.

In the final analysis, the *Buffy* auction constituted a unique event insofar as it marked a harmonic convergence of fandom, television production/consumption, entertainment marketing, and internet shopping. Just as important, however, the auction also compels us to reconsider the dimensions and boundaries of fan devotion, desire, and consumption, on the one hand, and of producer-fan relations, on the other. Certainly, the props themselves did not make their way into the homes of everyone who wanted one, but what the auction lacked in material gratification it made up for in opportunities for discursive resistance, critique, fantasy production, and play. What most fans consumed in the end was not the props from the show but the auction itself. And as one fan who wrote to the *New York Times* noted, "If it's sad to have one's favorite show go off the air, the secret truth is, it's also a relief. At last, we can start living in the past."[65] Thanks to BuffyAuction.com, not only could fans wax nostalgic about the show, they could hearken back to the days when they had 25-inch waists, wore an XS top, and honestly believed they could one day afford the second-hand clothes of a TV star.

NOTES

I would like to extend my thanks to *Cinema Journal*'s two anonymous readers and to Lesley Bogad, Claire Buck, Steven Cohan, and Ina Rae Hark, whose comments on earlier versions of this article were extremely useful.

1   In *Textual Poachers: Television Fans and Participatory Culture* (New York: Routledge, 1992), Henry Jenkins considers at length the multiple ways that fans engage in "active" readings and rewritings of television programs. Readers interested in learning more about the contours of television fandom will find the book instructive.

2   The group of core characters are often referred to as "the Scooby Gang" or "the Scoobies." The group originally includes Buffy, Willow, Xander, and Giles. Later in the series, other characters such as Riley, Tara, and, arguably, Faith and Spike become part of the group as well.

3   *Buffy the Vampire Slayer*, episode 1, "Welcome to the Hellmouth," first broadcast on March 10, 1997, by the WB, directed by Charles Martin Smith and written by Joss Whedon.

4   Boyd Tonkin, "Farewell Buffy, and Fangs for the Memories," *Independent*, May 21, 2003, 2–3.

5   Amanda Zweernik and Sarah N. Gatson, "www.buffy.com: Cliques, Boundaries and Hierarchies in an Internet Community," in *Fighting the Forces: What's at Stake in* Buffy the Vampire Slayer, ed. Rhonda V. Wilcox and David Lavery (Lanham, MD: Rowman & Littlefield, 2002), 241.

6   Gail Collins, "Buffy Rides Off into the Sunset," *New York Times*, May 21, 2003, A-30.

7   *Buffy the Vampire Slayer*, episode 18, "Halloween," first broadcast October 27, 1997, by the WB, directed by Bruce Seth Green and written by Carl Ellsworth.

8   *Buffy the Vampire Slayer*, episode 69, "The I in Team," first broadcast February 8, 2000, by the WB, directed by James A. Contner and written by David Fury.

9   *Buffy the Vampire Slayer*, episode 108, "Once More, with Feeling," first broadcast November 1, 2001, by UPN, directed and written by Joss Whedon.

10   *Buffy the Vampire Slayer*, episode 1, "Welcome to the Hellmouth."

11   Anne Millard Daughtery, "Just a Girl: Buffy as Icon," in *Reading the Vampire Slayer: An Unofficial Critical Companion to* Buffy *and* Angel, ed. Roz Kaveney (New York: Tauris Park Paperbacks, 2001), 152.

12   For more on the addled sexual politics of *Buffy the Vampire Slayer*, fan practices and media coverage surrounding the show and its stars, see Sherryl Vint, "'Killing Us Softly'? A Feminist Search for the 'Real' Buffy," *Slayage: The Online International Journal of* Buffy *Studies*, no. 5 (May 2002), www.slayage.tv/essays/slayage5/vint.htm.

13   *Buffy the Vampire Slayer*, episode 144, "Chosen," first broadcast May 20, 2003, by the WB, directed and written by Joss Whedon.

14   The hammer first appears in the episode "Triangle" (episode 89, first broadcast January 9, 2001, by the WB, directed by Christopher Hibler and written by Jane Espenson) and figures centrally in the season five finale episodes "The Weight of the World" (episode 99, first broadcast May 15, 2001, by the WB, directed by David Solomon and written by Douglas Petrie) and "The Gift" (episode 100, first broadcast May 22, 2001, by the WB, directed and written by Joss Whedon).

15   Matt Hills, *Fan Cultures* (London: Routledge, 2002), 28.

16   Hills, 35.

17   For more on Walter Benjamin's discussion of the "aura" of an original piece of art, see "The Work of Art in the Age of Mechanical Reproduction," in *Illuminations*, trans. Harry Zohn (New York: Schocken, 1969), 217–52, esp. 220–29.

18   Andrew, "Buffy Auction," www.PeterDavid.net, May 15, 2003 (downloaded February 16, 2004; author has copy of post).

19   Bill, "Re: Anyone checked out the official Buffy auction?" (message 5 in thread) posted to alt.tv.buffy-v-slayer newsgroup, May 20, 2003 (downloaded February 9, 2004).

20   In his chapter, "'Get a Life!': Fans, Poachers, Nomads," Jenkins outlines in very useful ways the dimensions and tensions of the fan-producer relationship, especially with regard to control over imagery, representations, characterization and narratives. For more on this, see pp. 24–33.

21   For more, see Sue Tjardes, "'If You're Not Enjoying It, You're Doing Something Wrong': Textual and Viewer Constructions of Faith, the Vampire

Slayer," in *Athena's Daughters: Television's New Women Warriors*, ed. Frances Early and Kathleen Kennedy (Syracuse, NY: Syracuse University Press, 2003), 67.

22   Mary Ann Doane, "The Economy of Desire: The Commodity From in/of the Cinema," in *Movies and Mass Culture*, ed. John Belton (New Brunswick, NJ: Rutgers University Press, 1996), 124.

23   Stella Bruzzi, *Undressing Cinema: Clothing and Identity in the Movies* (London: Routledge, 1997), 24.

24   Queen Anthai, "Buffy Auction," www.PeterDavid.net, May 15, 2003 (downloaded February 16, 2004; author has copy of post). Faith and Xander have a one-night stand in an episode called "The Zeppo," episode 46, first broadcast January 26, 1999, by the WB, directed by James Whitemore Jr. and written by Dan Vebber.

25   Mark Towns, "Re: I'm a fan, but sheesh!" posted to alt.horror newsgroup May 14, 2003.

26   *Buffy the Vampire Slayer*, episode 78, "Restless," first broadcast May 23, 2000, on the WB, directed and written by Joss Whedon.

27   This occurs during a flashback in a season 5 episode called "Fool for Love" (episode 85, first broadcast November 14, 2000, by the WB, directed by Nick Marck and written by Douglas Petrie), in which Spike kills a Slayer on a New York subway in 1977 and takes her coat as a trophy.

28   IronMaster, "Re: Willow-Vamp outfit!!!" (message 11 in thread), posted to alt.tv.buffy-v-slayer newsgroup, May 21, 2003 (downloaded February 9, 2004).

29   Dr. Bond, "Re: Willow-Vamp outfit!!!" (message 10 in thread), posted to alt.tv.buffy-v-slayer newsgroup, May 21, 2003 (downloaded February 9, 2004).

30   "The Wish," episode 43, first broadcast December 8, 1999, by the WB, directed by David Greenwalt and written by Marti Noxon; "Doppelgangland," episode 50, first broadcast February 23, 2000, by the WB, directed and written by Joss Whedon.

31   Episodes frequently regarded as a response to, or engaging, popular fan discourse and fiction include "Doppelgangland"; "Something Blue," episode 65, first broadcast November 30, 1999, by the WB, directed by Nick Marck and written by Tracey Forbes; "Superstar," episode 73, first broadcast April 4, 200, by the WB, directed by David Grossman and written by Jane Espenson; "Restless," episode 78, first broadcast May 23, 2000, by the WB; "Buffy vs. Dracula," episode 79, first broadcast September 26, 2000, by the WB, directed by David Solomon and written by Marti Noxon; and "Normal Again," episode 117, first broadcast

March 12, 2002, by the UPN, directed by Rick Rosenthal and written by Diego Gutierrez.

32   Justine Larbalestier, "*Buffy*'s Mary Sue Is Jonathan: *Buffy* Acknowledges the Fans," in *Fighting the Forces: What's at Stake in* Buffy the Vampire Slayer, ed. Rhonda V. Wilcox and David Lavery (Lanham, MD: Rowman & Littlefield, 2002), 229, 228.

33   For more on these episodes, see Larbalestier, "*Buffy*'s Mary Sue Is Jonathan," 228–31.

34   Slash fiction is a genre of fan fiction that develops a homosexual and/or homoerotic relationship between two characters within a media text, a relationship that typically is not developed explicitly within the official narrative of the media text itself, as in stories which explore sexual, romantic and/or erotic scenarios involving Kirk and Spock from *Star Trek*, or between Spike and Xander, or Buffy and Willow in *Buffy the Vampire Slayer*. Character pairings are indicated by the use of a slash [/].

35   *Buffy the Vampire Slayer*, "Doppelgangland."

36   Whedon originally posted this message to the Bronze discussion board on December 3, 1998. The Bronze is no longer maintained by Fox; however, the post can be viewed at several sites, including members.tripod .com/~buffyfaith/joss.htm (downloaded July 20, 2004).

37   Dr. Bond, "Willow-Vamp outfit!!!" (message 1 in thread), posted to alt.tv .buffy-v-slayer newsgroup, May 20, 2003 (downloaded February 9, 2004).

38   EGK, "Re: Willow-Vamp outfit!!!" (message 2 in thread), posted to alt .tv.buffy-v-slayer newsgroup, May 20, 2003 (downloaded February 9, 2004).

39   Rowan Hawthorn, "Re: Willow-Vamp outfit!!!" (message 3 in thread), posted to alt.tv.buffy-v-slayer newsgroup, May 20, 2003 (downloaded February 9, 2004).

40   Don Sample, "Re: Anyone Checked out the official Buffy auction?" (message 19 in thread), posted to alt.tv.buffy-v-slayer newsgroup, May 20, 2003 (downloaded January 23, 2004).

41   Joseph S. Powell, "Re: Willow-Vamp outfit!!!" (message 8 in thread), posted to alt.tv.buffy-v-slayer newsgroup, May 20, 2003 (downloaded February 9, 2004).

42   Shorty, "Re: Willow-Vamp outfit!!!" (message 14 in thread), posted to alt.tv.buffy-v-slayer newsgroup, May 20, 2003 (downloaded February 9, 2004).

43   Andrew, "OKAY, *NOW* WE'RE COOKING WITH GAS," posted to www.PeterDavid.net, May 17, 2003 (downloaded February 16, 2004; author has copy of post).

44   Juleen, "Re: Willow-Vamp outfit!!!" (message 21 in thread), posted to alt.tv
     .buffy-v-slayer newsgroup, May 20, 2003 (downloaded February 9, 2004).

45   Lee Parpart, "'Action, Chicks, Everything': On-Line Interviews with
     Male Fans of *Buffy the Vampire Slayer*," in Frances Early and Kathleen
     Kennedy, ed. *Athena's Daughters: Television's New Women Warriors* (Syr-
     acuse, NY: Syracuse University Press, 2003), 79.

46   Tom Galloway, "OKAY, *NOW* WE'RE COOKING WITH GAS," posted
     to www.PeterDavid.net, May 17, 2003 (downloaded February 16, 2004;
     author has copy of post).

47   Panic, "Re: NEED BETTER AUCTION ITEMS," posted to alt.tv.buffy-v
     -slayer newsgroup, May 21, 2003 (downloaded January 20, 2004).

48   Philip Chien, "Re: NEED BETTER AUCTION ITEMS . . . ," posted to
     alt.tv.buffy-v-slayer newsgroup, May 22, 2003 (downloaded January 25,
     2004).

49   DarkMagic, "Re: Anyone checked out the official Buffy auction?" (mes-
     sage 3 in thread), posted to alt.tv.buffy-v-slayer newsgroup, May 14, 2003
     (downloaded January 26, 2004).

50   Dstep, "Re: Willow-Vamp outfit!!!" (message 4 in thread), posted to alt
     .tv.buffy-v-slayer newsgroup, May 20, 2003 (downloaded February 9,
     2004).

51   The auction was not the first time this often latent tension has bubbled to
     the surface. In their work on "cliques, boundaries and hierarchies" in the
     Bronze posting board, Amanda Zweernik and Sarah Gatson point out in
     that the Bronze originally attracted so many fans precisely because, as a
     community, it strove to enact *Buffy*'s overall sense of equality. The Bronze
     and other fan communities strove to form similar "classless," nonhierar-
     chical communities. However, as Zweernik and Gatson learned, "[f]ully
     50 percent of respondents to our online survey of The Bronze member-
     ship admitted to seeking out a forum as a way to talk about a show their
     peers could not, or refused to, understand. What hooked them was the
     community that sprang up around the site. With that community, how-
     ever, came the very class structure Whedon sought to satirize." Zweernik
     and Gatson, "www.buffy.com," 242. Within the first year, the Bronze had
     established a category of VIP posters—a status that afforded certain fans
     more 'private' access to *Buffy* producers such as Joss Whedon and Marti
     Noxon and that manifested in real terms the (im)possibility of an equal
     playing field even in the idealized space of the web-based fan community.

52   PimpDaddy, "Buffy auction!!!" posted to Tangent 21—Buffy auction!!
     May 22, 2003 (downloaded February 15, 2004), www.tangent21.com/it
     .php?node_id=104&topic_id=4243.

53 Acker, "Buffy auction!!!" posted to Tangent 21—Buffy auction!! May 22, 2003 (downloaaded February 15, 2004), www.tangent21.com/it.php?node _id=104&topic_id=4243.

54 Dr. Bond, "Re: Anyone checked out the official Buffy auction?" (message 9 in thread), posted to alt.tv.buffy-v-slayer newsgroup, May 20, 2003 (downloaded February 9, 2003).

55 Dr. Bond. It is worth noting that with little exception, these items tend to be ignored by the broader fan community, which either out of conscientious objection or simple disinterest, typically refuses to bid on them.

56 For more on the relationship among theme restaurants, entertainment culture and consumption, see Josh Stenger, "Consuming the Planet: Planet Hollywood, Stars, and the Global Consumer Culture," *Velvet Light Trap* 40 (Fall 1997): 42–55.

57 Ben Fritz, "Bidding Biz: Auctions thrive on hunger for memorabilia," *Variety*, August 31, 2003 (downloaded September 1, 2003), www.variety .com/story.asp?l=story&a=VR1117891746&c=1308 (URL inactive).

58 Tjardes, "If You're Not Enjoying It," 68.

59 For more information on Fox's cease and desist order, see Lynn Burke's "Fox Wants *Buffy* Fan Sites Slain," *Wired*, March 1, 2000 (downloaded July 22, 2004), www.wired.com/news/business/0,1367,34563,00.html (URL inactive).

60 For more on the blackout and the Buffy Bringers, see Ellen Ross, "Bringing on the Blackout," May 12, 2001 (downloaded March 1, 2004), www .suite101.com/article.cfm/buffy_and_angel/39263 (URL inactive).

61 Ross, "Bringing on the Blackout."

62 mp405, untitled online posting to *Buffy the Vampire Slayer* forum at "Television Without Pity," June 10, 2003 (downloaded February 18, 2004), forums.televisionwithoutpity.com/index.php?showtopic=2285021&st= 330 (URL inactive).

63 Beren, "Bummer about the Buffy Auction" (message 1 in thread), alt.tv .buffy-v-slayer newsgroup, May 28, 2003 (downloaded February 9, 2004).

64 Claris, "A Letter to Salon.com: Who Is Your Money Going To?" June 11, 2003 (downloaded February 21, 2004), www.themusesbitch.net/?&article =37 (URL inactive).

65 Emily Nussbaum, "Sick of 'Buffy' Cultists? You Ain't Seen Nothing Yet," *New York Times*, June 8, 2003, 2.

CONTRIBUTORS

LUCY FISCHER is a distinguished professor emerita of English and film and media studies at the University of Pittsburgh where she directed the film studies program for thirty years. She is the author or editor of fourteen books: *Jacques Tati* (1983), *Shot/Countershot: Film Tradition and Women's Cinema* (1989), *Imitation of Life* (1991), *Cinematernity: Film, Motherhood, Genre* (1996), *Sunrise* (1998), *Designing Women: Cinema, Art Deco, and the Female Form* (2003), *Stars: The Film Reader* (coedited, 2004), *American Cinema of the 1920s: Themes and Variations* (2009), *Teaching Film* (coedited, 2012), *Body Double: The Author Incarnate in the Cinema* (2013), *Art Direction and Production Design* (2015), *Cinema by Design: Art Nouveau, Modernism, and Film History* (2017), and *Cinemagritte: René Magritte within the Frame of Film History, Theory, and Practice* (2019). She has held curatorial positions at the Museum of Modern Art (New York City) and the Carnegie Museum of Art (Pittsburgh) and has been the recipient of both a National Endowment for the Arts Art Critics Fellowship and a National Endowment for the Humanities Fellowship for University Professors. She has served as president of the Society for Cinema and Media Studies (2001–3) and in 2008 received its Distinguished Service Award. In 2016, she received the Chancellor's Research Award for Senior Scholars at the University of Pittsburgh.

KARA LYNN ANDERSEN is an associate professor of cinema studies at University of North Carolina School of the Arts with research interests in representations of collecting, American animation history and theory, and video games. She has written about racialized voice acting and 3D cinema on the blog *animationstudies 2.0* and has published entries on *The Sims*, *Animal Crossing*, and girls' games in the *Encyclopedia of Video Games: The Culture, Technology, and Art of Gaming* (2021).

ERIKA BALSOM is a reader in film studies at King's College London. She is the author of four books, including *After Uniqueness: A History of Film and Video Art in Circulation* (2017, Columbia University Press) and *Ten Skies* (2021). Her criticism appears regularly in venues such as *Artforum* and *Cinema Scope*. She is the cocurator of the exhibitions *No Master Territories: Feminist Worldmaking and the Moving Image* at the Haus der Kulturen der Welt, Berlin (2022) and *Peggy Ahwesh: Vision Machines* at Spike Island, Bristol (2021). In 2018, she was awarded a Philip Leverhulme Prize.

JOANNE BERNARDI is professor of Japanese and film and media studies at the University of Rochester. She is author and editor of *Re-envisioning Japan: Japan as Destination in 20th Century Visual and Material Culture*, a multimedia digital humanities project and original collection of tourism, education, and entertainment ephemera. Her publications include *Writing in Light: The Silent Scenario and the Japanese Pure Film Movement* (2001), *Provenance and Early Cinema* (coeditor, 2021), and *The Routledge Handbook of Japanese Cinema* (coeditor, 2020), as well as book chapters and journal articles on Japanese cinema, the moving image and media history, historiography and preservation, Godzilla and nuclear culture, and digital humanities scholarship and pedagogy. She is currently writing *Films for the Living: The Cinema of Juzo Itami*. Initial development of the Re-envisioning Japan digital archive was funded by grants from the University of Rochester.

MARK BEST is a senior lecturer in film and media studies in the Department of English at the University of Pittsburgh. He teaches courses in subjects including film genres such as superheroes, science fiction, and the Western; the graphic novel; American popular culture; the Bible as literature; horror literature; postmodern literature; and others. His research interests include Japanese science fiction film and television, toys as cultural artifacts and art, the Bible in popular culture, and the American superhero genre and gender in the Cold War era. He is currently working on a book project on Japanese giant monster movies, specifically the history of the *Gamera* film series from the 1960s to the present.

BLAIR DAVIS is an associate professor of media and cinema studies in the College of Communication at DePaul University in Chicago. His books include *The Battle for the Bs: 1950s Hollywood and the Rebirth of Low-Budget Cinema* (2012), *Movie Comics: Page to Screen/Screen to Page* (2017), *Comic Book Movies* (2018) and *Comic Book Women: Characters, Creators and Culture in the Golden Age* (2022). He has written about comics and pop culture for *USA Today*, the *Washington Post, Saturday Evening Post*, and *Ms.* Magazine and has comics-related essays in numerous anthologies, including *Comics and Pop Culture* (2019), *Working Class Comic Book Heroes: Class Conflict and Populist Politics in Comics* (2018) and the Eisner Award–winning *The Blacker the Ink* (2015). Davis serves on the editorial advisory board of the journal *Inks*, for which he edited a roundtable on comics and methodology in its inaugural issue, and he served on the executive board of the Comics Studies Society. He has been interviewed about comics and cinema for AMC, ABC, CBC, the *Chicago Tribune, USA Today, Voice of America* and the *Wall Street Journal.*

KRIN GABBARD teaches the occasional course in the Jazz Studies program at Columbia University. In 2014, he retired from Stony Brook University where he had, since 1981, taught classical literature, film studies, and literary theory. His books include *Psychiatry and the Cinema* (1987), *Jammin' at the Margins: Jazz and the American Cinema* (1996), *Black Magic: White Hollywood and African American Culture* (2004), *Hotter Than That: The Trumpet, Jazz, and America Culture* (2008), and *Better Git It in Your Soul: An Interpretive Biography of Charles Mingus* (2016).

BARRY KEITH GRANT is a professor emeritus of film studies and popular culture at Brock University in St. Catharines, Ontario, Canada. He is the author or editor of more than thirty books and dozens of essays. Among his books are *Invasion of the Body Snatchers* (2010), *Shadows of Doubt: Negotiations of Masculinity in American Genre Films* (2011), *The Hollywood Film Musical* (2012), and *Monster Cinema* (2018). Several of his books—*Film Genre Reader IV* (2012), *Documenting the Documentary* (2014), and *The Dread of Difference: Gender and the Horror Film* (2015)—have been widely used as course texts across North America and abroad. His work has been translated into several languages, and he has lectured around the world. Grant has always been a collector and first presented work on the subject of collecting and his own obsession with it at a Popular Culture Association conference in 2005. An elected fellow of the Royal Society of Canada, he has been a pioneer of film and popular culture studies in Canada.

TAMAR JEFFERS MCDONALD is a professor of film history and dean of the School of Art and Media at the University of Brighton. She read English at Somerville College, Oxford, before being awarded her PhD in film by the University of Warwick. A Hollywood historian, Professor Jeffers McDonald is the author of several monographs on romantic comedy, film costume, stardom, and movie magazines and wrote the BFI Film Classic on *When Harry Met Sally*. Her most recent publication is a coedited collection, *Star Attractions: Twentieth-Century Movie Magazines and Global Fandom* (2019), while her current writing project traces the history and impact of the Hollywood movie magazine from 1911 to 1976.

LEAH M. KERR is an archivist, writer, and researcher who highlights the lives and accomplishments of Black and underrepresented people. She cofounded the Mayme A. Clayton Library and Museum, and is the project archivist at Duke University's John Hope Franklin Research Center for African and African American History. She collected Pearl Bowser's papers for the National African American Museum of History and Culture and processed Robert A. Hill's Marcus Garvey and the United Negro Improvement Association papers, the Joint Center for Political and Economic Studies records, and Alan Gurganus's papers for the David M. Rubenstein Rare Book and Manuscript Library. She also cowrote the screenplay "For Hire" and is the author of *Driving Me Wild: Nitro Powered Outlaw Culture* (2000).

ADAM LOWENSTEIN is a professor of English and film and media studies at the University of Pittsburgh, where he also serves as director of the Horror Studies Working Group. He is the author of *Shocking Representation: Historical Trauma, National Cinema, and the Modern Horror Film* (2005), *Dreaming of Cinema: Spectatorship, Surrealism, and the Age of Digital Media* (2015), and *Horror Film and Otherness* (2022). He is a member of the board of directors for the George A. Romero Foundation.

JOSH STENGER is a professor in the Department of Film and New Media at Wheaton College in Norton, Massachusetts. His research interests include fandom, particularly the professionalization and monetization of fan labor and participatory fan cultures, creative industries and creative labor, transmedia franchises and storytelling, digital humanities, and the future of higher education. Most recently, his work has advocated for the development of new quantitative tools and methodologies for studying fan works and their reception, particularly as media industries and digital platforms increasingly define and measure audience engagement via algorithms and the resulting datafication of users and user experiences.

INDEX

CPSIA information can be obtained
at www.ICGtesting.com
Printed in the USA
BVHW030445130323
660215BV00005B/24

9 780814 348550